A PEOPLE'S GUIDE TO PUBLISHING

T0182662

A PEOPLE'S GUIDE TO
PUBLISHING

*Build a Successful, Sustainable,
Meaningful Book Business from
the Ground Up*

JOE BIEL

MICROCOSM PUBLISHING
Portland, OR

A PEOPLE'S GUIDE TO PUBLISHING
Build a Successful, Sustainable, Meaningful Book Business from the Ground Up

© Joe Biel, 2018
This edition © Microcosm Publishing, 2018
First edition, first published December 10, 2018
Second Printing, December 2019

ISBN 978-1-62106-285-1
This is Microcosm #300
Edited by Elly Blue
Cover illustration by Cecilia Granata
Book design by Joe Biel

"Organizing a Bookstore Release Event" (pages 333-339) © Laura Stanfill, 2018

"Working with the Author" and "Social Media" (pages 319-329) were written by Elly Blue and published as online articles called the "Business of Publishing."

"Is It Public Domain?" (page 267) is © Erika Schnatz, 2016-2018

For a catalog, write or visit:
Microcosm Publishing
2752 N Williams Ave.
Portland, OR 97227
Microcosm.Pub

To join the ranks of high-class stores that feature Microcosm titles, talk to your local rep: In the U.S. **Como** (Atlantic), **Fujii** (Midwest), **Travelers West** (Pacific), **Manda/UTP** in Canada, **Turnaround** in Europe, **New South** in Australia and New Zealand, and **Global Publisher Services** in Asia, India, South America, and Africa.

If you bought this on Amazon, I'm so sorry because you could have gotten it cheaper and supported a small, independent publisher at **Microcosm.Pub**

Global labor conditions are bad, and our roots in industrial Cleveland in the 70s and 80s made us appreciate the need to treat workers right. Therefore, our books are MADE IN THE USA and printed on post-consumer paper.

Library of Congress Cataloging-in-Publication Data

Names: Biel, Joe, author.
Title: A people's guide to publishing : build a successful, sustainable,
    meaningful book business / Joe Biel.
Description: Portland, Oregon : Microcosm Publishing, [2018]
Identifiers: LCCN 2018024076 | ISBN 9781621062851 (pbk.)
Subjects: LCSH: Publishers and publishing. | Booksellers and bookselling.
Classification: LCC Z278 .B49 2018 | DDC 070.5--dc23
LC record available at https://lccn.loc.gov/2018024076

This book is dedicated to Sidnee Grubb, whose enthusiasm and curiousity for all things publishing inspired me to write it. Elly Blue pushed me to make it happen as did many strangers, whose confusion and misinformation was deeply disheartening. If Sidnee had never asked me what to read for her continued education after finishing her internship, and Elly had never pushed me to do it, this book would not exist.

MICROCOSM · PUBLISHING

Microcosm Publishing is Portland's most diversified publishing house and distributor with a focus on the colorful, authentic, and empowering. Our books and zines have put your power in your hands since 1996, equipping readers to make positive changes in your life and in the world around you. Microcosm emphasizes skill-building, showing hidden histories, and fostering creativity through challenging conventional publishing wisdom. What was once a distro and record label was started by Joe Biel in his bedroom and has become among the oldest independent publishing houses in Portland, OR. In a world that has inched to the right for 80 years, we are carving out a place in the center with DIY skills, food, bicycling, gender, self-care, and social justice.

CONTENTS

FOREWORD

The Underground is Bigger than the Mainstream

In 1970, there were about 3,000 indie publishers. By 2006, there were 82,000. Today there are hundreds of thousands of specialized independents, and probably over a million if you include bedroom operations. Even with so many presses, that's still an average sales of $120,000 per publishing house. In 2016, 66% of book sales were from independent publishers, so we are now selling more books than the majors! While The Big Five, major publishing houses that dominate the industry, have lost 27% of their market share since 2012, small presses continue to grow and find new opportunities at a manageable scale.

There has never been a better time to become an independent publisher.

Still, there are over 500 new books published every single hour with millions of new books being released every year, and tens of millions of books already in print. There are more books in print today than at any point in history. At the same time, conventional book outlets (collectively known as "the book trade") like Barnes & Noble, Books-A-Million, Amazon, independent bookstores, and libraries have neither grown, shrunk, nor added capacity in any significant way for the past 40 years. Instead, they endlessly take little bites out of each other to compete for the same customers and dollars, and the stores make publishers squabble over precious shelf space.

Fortunately, there are better options for book sales than competing for bookstore space until you've created some demand for your work. If you're focused and smart about what you publish, you can be quite successful.

As an indie publisher, you must be careful and deliberate about your focus, process, and growth. You can ignore Amazon completely or build your brand around their services (though I wouldn't recommend the latter). You can use digital printing to create one copy of each book at a time or print thousands in a (much more economical) offset print run. You can compete on a relatively even playing field and make changes quickly and easily, while the dinosaurs are trying to discover how to manage their sprawling size, fight entrenchment, and become relevant again. You can research your problems thoroughly and implement your decisions quickly. Even better, the road to success is also more fun than it's ever been before.

One major advantage for small presses is that branding is not an important part of a reader's book shopping. Most readers do not purchase a book because of who published it. They purchase a book because the subject is interesting to them, they are seeking the emotional payoff that the book promises, or the book is helping them to solve a problem in their life. Sometimes they will be familiar with the author or perhaps have read a review or article about the book. But otherwise as long as your books look as credible and professional as the ones next to them, they will receive honest consideration from people deciding what to buy.

That said, while your press's identity will not be important to most readers, it will be important to people who work in the publishing industry. And the fact that most readers will buy your books without knowing about your press doesn't mean that you shouldn't build an identity around your publishing.

I founded Microcosm Publishing 24 years ago as an autistic, 18-year-old, at-risk youth who ran away from my parents. As a teenager, I had very few tools or resources at my disposal. My upbringing had been violent, my education had been absent, and punk rock gave me a set of morals and principles that saved my life. I set about creating books to fill these gaps, and today we've sold millions of these books and have the next four years of our publishing schedule booked solid. My meaning and purpose is still to create resources and self-empowerment for others so that they can have the lives that they want and change the world around them. By telling our story and connecting it to our books, we've made our readers feel closer to us and feel strongly about evangelizing our work.

Publishing Is Movement Building

A publisher has the vision to see a different world and the determination and grit to make it happen. The best part of publishing is that you get to be who you are, open and honest on the page. Make your publishing an honest, fundamental expression of yourself and your interests. In his book *Growing a Business*, Paul

Hawken instructs the reader to build a business so uniquely their own that even if everyone else tried to steal their concept, no one else could succeed because they wouldn't execute the strategy the same way as the creator.

The number one mistake that I see publishers making is not having a fundamental understanding of who they are and why they exist.

Let's drill down and build your movement:

- Dig deep to find your meaning and purpose.

- Get a brand new notebook and draft your vision until your mission is crystal clear.

- Write it in sharpie on the inside cover and workshop it into your single-sentence tagline.

- Your statement of purpose will ground you during uncertain times, hard decisions, and financial peril.

Publishers are often afraid to express themselves in this way. Fight the desire to be plain. You need to have a backbone and should be drawing a line in the sand around your values. Nobody eats plain, nonfat yogurt because they love the taste. They eat it because there is something fundamental about themselves that they don't embrace, and they've been sold plain yogurt as a solution to that supposed problem. As a small publisher, you don't have enough of a marketing budget to market yourself as plain. If you do, cut your marketing budget and go back to reflecting on what you care the most about.

Some publishers fear that by having a clear identity, set of interests, and even political opinions, they will repel customers, authors, and retailers. This fear is partially founded. It will absolutely repel everyone that you want nothing to do with and save you quite a bit of time navigating those people. Even better, a strong identity will attract exactly the kind of people that you *want*.

Having a strong identity as a small publisher will achieve most of the hard work that larger publishers spend hours in boardrooms trying to figure out, like how to attract the right new authors, how to reach an audience, how to be interesting to young people, and how to stand out from the crowd.

Think of your publishing company like a grassroots political campaign. Write down the answers to these questions to understand the big picture:

- Who are you?

- What do you want?

- Who is on your team?

- Who can you count on to help?

- Where do people who are excited about these things spend their time?

- What are their other interests?

- What are some badass slogans?

- What are your ultimate goals?

- What could you accomplish that would make your existence obsolete?

- What bigger goals could you brainstorm then?

You need to create more than great books. Frame your message around what you believe in rather than what you oppose. Build your movement so that it can grow around you rather than behind you. You want other people to be invested in it too. Create opportunities for other people to talk and offer input. But when other people are talking, always remember the core mission so that you don't fall down a tangent or get lost on a mission that isn't your own. In the end, you'll have a community and a movement.

In 2012, I went to Memphis and did a presentation. A fan came wearing a Microcosm t-shirt that I had printed in my basement in 2001. He told me that he only wears it for special occasions. We took a photo together at his request. The interaction took a few minutes, and he apologized for "interrupting" me, but that is a moment that neither of us is ever going to forget because it bonded us together. Moments of common connection like that are the reason that people become publishers and travel the country.

People can tell when you're having fun and will gravitate towards you. You can have a bad day sometimes, but make sure that you're having fun more often than not. You're a movement leader!

Most independent publishers focus on a single subject: business, mysteries, photography, science fiction, children's books, self-help, adult coloring books, politics, or literary fiction. Having a specific focus simplifies many aspects of being a publisher. Once readers find one of your titles, it's easier for them to latch onto the rest of your catalog, and it's more likely that they will be interested in other books that you publish. Authors will come to you that write the kind of books that you are interested in publishing. It's easier to approach stores with a whole thematic catalog because the work makes sense together. It becomes much easier to dominate a subject or category and be seen as a leading thinker in that area. For example, CompanionHouse Books has published hundreds of books about dogs, so when you research books about dogs, you would easily end up at CompanionHouse. But as a consumer who is interested in books about dogs, it's likely that you will find yourself owning some of their books without noticing what publisher they came from. Dominating a category like this is great for business, but imagine the increased sales if CompanionHouse was more of a household name among readers and did more marketing to consumers and appearances at consumer events!

Your website, books, catalogs, mailing list, and your own writing should always tell people who you are and what you believe in. They should always be an invitation to join your movement with your next books. This kind of investment will keep people curious and interested in what you do. Even if they don't like everything that you do, they'll be thoughtful and motivated to talk about you to people who will.

Give people a reason to stick with you, and they will.

INTRODUCTION

What a Publisher Does

As a publisher, you will solicit books from authors, read submissions, work with authors to produce the best book possible, pay for and coordinate the manufacturing of books, and work hard to market, sell, and distribute those books as far and wide as possible. Here are the various jobs involved:

• ***Marketing and development***: This is the most important part of publishing. Spend a few hours considering the benefits that a proposed book offers to the reader and research the books in print from the past five years that a reader might purchase in addition to the book or instead of it (known as "comps"). If there is need for another similar book, look closely at the titles, subtitles, descriptions, prices, and cover designs of the comps. Sometimes this process is immediate and obvious, other times it takes months of back-and-forth and doubt. Then create a profit and loss statement (see page 244) to determine the likely outcome. The end goal is to make sure that each book is described accurately, and that it fills a wanted and empty niche in the world of books so that excited readers can happily discover it.

• ***Editing***: While the myth is that most publishers' effort seems to go into grammar and comma placement, editing is really about big-picture development, ensuring that the book in stores matches the one described on the cover and is as awesome as it can possibly be.

• **Production**: When the edits are finished, you design the book and send it to the printer. The development process informs each book's size, color, design, paper type, how many copies are printed, when it is printed, when it is released, and where all the copies are warehoused. Budget the production and promotional costs and make a plan to recoup the investment quickly.

• **Publicity**: Books are promoted with catalogs, flyers, events, reviews, interviews, articles, YouTubers, bloggers, web and print advertising, and in every creative way you can imagine. Some publishers print advanced reader copies (ARCs) for reviewers six to twelve months before the book is printed. In most cases, a Kickstarter campaign (see page 307) is the best way to combine marketing, publicity, sales, and distribution all at once with immediacy for your fans. Involve the author in every step of this process in order to have the best chance of success.

• **Sales and distribution**: Behind marketing and development, this is the second most important step, but also the last one. Once your vision is committed to paper, you'll be selling the ideas behind it. Books are sold to:

- The trade (20% of industry, highly competitive, Internet and brick bookstores)

- Academic (20% of industry but dominated by key players already, such as Routledge, University of Chicago, Houghton

Mifflin, Wiley, and others who produce extensive textbooks and reference titles)

- Gift sales (20% of industry, boutiques who use books as impulse items instead of telling a composite story about the organization)

- Specialty market (15% of industry, places that sell a single type of product where books are fringe, telling a story about their mission to their customers)

- Libraries (15% of industry)

- Mass market (5% of industry, big box stores)

- Institutional sales (3% of industry, customers that don't resell the books but use them with their staff or programs)

- Fans and readers—on your own website, at events, and in person (2% of industry but tremendously valuable for you).

Think Like a Publisher

Now that you understand your role as a publisher, it's important to get in the proper mindset. Almost everyone in the world believes themselves capable of writing a book. Your job is to sort out which authors and books are a good fit for your house.

I find that almost everyone I meet in any environment or context has the goal to write a book. When random strangers learn that I am a publisher, they corner me and begin pitching. I try to be polite, give them my card, and walk them through how we take submissions. I also explain that while even though one million new books will be published this year, tens of millions of people believe they could or should be writing books. I receive twenty times more proper submissions than I could even consider. And thus there's no reason to stand around entertaining these pitches when I'm trying to socialize. Nobody likes to hear hard realities, and I find that the actual best solution is not to talk about my profession.

WHY THE BOOK MARKET IS CROWDED

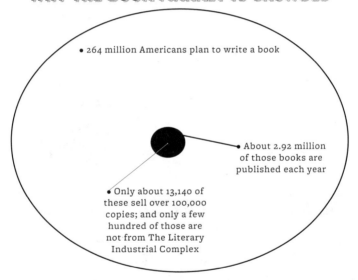

- 264 million Americans plan to write a book

- About 2.92 million of those books are published each year

- Only about 13,140 of these sell over 100,000 copies; and only a few hundred of those are not from The Literary Industrial Complex

Publisher Peter Workman, according to popular anecdote, believed that successful publishing relied upon a sturdy "three-legged stool:"

1. The book must have the right price, format, and trim size for its shelf and subject.

a. The content must challenge existing wisdom.

b. It should be the best possible book in its category and become a "category killer."

c. It should be an attractive value with emotional appeal.

2. The author and publisher must have a great relationship, and the publisher must have an authentic relationship with the book's audience.

   a. Content is created.

   b. Book is introduced to professionals and the trade.

   c. The author and concepts are introduced to the audience.

3. Commerce at every level: the book must benefit everyone who touches it.

   a. Author, publisher, sales rep, account, and reader must all benefit from "value stream."

   b. This prevents disruptions in the supply chain and keeps deep discounting from retailers like Amazon from undermining a book with a community behind it.

If any of these legs were missing, Workman believed that the stool would collapse and the book would fail.

In 1984, Workman Publishing Company released *What To Expect When You're Expecting*, one of the first books about pregnancy for new mothers. The primary author, Heidi Murkoff, had no medical expertise or credentials to write the book and was motivated by the lack of resources available when she had a baby. Worried about the credibility of the author, Workman strengthened Murkoff's second leg by pairing her with medical experts and specialists to check the risks and accuracy of her advice and began sending her as a speaker to professional conferences. *What To Expect When You're Expecting* is now read by 93% of people seeking a book on pregnancy and has become Workman's flagship title. More importantly, the book has entered the cultural fabric of the U.S. When a movie wants to convey that someone is pregnant, the director puts the book on screen. The book is so authoritative that it visually embodies a common emotional experience and has sold nearly twenty million copies.

What Kind of Publisher Are You?

Understanding the volume of unpublished and unpublishable authors out there leads many would-be publishers to go into the service side of pay-to-play or vanity publishing, which is now called hybrid publishing (see page 34). The business model of hybrid publishers is to take authors' money up front instead of earning income through book sales. While the money can seem appealing at first, if you work in hybrid publishing you cannot also be a respectable publisher because you will lack credibility. Worse, the failure of hybrid publishing is that while there are professionals involved, they aren't empowered to make the important decisions. The onerous development decisions are handled by the author, whose ego makes emotional decisions until their wallet cannot handle it any longer. This sounds fine to most authors in theory, until they have spent $20,000 for a book that sold 100 copies

Mass production model
ex. Trade book publisher with
small profit margins
Advantage: Scalable

Automation model
ex. Setting up and owning
a business with outside
management
Writing books published by
other people
Advantage: Passive income

**Service-oriented/Labor-
intensive model**
ex. Custom publishing,
Consulting, author services,
technical publishing
Advantage: Bigger profit
margins

because there is no market for it or it is misdeveloped. An author is too close to the project to make decisions responsibly.

So let's spend a few minutes studying this business model triangle. The triangle will help you understand the kind of services that you provide and that you cannot be all things to all people.

There are three distinct ways of approaching an organizational model.

- The most common type of publisher, trade books publishing, typically involves small profit margins that you make up for by selling lots of copies and publishing lots of titles.

- Publisher services include hybrid publishing as well as custom publishing, where you create a custom book for an author, a wedding, family, celebrity, or corporation. This model offers bigger margins but with fewer customers because each one consumes so much of your time and focus.

- Licensing involves automation; you essentially create something and the work is handled by others. Automation could mean writing a book for a different publisher, owning a business but hiring outside management to run it, or selling the rights to your books to publishers in other territories, languages, or formats (audio book, French edition, hardcover rights, etc).

There's a tendency for a new publisher to want to place themselves in the middle of this triangle and awkwardly try to offer all three types of products and services. The idea is that by not choosing a side, they can have the best of all worlds. But in reality, it becomes unclear what services they offer and why someone would go to them for those services.

Joe Matthews, CEO of Independent Publishers Group, shows how this conflict plays out in practice: "Small publishers have trouble distancing themselves emotionally from their projects and making rational, critical decisions. This often leads to regrets...Every time we get a submission from a publisher, we go straight to the submission page of their website. If they offer 'services' or have 'fees to help authors succeed,' we run away from it. If it says 'Mail submissions here for us to review them,' we know that it is a real publisher. The problem is that vanity publishing has been rebranded as 'hybrid publishing."

You can move between two points on an outside line but try to avoid the middle of the triangle. For example, our bookstore receives phone calls from people that want us to make photocopies or send faxes for them because we are a "publisher" and that's what they believe a publisher does. We also receive requests from customers who want to pay us to print short runs of their books. But we don't own any printing equipment, and offering these services would harm our reputation and place us awkwardly in the center of the triangle. While we could earn a little extra money this way, it distracts from the actual work that we are focused on, and adding the extra service would be yet another thing to market and advertise. We just want to sell books.

To help decide your model, think about what would be most exciting and fun for you in the day-to-day sense. From there research the least crowded aspects of your specific area of the industry to make sure there is room and demand for you. Visit a few regional conferences to help decide what is sought after. Once you have a clear model, to succeed in publishing only requires being willing to work hard every day and thinking critically and analytically to find the shortest path towards every goal.

Approach Publishing as a Passionate Hobby

Your publishing is best when it's a natural extension of your existing passions and interests. Fellow publishers that I meet are shocked that our company is financially solvent and that our staff and I are paid for our work just like any other job. On the other hand, business people that I meet are equally surprised when I explain to them that our profit margin is 3.01% and that even the most profitable publishers have a profit margin around 10%. In short, you don't go into publishing for the money, and, if you do, you won't last long.

Almost all businesses lose money for their first five years and most fail, but publishing comes with the added bonus that even if you succeed, the salary is not one to brag about. This is why it's much better to approach publishing like a passionate hobby where you access your meaning and purpose. Just like knitting, yoga, or fixing old cars, you'll invest some of your money because you believe in what you're doing and enjoy the process. If you don't, publishing likely isn't for you.

Since your publishing is built around you and your interests and hobbies, there are benefits besides being popular at parties. You can deduct every movie you see and every book you purchase on your taxes. When you attend conferences or stay in hotels that you would have anyway, they are now a business deduction. When you pay for classes or pay dues, those are deductible, as well.

Treat It as a Business—Think About Profit Centers and Cost Centers

Be mindful of the best and worst outcomes of each dollar spent. When you spend money, save your receipts. Planning ahead is the most important part of publishing. I met someone at a festival who told me that she was intending to write a very niche tourist guide, had not done any research about comparable titles, and had begun by hiring a graphic designer for a few thousand dollars. I asked what her total budget was for the project and how many she expected to sell. She didn't know and was surprised when I explained the difficulty she would have printing and distributing her book and how small the audience was.

In doing research for this book, I cannot tell you how many publishers have told me stories about spending $50,000 on a book that would yield, at best, $40,000 in income—and often results in much less.

Make informed decisions and create a budget for each project so that you at least have the possibility of being able to invest any leftover income on future projects. After a few years, you should have a clear idea of where you are making and losing money.

Understand the Publishing Ecosphere

Around one hundred and twenty billion dollars[1] is spent annually on books worldwide! If you are interested, there are dozens of publishing blogs where industry stats are disputed to point out unreported book sales and argue about emergent trends. As you find your place in the industry, understanding the scale of these operations is important in order to understand how small you are and appreciate your corresponding ability to turn on a dime and be innovative.

While there are now hundreds of thousands of microscopic presses dotting the globe that comprise about 42% of those sales, most people are familiar with The Big Five, a handful of household names

1 Based on total 2016 reported trade sales of $42.49B, estimating unreported specialty markets and gift sales plus technical, professional, academic, eBooks, self-publishing, etc.

that control so much of the playing field:

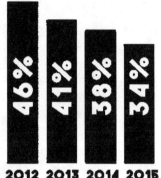

1. ***Penguin Random House*** ($9.2 billion U.S. sales in 2016, operated by global media giants Bertelsmann and Pearson)

2. ***Hachette*** ($2.4 billion U.S. sales in 2016, formerly Time Warner Book Group)

3. ***HarperCollins*** ($1.6 billion in 2016 U.S. sales, owned by News Corp)

4. ***MacMillan*** ($1.2 billion in 2016 U.S. sales, owned by German media company Holtzbrinck)

5. ***Simon & Schuster*** ($767 million in 2016 U.S. sales, owned by CBS Broadcasting)

While most publishers tend to think of the U.S. as their biggest market, the majors do tens of billions of dollars in sales in other countries, languages, and markets. I had a grand plan to translate currencies for each of the foreign market sales for these companies but this proves remarkably complex. Fluctuations in currency exchange rates can spell the difference between making and losing money for these companies. Hachette, for example, does more business in France than in the U.S. In fact, 80% of their sales are outside the U.S.

I'd like you to wrap your brain around all of these factors to truly understand how massive the publishing industry is and how much room still exists within it.

Up until 1989, these companies had been run like independents, publishing work of a literary nature. Even if a publication didn't yield much profit, the thinking was that it was enriching the culture. The late 1960s had seen the rise of the midlist, books that sell 3,000-10,000 copies:, more than enough to economically justify their publication for a small publisher but not enough to sustain the Literary Industrial Complex's needs. These include titles like women's literature, Black liberation literature, and gay rights literature as well as work speaking to the perspectives of many people on the margins, or people of peripheral political perspectives. But gradually this thinking yielded to business consolidation.

In 1965, G.P. Putnam acquired Berkeley Books. Both companies were then sold to Music Corporation of America (MCA) in 1975, who in turn sold the company to British multinational conglomerate Pearson, forming Penguin Group in 1996.

In 1975, Gulf and Western Industries bought Simon & Schuster, and it has changed hands between several multinational television corporations since then. Time, Inc, and Warner Communications merged in 1989 to create the Time Warner corporation and eventually sold its book group off to the French corporation Hachette Livre in 2006.

In 1989, Rupert Murdoch entered the public consciousness when his News Corporation bought HarperCollins. Holtzbrinck bought MacMillan (formerly St. Martin's Press) in 1995. In 1998, the German

Bertelsman group, whose major asset was America Online, bought Random House and merged it with Bantam Doubleday Dell, which rapidly created the largest publishing company in the world. In 2013, they merged with Penguin Group to create Penguin Random House (PRH).

This chain of events launched the Literary Industrial Complex, a series of consolidated conglomerates who began to treat books more like commodities than culture.

By the 1990s, the publishers that were once run as professional hobbies of independently wealthy people were suddenly being pushed into only focusing on profit centers. Once bastions of ideas, they were now being run by accountants instead of tastemakers, who quickly axed the aforementioned "midlist" titles as a matter of simple economics. You can see the difference if you take a look at books published by major houses before and after their biggest mergers. Today, major houses focus strongly on celebrity memoirs and other books that have virtually guaranteed sales. This has created room for the independent publishers of today to fill in that midlist, and this is where you come in. Books that are expected to sell 5,000 copies aren't sufficient for a company with annual revenues of three billion dollars. But to a small or midlist publisher like yourself, those are perfectly wonderful sales.

These are all trade publishers, meaning that they primarily produce books for the general public that are designed to be sold through conventional channels like bookstores. Each one of these companies publishes over a thousand new books per year and maintains a back catalog (the industry term is "backlist") bigger than a phone book. They frequently acquire new divisions and merge with other companies strategically to maintain their volume and upper hand.

Outside the Big Five, there are numerous other publishers with income over $100M: Scholastic, Thomson, McGraw Hill, Workman Publishing, John Wiley & Sons, and Quarto Book Group. Other publishers who sell millions of dollars of books each year include Abrams Books and Chronicle Books.

Initially, your sales will be in the thousands of dollars per year. It took Microcosm four years to reach $100,000 annually, which felt like infinite success until I researched sales of other publishers. Today, our sales hover over one million dollars per year. Midlist presses of a similar size include PM Press, Feral House, Haymarket Books, Fantagraphics Books, and Bazillion Points.

There are also literally hundreds of thousands of publishers so small that they don't have staff or even an office. This tiny size is a good place to start—with a small desk in your living room and a clear idea of what you want to publish.

Let's look at some more terms to help you understand the wide breadth of the ecosphere:

Division/Imprint: The Literary Industrial Complex buys so many formerly independent companies and launches so many new lines that they distinguish them as "divisions." Within those divisions are independent imprints. There are around two thousand imprints. These presses are often run independently of their parent companies but with a strong financial imperative (read: if the editors' books aren't selling well enough, they get canned). For example, Threshold

Editions, which infamously purchased the rights for Breitbart commentator Milo Yiannopoulos' *Dangerous,* is an imprint of major house Simon & Schuster. Their editors worked independently of the top brass so they didn't need to approve this decision with their bosses' bosses. Still, when the controversy heated up, they fled from the book like a time bomb. These companies often appear to be independents but are not because they have the financial backing of their parent companies.

Technical Publisher: Even though Houghton Mifflin Harcourt has an income over one billion dollars per year, they are not part of the "Big Five" because their primary focus is on technical books and textbooks, which are not developed as trade books. A non-trade publisher focuses their effort not on creating products for the general public but on developing books for academics, experts, professionals, and students—technical books, textbooks, reference titles, and things only professionals would need. For example, most people wouldn't be purchasing a $250 book about architecture or psychology or fabricating bicycles written in jargon that only experts understand. The prices on these books are higher because the sales potential is much lower. The audiences are small and the authority of the author is a given. There are also many non-profit textbook and University-affiliated presses creating peer-reviewed academic books like Houghton Mifflin, albeit on a much smaller scale.

Independent Press: A press that is often owned by the publisher that can make decisions independently and without oversight. An independent press is self-financed and receives the consequences of its actions. Confusingly, self-published authors are trying to co-opt this idea by referring to their self-publishing companies as "independent presses." Since the barrier to entry is so low, there are roughly one million independent presses in operation today.

Small Press: A small press typically has a staff of one to five, often including the owner who tends to double as the editor and publisher. Small presses tend to have a specific focus, like literary fiction, empowering children's books, radical politics, photography how-to, medical reference, psychology, or business management. Except in rare cases, a small press does not exist only to release books by the publisher, which is where its credibility comes from. There are roughly 100,000 small presses in existence today.

Midlist Publisher: An independent publisher with established credibility in a certain subject or genre and a distribution network. Most midlist publishers have a staff of 3-10 employees and income in the hundreds of thousands, or millions, of dollars per year. Midlist publishers are respected throughout the industry and will often be purchased and absorbed by the Literary Industrial Complex or be distributed by them.

Vanity Publisher: Vanity "publishers" charge fees to an author before publication and create a book-shaped object without contributing to its professional development. Vanity publishing goes back to the beginning of private wealth, where an "author" could pay exorbitant fees for a "publishing" company to "publish" their book without the difficulties of writing something worth reading.

Indie Author: Authors who have rebranded vanity publishing but still self-publish their work, typically through Amazon's Kindle and CreateSpace programs. The oddity here is that none of the companies that indie authors use are remotely independent. They are the same companies that control the vast majority of retail distribution in the publishing industry.

Authorpreneur: Graduating from the deprecating depths of being an indie author, "authorpreneurs" have rebranded vanity twice to distinguish themselves from indie authors. They are indie authors who pay other people for services that a publisher would normally perform for them for free, like cover design, editorial, development, sensitivity reading, and publicity.

Author Services: Some companies confusingly market themselves as publishers that offer printing services with "author services," essentially charging authors fees for tasks normally performed by the publisher. Most of these companies sell packages from $799 to $9,999 for services that authors often think they need, like having their book sold on Amazon, making it available to bookstore buyers, or marketing it for potential TV and radio publicity spots. Buyer beware: often such companies abuse the would-be self-published authors' trust and lack of knowledge to sell expensive services that do not actually have much value.

Hybrid Publisher: At hybrid companies, downsized industry professionals are mildly selective about which authors' money they will take and create a professional book that is completely financed by the author. This small step up from self-publishing can masquerade as being traditionally published, by combining the best aspects of vanity and traditional publishing—though the book is almost always left without distribution and does not follow industry standards of publication. Ultimately this is a failed proposition because the author has the final say and—even with the help of industrial consultants—is too emotionally close to their own work to make decisions that would allow it to thrive on the shelf.

Clear Topic + Reputation = Sales

Know what you love and publish it so clearly and repeatedly that your readers will pick up on it. You will be tempted to try new things periodically, but it's vital to remain consistent.

A few years ago, Microcosm published *Amica's World,* a book by Jane Goodall and Washo Shadowhawk, her first youth award winner. The book was about adopting a giant flightless bird and had all of the trappings of a successful title...for a nature publisher. We are not a nature publisher, and this title was met with much confusion. One reporter was polite enough to point out "This does *not* seem like a Microcosm book." Our sales staff said nice things like "This could be a major bestseller" but only implied the subtext "for a publisher who typically handles books of this type." And it's true. We lacked the relationships and reputation to make the title work.

By contrast, our bestselling book, *Make Your Place: Affordable, Sustainable Nesting Skills* is a DIY book about how to turn your house into a home without chemicals. The book feels like a throwback to the Whole Earth catalog of the 1970s. *Make Your Place* was published right as the recession hit in 2008 and has since sold over 125,000 copies. As a result, this is the kind of title that stores, the industry, and reviewers expect from us. We are too small of a company to also create a gift book about nature that has completely different standards in terms of price point, production, trim size, value, and page count.

On the other hand, when we released *Homesweet Homegrown*, a book about how to garden inside a small apartment and cook and preserve the vegetables, it was a success and has sold about 15,000 copies. It's because *Homesweet Homegrown* and *Make Your Place* are both understood by the same audience. The likelihood of the same person enjoying both of them is much greater. Over many years, repetition and consistency have built our reputation in this category of producing small trim paperbacks that sell well beyond the industry average.

Find your niche and stick with it. Expand slowly into adjacent categories in a way that makes sense to your audience. Otherwise you have to reinvent the wheel with each new area of specialty.

Start Small, Make Mistakes on a Smaller Scale

Your first few books are your least likely to be successful and you're most likely to have embarrassing errors that communicate your amateurism to people who are familiar with the industry. That's okay. Start small and grow gradually. It's much better than amping yourself up on your first project and being disappointed when it doesn't have the huge successes that you are counting on it to achieve.

When I founded Microcosm, I put away $100 from each week's paycheck to invest in the press. At the time that felt like a lot of money to me. Gradually I used this money to print zines and order from other publishers. As those items sold, I put the money back into ordering and grew sales by 10-25% each year. Zines are a wonderful way to see if there's interest in a subject before you sink your fortune into it. For the cost of $40 and a few hours, you can get some solid feedback and know if you have a dud on your hands.

To be fair, if I was starting out today, I don't think it would be possible to grow to our size and scale without considerable resources doing it the exact way that I did. But there's a new path waiting for you. You'll just need to identify it and carve it out.

When I needed $4,000 to print my first book, I had a large enough platform that I could go to my audience, state my intention to publish something that was a bit more expensive and ask for preorders and regular orders to bring in the revenue. Nowadays, this is exactly what Kickstarter is for. I constantly read about companies investing "only" $10,000 into their publishing startup, and I wonder who can afford to sink that much money on a creative scheme in a small-margin industry. Today, I would recommend graduating from zines to adapting the ones that sell best into paperbacks. Testing with zines first will also give you a sense of which authors are willing to hustle on behalf of their books. If you are still apprehensive or risk averse, companies like Lightning Source or Lulu.com can produce books a single copy at a time and, while the production isn't as nice as offset printing and the unit cost is much higher, it's part of a steep learning curve where you can afford to learn from your mistakes without getting frustrated and throwing in the towel.

PRINT BESTSELLERS, MIDLIST, AND FLOPS
THE DECLINE AND RISE OF THE BESTSELLER

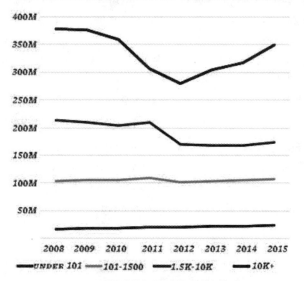

UNDER 101 — 101-1500 — 1.5K-10K — 10K+

UNITS SOLD BY YEAR

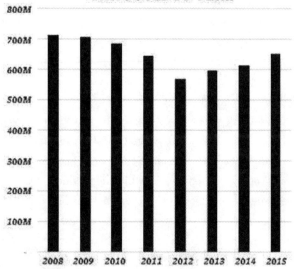

In the technology world, this is called "proof of concept." If an idea can demonstrate sufficient interest and can sufficiently scale up to the necessary size to support the company, it works. This method will allow you to learn all aspects of development, production, marketing, sales, and distribution without losing your home while also building and maintaining relationships with stores and reviewers that become very valuable within a few years.

Haymarket Books, a Chicago nonprofit publisher that equips activists to take ideas, history, and politics into social justice struggles, began small with two people and an idea in 2001. According to publisher and co-founder Julie Fain, "We started with a commitment to the premise of 'books for changing the world.' As people directly involved in social movements, we knew how important it was for other activists to have books that spoke to the questions and debates happening." Since then, Haymarket has sold over one million books, including over 100,000 copies of Rebecca Solnit's *Men Explain Things to Me*. Julie explains that the future can be surprising. "We didn't know that over ten years later we'd be putting out almost 50 books a year and publishing some of our political and literary heroes. I still have to pinch myself about that all the time!"

Adam Gamble, publisher of the now very successful children's picture book company Good Night Books, began his publishing company with an ambitious investment. While working as a journalist, he self-published 5,000 copies of a guidebook to Cape Cod, *In the Footsteps of Thoreau*, because "I didn't think I would get paid enough by local publishers or have enough control. I financed it and my next 40 or so titles by other authors with credit cards. I sold about 4,000 copies in the first six months and began making money leading nature walks and doing slideshows. I had had no idea what I was doing, but the results were far better than I could have hoped, so much so that I never went back to being a reporter and have only had a couple of short stints of being employed by someone else. I discovered I have a somewhat unusual aptitude at both business, sales, and being creative—writing, design and an eye for art. I honestly wouldn't change a single thing about that book."

You may not have the skills, timing, circumstances, or luck that Adam did. So unless you have money that you can afford to lose, it's better to start very small. Or as Per Henningsgaard, former director of publishing at Ooligan Press, advises, "If you sink a lot of money into printing with the wrong paper, binding, ink, or margins, those decisions and mistakes can make the difference between your first five books becoming a write-off or not."

Asia Citro, publisher of The Innovation Press, learned this lesson in a major way. She published an oversized children's gift book where every page was printed on very heavy paper with a special binding that would lay flat when the book was open. The comparable titles had sold millions and critics loved Asia's book. But everything that could go wrong, did. She printed 5,000 copies and after all of her costs, she had spent $9 per copy. The book sold fewer than 1,000 copies. Her primary sales channel is her trade distributor so even if she had sold them all, her net earning on those first 5,000 that retail for $21.95 each would be $8.12 per book. So even if she sold every copy she would be *losing 88 cents per book*. Her cost per unit was too high. She would have to sell 10,000 copies for the book to be slightly profitable.

Evaluate the worst case scenario and only take risks you can stomach and recover from, and create some distance from emotional decisions. Adam Gamble advises to "avoid listening to other people too closely, as few others are risking their own money, yet many others will benefit from risking mine."

Ignore the parts of the industry that you cannot afford to compete with. You won't launch the next Amazon. (If you do, please write to me and tell me that I'm wrong and how you did it.) But you might control a niche of books about gardening or invent a new genre of fantasy books that HarperCollins hasn't even considered. Small presses' strength is in the niche—a successful book sells 5,000 copies, not 50,000. At this volume, you can take on different books that the majors cannot and slowly build your own industry in parallel to theirs. And by focusing on direct sales, specialty markets, and gift accounts first, you can shed much of the highly contextual and competitive aspects of publishing.

So How Do I Succeed?

The hip hop artist Jay-Z, who has sold over 100 million albums and is worth over $800M offers business advice in his book, *Decoded*, that he says he learned as a street drug dealer. Roughly paraphrased, he believes that there are three things that make a person good at business:

1. **The ability to do math in your head**

2. **Being a good judge of character**

3. **Making quick decisions**

When I read this, I immediately thought that these are the basic building blocks of a publisher. I would add critical thinking skills and a willingness to work hard, which Jay-Z also exhibits in force. I've always been quite good at #1 and #3 and mastered #2 later in life. But again, by being loud and proud about my values and politics, I've been able to naturally repel the kind of people that I don't want to deal with. With time, I learned to trust my gut and realized that I was an instinctually good judge of character. Even if you have these skills naturally, you will likely need to practice and hone them as you find yourself in unfamiliar social situations with highly skilled negotiators.

My "Rules" for Publishing (in Brief)

In 2012, after having outside management for six years, I returned to my role as the publisher and general manager. The staff and I jokingly wrote down these on our office chalkboard and someone wrote "The Rules" on top. Over time they became less of a joke and increasingly vital.

1. **Believe in yourself:** You can't do anything if you have constant imposter syndrome. You're the boss. You're the publisher. You have to make good decisions, and to do that and to have others believe in you, you have to believe in yourself.

2. **No accidents:** Do things intentionally. Don't fall off a ladder packing shelves. Be conscious of and consider the possible impact of your actions so you aren't surprised when something plays out differently than you intended.

How to Make a Decision

What is my desired outcome?

What is the simplest solution to achieve it? Is there an easier way?

Does my idea work for everybody involved?

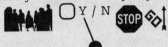 Y / N STOP GO

Are the costs & consequences acceptable?

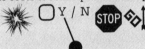 Y / N STOP GO

What are the worst, best, and likely outcomes? Can I manage them all?

 Y / N STOP GO

Does this decision cause harm to anyone I care about and/or our relationship?

STOP GO Y / N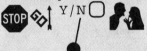

Does this decision take too much time and energy
from the things I want and need to do?

STOP GO Y / N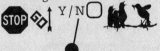

Could this decision cost more money than I can afford? Is there a cheaper way?

STOP GO Y / N

DO IT!

3. **Talk about your problems:** This is how problems are solved. Find people that have been reliable to you in the past and that you can trust. Find a mentor who has been down this road before. If you have something that you can easily explain and need a quick answer, shoot me an email. Sometimes just asking the question out loud is enough to realize the answer, even when there's nobody to ask.

4. **Respect others but don't let haters get you down**: Not everyone is going to love what you do. Reviewers are not always going to "get" your books and will sometimes tear them apart. Sometimes a stranger will develop a vendetta against you because your vision gets under their skin in just the wrong way. It doesn't matter. They aren't going to support you, so focus instead on the people that love what you do. At the same time, don't stoop to their level or develop a reactionary relationship. Respect them. Oftentimes years later you'll meet and become friends. But that cannot happen if you aren't respectful or if you develop an adversarial relationship.

5. **Complain as necessary**: Get it out. You need to offload periodically. You don't need to have an audience around for your complaints, but things will go wrong and your feelings will be hurt and you will need to express yourself. Don't do this on social media as it just looks grumpy and bitter. Talk to people who care about you. More importantly, keep a gratitude journal. Each day write down three things that happened in your publishing career that you are thankful for. Doing so will give you a positive outlook and the good things that are happening to you will outweigh the negative ones.

6. ***Drink iced tea (or other suitable beverage)***: Having routines and comforts around is important. You need something to reward yourself with when you achieve a goal or finish a major project. Caffeine runs in the veins of the industry, so don't let your habit get out of control but keep things around that make you feel better.

7. ***Don't stop believing***: Again, things will go wrong. In 2006 our printer used the wrong line screen on 4,000 copies of our most expensive book ever. It cost us $18,000. They refused to reprint and told us that we would have to get a lawyer to negotiate the issue. We walked away from that printer and passed out the books for free. Friends still mention this incident and tell me that they cannot believe that I kept publishing after that debacle. Six years later the printer came under new ownership and they offered us a credit to come back. We've been working with them ever since and still are seven years later. Sure, you could walk away and burn the whole thing down, but conflicts have a wonderful way of resolving themselves if you keep your eye on your goals and values.

For Now, Let's Do Some Homework:

- What are your values?

- What is your mission?

- What is your vision?

- What are your goals?

- Who is your competition?

- Who is your audience?

- How do you talk to them?

- What does your success look like?

THE LIFE CYCLE OF A BOOK

IDEA
- Author or publisher comes up with a concept! Everyone is hesitant, yet excited.

RESEARCH
- Investigation into existing books in print, available niches, and best practices. P&L is created.

CONTRACT
- Author and publisher come to agreement, plan the release.

EDITORIAL
- Editor reviews author's work, offers insight to create best book possible.

PRODUCTION/DESIGN
- Book is designed for proper trim size and page count as well as having an appropriate cover created!

SALES/PUBLICITY MEETINGS
- Publisher begins talking to wholesalers, bookstores, reviewers, and media.

PRINTING/MASS PRODUCTION
- Print size is determined. Book is printed!

WAREHOUSING/FULFILLMENT
- The books are stored somewhere. The orders are sent out as they come in! Peak momentum is reached!

ROYALTIES
- Author gets a fat check! P&L is updated to show how first year of selling went.

PULPING
- Sales slow down. Remaining books are turned into paper so they aren't taxed.

RIGHTS SALES
- Sell the book to a new publisher!

REMAINDER

HALF PRICE BOOKS
- Sales less than expected. Copies are sold on the cheap to re-seller.

NEW EDITION / REPRINT
- It keeps selling! Hurry! Make more!

47

HOW TO *STARVE*

 Compare self to others on Facebook every day

 Punch down/Criticize

 Fear change

 Hold a grudge

 Talk about people

 Know it all

 Blame others for failures

 Feel entitled

 Never set goals

 Dictate others' experiences

 Internalize criticism

48

HOW TO *THRIVE*

 Read every day

 Respect/Compliment

 Embrace change

 Forgive

 Talk about ideas

 Learn daily

 Accept responsibility

 Feel gratitude

 Have a long-term plan towards real goals

 Learn from people with different experiences

 Embrace meaning and purpose!

1. BUILD YOUR MOVEMENT

Make Books that Need to Exist

Starting around 2007, I began to hear nothing but doom and gloom from the publishing industry: print is dead, readers only want digital, some corporation bought so and so, it's all over, yada yada.

I had watched as even Loompanics Unlimited closed up shop for good in 2006. Loompanics was Michael Hoy's mouthpiece for anti-government screeds that attacked libertarians for their corporatism as much as mainstream Republicans and Democrats. They had titles about how to pick locks, perform lewd acts, and espousing anti-government views that they had published steadfastly since 1975. They were the last company that I expected to close.

Publishing sales dipped in 2012 after a period of sustained growth. Investments and expenses dropped as publishers began to anticipate the takeover of digital products. Unit sales faltered, especially for small publishers who were investing less in fewer new titles. There was tremendous uncertainty about the future of publishing.

The rise of eBooks hit the public in 2007—just as the U.S. was hitting the stock market recession. In order to introduce the new technology and attempt to convert readers to it, many eBooks were given away for free or priced at 99 cents. Readers came to see eBooks as having little or no value. In an increasingly competitive market, underpriced and underdeveloped eBooks began cannibalizing sales from all books and lowering the tide for all ships.

Still, there are exceptions: books that people would be embarrassed to be seen reading on the bus—romance, thriller, murder mystery, throwaway science fiction, or serialized fantasy novels—did very well in digital formats. You and I could wax philosophical all day about the tangible nature of books, but let's face it, it's much harder to build a movement digitally when you are reliant upon artificially underpriced content and major corporations that are working in their best interest, not yours.

With fear on the industry's horizon that digital would usurp and destroy publishing one book at a time, 2013 was Microcosm's second-best year behind 2006. Through business savvy and hard work, we paid off our old debts, re-instituted raises and a year-end bonus for our staff, published twenty new titles, and moved into a new, larger office that we are working towards owning. And we did all of this without a single book selling over 5,000 copies that year. Since then, several other publishers have quietly told me that the dark years during the recession were also their best for sales. Bookstores were struggling during this time, but our survival came down to developmental styles and situating titles for specialty markets like pet shops, urban homesteading supply stores, and record stores. The fact that we were publishing low-cost books that taught tangible skills on how to survive a recession probably didn't hurt either. As consumer spending habits climbed again, so did our prices.

Publishing is like gambling. Some bets are better than others, but in the end it's still a gamble. Prior to 2013, we relied upon a single title to sell over 10,000 copies each year and pay the bills. So we shifted gears and now focus on having a positive relationship with the right printer, keeping around 400 books in print that each give us a steady trickle year after year, constantly rechecking the math on our spreadsheets, keeping track of who is buying our work and what kinds of things they like best, working with authors who are great self-promoters, building relationships with blogs, and putting attention into production, design, and all of the little details. This strategy has allowed us to be successful on our own terms while having the privilege of avoiding Amazon's creepy influence on books.

Because my roots are as a teenage punk rocker working out of a bedroom, this approach made perfect sense to me, and we have chosen to stay independent of outside financial pressure and influence and continue to publish twelve to twenty new titles per year.

I took more cues from how indie record labels like Dischord, SST, or Lookout Records interact with the music industry than from how small publishers like Soft Skull Press or Seal Press operate within the publishing industry. We have always operated slightly outside of, but parallel to, The Literary Industrial Complex. By ignoring aspects of the industry that we couldn't afford to compete with and building interest outside of traditional channels, we quietly appeared as a formidable force. In 2011, a confused Calvin Reid from *Publisher's Weekly* exclaimed, "Why have I never heard of you?" when we were signing with a new distributor.

We did not use a proper trade distributor for our first fifteen years, mostly because we didn't need one. Instead, we built our ground game, doing tours through small towns with a pop-up bookstore. Fans passed out our catalogs in far-away cities. We sold books at events where there were no other books in sight.

Today, we still focus 95% of our efforts on print because it is more environmentally responsible and gives us much more freedom in keeping our money in the U.S. manufacturing economy—and also because nonfiction books like ours just don't sell in electronic formats. We actively build a movement of people who believe in the work and subjects that we promote, like self-empowerment (based on lived experiences more than experts), gender (in the most subversive way possible), punk rock (what's interesting culturally about it, besides the nostalgia), and bicycling (culture and transportation, not exercise or sport). I created a successful press that never made it onto the radar of the Literary Industrial Complex because I was playing their game but ignoring their rules.

Despite popular misconceptions, print books are still the preferred choice among readers. Around 2011, digital products and eBooks peaked at around 8% of total book sales and continue to shrink to their current state of around 4% of market share. Amazingly, eBooks only comprise about 1% of total sales at Microcosm.

Ian Christe founded coffee-table music book publisher Bazillion Points after publishing *Sound of the Beast: The Complete Headbanging History of Heavy Metal* with HarperCollins. Despite selling hundreds of thousands of copies in the U.S. and a dozen foreign editions, he could not get a contract for a follow-up title.

He was receiving frequent inquiries from people asking how to get books published about various music movements and the lack of interest he received from the Literary Industrial Complex for this kind of work even after such a successful book led him to the only logical solution: starting his own publishing company. He has maintained unique production values and credibility for the quality and consistency of his work. People who want authentic and thorough examinations of a music scene know to look for the gothic "B" on the spine of an oversized hardcover. His is the only functional way to approach publishing in the modern era, meaning that he recognized there is an audience under the surface hungry for work like his, and he hustles relentlessly to get books to readers.

Even so, the focus of many new publishers is on literary quality rather than what readers are actually looking for. Microcosm offers three intern positions every quarter. Often these are filled by aspiring editors; young people who want a job that largely doesn't exist anymore. We do our best to explain that editorial jobs have more to do with occupying niches than creating literary masterpieces. We tell them the story of a friend who began volunteering at a local small press many years ago, after dropping out of high school. He was more interested in the press's political mission than their literary merit and was soon put to work as a proofreader. Knowing nothing about the correct use of grammar or placement of punctuation, he suggested that another task might be more appropriate. The staff assured him that they weren't concerned about his ignorance and, predictably, one book came back from the printer with innumerable typos throughout, including an egregious one on the front cover. Rather than harming the book's credibility, the typos cemented the identity of the publisher as a struggling underdog that was deserving of financial support, and the book went on to sell out of several printings.

Still, each and every intern will protest, "But don't the books have to be *good?!*" To which I merely point to the example of *50 Shades of Grey*. It was originally published in 2009 as *Twilight* fanfiction under the title *Master of the Universe* on FanFiction.net. Author E.L. James was an aggressive promoter that knew how to drive traffic and capture over 50,000 reviews in her first two years on the site. Even then, community members found the writing to be derivative and borrowed heavily from other fanfiction writers of its era. *50 Shades* was too sexually explicit for FanFiction.net's community guidelines and was removed. The Writer's Coffee Shop, a tiny press specializing in works too explicit for FanFiction.net, picked up the book for publication in May of 2011. The editors changed the names of *Twilight* characters and fans were excited to be able to share this work in a format that was more credible with readers outside of their community. Even though they were digitally printing one book at a time, the book was outselling *Harry Potter* in England and the rights were bought by Vintage, a division of Random House, for forty million dollars. Vintage was careful to maintain the same editorial work and amateur cover design as to not lose the value of their new property. The book was hated by critics for its lack of literary style, and Salman Rushdie was quoted saying that he had "never read anything so badly written that got published. It made *Twilight* look like War and Peace." Regardless, the book went on to sell over 125 million copies.

Penguin Random House is the largest publisher in the world with sales of over $9.2 billion in 2016 and over 250 imprints. Why would they need to buy a book from a tiny publisher that virtually no one has never heard of, let alone for so much money? Because resources are the most common enemy of innovation and creative thinking. Consumer habits are not controlled by the opinions of critics or experts, and *50 Shades* teaches us that the emotional payoff and concept are more important than the editorial quality of a successful book. There was an available niche so big that mainstream publishing houses were blinded by it. The book was so influential that it changed consumer habits for lingerie and sex toys and was the fastest selling book *ever* in the UK. Indeed, the underground is bigger than the mainstream.

The idea that "well-written" books are what is sought is a fallacy born of the Literary Industrial Complex and MFA writing programs that convince authors to prioritize well-developed narratives and complex characters. But in reality this writing is just another type of marketing that strategically limits your work to a very specific readership. Perpetuating this myth isn't helpful to anyone. Publishers seek books that tap into the niches that they know how to speak respectfully to. Believe it or not, many wide niches still exist even as more mainstream/literary genres continue to be completely saturated. Per Henningsgaard, publisher of Ooligan Press, explained "Good niches come from very particular kinds of passions. Not just science fiction. What kind of science fiction? You really need to dig and read widely enough to determine where there's an unmet need. Where is there a lack of representation that you identify with and feel passionately about the niche?"

How to Create New Audiences for Books

Mary Applehof was a pioneer in vermicomposting, the practice of breaking down garbage with worms. A student of biology in the 1950s, Applehof taught the world how to recreate nature's ability to break down waste in our backyards, especially to recycle food waste. By the 1970s, she had taught thousands of children how to compost with worms. Following her passions and paying little regard to money, she bought a mimeograph machine and self-published her book *Worms Eat My Garbage* in 1982, naming her operation Flower Press. This book became the definitive resource on the subject for children *and* adults and consequently sold hundreds of thousands of copies. She passed away in 2005, and her family has fought over the rights to her work, which was eventually acquired by Storey Publishing for a proper new edition in 2017.

Many people who were inspired by Applehof's legacy wrote vermicomposting books that sold relatively well. She is responsible for creating a niche based on her passions and expertise that effectively made many others just as excited about worms as she was. That's the best success one can hope for because passionate readers continue to sell books and stir passions long after she's gone!

You should focus on publishing books that fit your mission and politics, that you know how to sell, and that meet your personal definition of "good."

C. Spike Trotman, a Black female comics artist with a mohawk and facial piercings, sports a handwritten sign at events proclaiming "I was told there was no room for the kind of comics I love. So I built one. I am non-compliant." Trotman has since raised over one million dollars on Kickstarter for publishing comics on diverse topics from erotica to how-to. Just like Christe, Trotman functionally approaches publishing by recognizing an audience excited for her work and is willing to work hard to reach them.

Similar to Spike Trotman's rejection from traditional publishers for her vision of erotic comics with diverse protagonists, science fiction has long been dominated by male writers with male visions writing about male subjects. In 1975, seemingly in response to the men who had been elbowing women out of publishing scenes for hundreds of years, Janice Bogstad created *Janus*, a feminist sci-fi zine that featured writers including Octavia Butler and Joanna Russ. Bogstad brought a feminist edge to science fiction and cultivated a generation of women sci-fi authors that thrived in its community. The zine was nominated for a Hugo Award in 1978, 1979, and 1980 and was subsequently taken over by an editorial committee who later founded WisCon, the leading feminist science fiction convention that continues to this day. Bogstad created an entire generation of women sci-fi authors and publishers. More recently, queer and intersectional sci-fi writers launched their own movements. And Elly Blue, co-owner of Microcosm, is quietly birthing the bicycle feminist sci-fi scene.

How do you find a vacant niche? Use Amazon as your research tool. Find subjects and categories where the top four titles are ranked in the top 100,000 of all books. If none of the books in that subject are in the top 100,000, not enough people are looking for books on this subject. If the top four books are in the top 100,000, see if one expert or celebrity author dominates the field. If they do, it will be difficult for you to break in. You can't compete with a credentialed famous person unless you have the same strength or are smarter or lucky. Move on until you find a subject with lots of demand where there is room for you to add your voice.

Major publishers perform similar research with NPD Decision Key and expensive software like Acumen, Trilogy, or CoreSource interpreted by experts. They use profit and loss statements (see page 244) to determine probable sales, expenses, and figure out how much a reasonable royalty advance is. Using the free, public data on Amazon, you can work the system backwards and find genres and types of books that could sell enough based on the size of the niche and demand for it.

Alternately, you can find a niche within a niche or use similar subject matter to reach a different audience. For example, since the late 1970s, crafting books were thought of as a market for women over 50. Around 2006 knitting books aimed at women in their early 20s were published and became quite successful. Naturally, within a few years the market for knitting books for young women was also saturated as many publishers made imitations of successful pack leaders. Similarly, queer Mormon erotica might surprise you in the size and scope of its readership. A niche within a niche is often the amount of specificity that can allow your books to stand out in a crowded market.

The most important question to ask yourself is "Why would people read this book?" Strangers will not care that your books are notable to you but rather how they apply to their life, experiences, or people that they care about. Figure out what is unique about your books compared to similar ones on the same topics and how you can better inform the lives of others.

But remember: upwards of 10,000 new books will be published tomorrow. And the same on the following day. And the same on the day after that. That adds millions of books to the market each year on top of the tens of millions of books in print and perennial bestsellers. Build an authentic relationship with your audience and stand above the competition by clearly defining your book and its reason for existing.

Homework:

- What is my niche?

- Why would people read this book?

- How will I connect authentically with my audience?

- How do I stand out?

- Do I know my audience or am I going to create them? How?

- What am I most excited about?

2. TITLE DEVELOPMENT

How To Make Books that Readers Will Find & Relate To

There are two statistics that are vital for understanding publishing. First, Jeff Bezos earns more in the time that it takes you to read this sentence than the average Amazon employee does all year. Second, NPD Decision Key reports that 93% of books in print sold fewer than 50 copies in 2018. The system serves the top so now that you've identified your niche, it's time to learn how to continually land in the top 7%!

Good books cause strong feelings. Title development is what makes those feelings click. Title development is the vital leg on your stool; it is where you create the perfect title, subtitle, cover design, trim size, cover price, production values, and promised emotional payoff to the reader.

Title development is the most important part of publishing. Remember, there are thousands of books being published today and you have four seconds to capture the reader's attention. Proper development is how you stand out and establish credibility. Your development for the title should be referred to at every step of your decision making process. Development is the most vital leg of the stool because it conveys subconscious information about the credibility of the book that informs a potential reader's decision when standing in a bookstore or hovering over a Buy button online.

The short formula for good development is Niche + Price + Quality = Success!

Mark Suchomel, Senior Vice President of Sales & Client Services for Baker & Taylor Publisher Services and founder of Legato Publishers Group, explains, "You can't expect a good book to sell. There has to be a reason that is expressed through a good cover that communicates what the consumer gets out of the book. What's it going to do for me?"

You want your book's development to make the most compelling proposition: "What if there was life on Mars?" or "How to create the most fuel-efficient vehicle on the planet." If your book is ultimately about you or your life, this isn't of interest to people unless you are an A-List celebrity. (If you are, congratulations, and please get in touch!) For everyone else, readers want to know how your book relates to them and what it has to do with their life, interests, and experience. Michelle Tea's memoir *How To Grow Up* answered this question clearly and thus was more successful than it would have been without reader-orientation.

Most publishers orient their development around their biggest accounts. In the 1980s and 90s, publishers developed books that would entice large sales to Borders and Barnes & Noble. If the order wasn't sufficiently large, the publisher would cancel publication. For obvious reasons, the results made publishing less diverse in terms of focus and scope, as well as creating a fairly myopic publishing industry where a painful majority of authors were neurotypical, upper-class, white men. This closed-minded and fearful approach is ultimately what created so much space for small presses to challenge the status quo. We don't need to sell anywhere near the quantities that the majors do to make money and as a result, our catalogs are more interesting and innovative.

Develop the Nuts and Bolts of Your Book

After Asia Citro had a child with severe colic, she began inventing sensory-based activities as a way to engage and distract both her children and herself. Her friends convinced her to start sharing the activities on a blog. Soon, Ashton Kutcher and George Takei were sharing her writing, she had fifteen posts go viral, and 40 million visits to her blog. She published a book with a Simon & Schuster imprint which sold around 100,000 copies. After that experience she wanted to be in charge and launched The Innovation Press to publish her own books. She has a master's degree in science education, and could only find books about science inquiry for teachers, so she created one for parents. She began writing a series of books that could be used in conjunction with each other. She wanted to create books full of activities that were fun for the parents as well as the children. She adorns her covers with pictures of girls instead of boys, and the protagonists on the cover of *Zoey and Sassafras* are Black. She features kids wearing hijabs in *Mossby's Magic Carpet Handbook*. The amazing thing about her niche is that her biggest customers are still the major industry accounts like Books-A-Million, Barnes & Noble, and Amazon. More importantly, her approach was based in what the market was lacking rather than what these major accounts said they wanted. Citro identified a major gap in the market that she wanted as a reader. She correctly surmised that there were other parents who wanted educational outdoor activities with their children. As a result, she sold 125,000 books in her first two years. Scholastic, who controls 33% of all children's book sales, began making offers to license her titles.

In a similar example, Laura Stanfill, publisher of literary fiction powerhouse Forest Avenue Press based in Portland, Oregon, received a pitch from her graphic designer, Gigi Little, for a collection of sci-fi stories riffing on the popular "Keep Portland Weird" theme. *City of Weird: 30 Otherworldly Portland Tales* has been on the bestseller list of the largest bookstore in the world, Powell's Books, for over a year and is now going into its fourth printing. Its sales have surpassed Stanfill's previous bestsellers by a wide margin. Often, fiction titles sell while the authors are touring and reviews keep popping up, but *City of Weird* has kept selling long after its active publicity pushes have dried up. This type of book is called an evergreen. The eye-catching octopus monster on the cover, a low price of $15.95 for 312 pages, and the catchy subject matter have definitely helped, but so has the attention this book has received from independent bookstores in the Northwest. Powell's featured it for multiple major promotions and it continues to receive high-profile shelf space at many regional stores. There will always be new readers for this book as tourists and residents come and go and want a literary keepsake.

Forest Avenue featured other anthologies in 2012 and 2014, but they did not result in anywhere near the level of *City of Weird*'s sales record. Laura suggests having a really focused theme and aesthetic direction for books like this with a strong regional angle so that the book can sell itself.

Develop all of your books to have very long lives. You've probably noticed that many Big Five titles are focused on rapidly changing current events like the current state of climate change or an insider's look at the President or a natural disaster or a celebrity who is hot in the news. There were thousands of books about how George W. Bush was a terrible president. These titles burn hot very briefly and then get remaindered or pulped. You can't afford to publish books like this. You want to create the opposite kind of book: an evergreen. You want your book to be as relevant tomorrow as it will be in ten or twenty years. Some time-sensitive information is okay, but you want to avoid including dates or current event references on the cover, unless it's a history book, so it doesn't look outdated quickly.

A successful example of a well-developed book is Howard Zinn's *A People's History of the United States: 1492-Present.* Priced at $19.99 with various editions packaged with either a plain white cover and gothic type or a photograph with an inset title, the book resembles most pieces of assigned school reading but with a radical edge. When it was published in 1980, history books were assumed to be unbiased and centrist, as if neutrality were possible while telling the story of the victors. The premise and title of Howard Zinn's book challenges this assumption and communicates that it's a retelling of American history with a left or radical, disenfranchised perspective. Hundreds of thousands of copies later, the audience still finds the book compelling, and it's clear that this approach has worked.

Now for Examples of Less-Successfully Developed Titles

Major houses make developmental mistakes too! Take a look at the cover of Eric Schlosser's sophomore slump, *Reefer Madness.* I see you rolling your eyes and well you might. But give the book a chance. It's not a story about stoners or a laugh at antiquated anti-marijuana campaigns or an argument that we should all smoke weed. It's actually an economics book, examining the history of some of the biggest black markets in the U.S.—including strawberries, pornography, and, yes, cannabis. But while the book is absolutely fascinating to read, there are some serious packaging errors here. If you picked it up and wanted to read something about weed or thought it might relate to or rebuke the 1936 scared-straight film with the same name, you'd be disappointed. And if you wanted to read a serious history of underground economies and didn't have a friend to tell you what this book was actually about, you'd pass by it every time.

So don't make the mistake that Simon & Schuster did. Realize and accept that as a small independent publisher you will likely have the smallest marketing and publicity budgets of all similar books. Your packaging must compensate, so you will need to spend extra effort developing your book to clearly dictate—visually, emotionally, and linguistically—exactly what benefits it will offer the reader. Be straightforward, but don't forget to have fun with it, too—puns and humor tend to work well. Readers tend to be wiser than your average person and respond well to feeling like they are on the inside of the joke.

Many publishers don't understand book development. An academic doctor self-published a highly specialized technical non-trade (developed to be sold to experts and colleagues rather than in bookstores) book about death. She hired a professional design team who created a beautiful cover of a woman lying face-down on the ground in a manner suggesting that a struggle had occurred. The design takes a serious, professional book and invokes the iconography of a murder mystery. Anyone looking for her book would not find it with this cover, and anyone looking for a murder mystery would he quite shocked to read a highly scientific book about dead people.

At our regional trade show, a local self-published author who became upset when I talked about the need for development and a defined audience told me, "Some writers don't need a niche." She told me about how she does local readings at her library and bookstores and claims to sell her books like hotcakes. Looking at her covers, I couldn't discern if they were fiction or nonfiction, what her books were about, or what the benefits of reading them were. Obviously, she was very skilled at hand-selling but neither an author nor publisher can be present to hand sell every copy of a book and even if they could, it would severely limit the size of the readership. If a stranger can't determine the emotional payoff of your books from looking at the covers, then someone must be present to verbally offer these details to each person who might be interested. It's horribly inefficient and exhausting. Worse, you are losing your passive sales since every copy sold requires quite a bit of individual effort.

The most frequent things that ruin the chances of success with a good book are:

1) There is already a book just like it with a bigger marketing budget.

2) There is not adequate interest in the topic.

3) The development makes it unclear what benefit, if any, the book offers to the reader.

4) The field is crowded with relatively similar books that offer the same thing at relatively the same price and value. So everyone gets

a piece of the pie, but no one's piece is large enough to satisfy their needs.

6) The way that the book is packaged turns off the kind of reader who would enjoy the book.

Develop Before the Book Has Been Written

When working on book development, start by relentlessly reading—or at least researching—the existing books in your niche and genre. Next, spend a few hours in your head defining the benefits of your book to the reader. Write down your brainstorms. Go to two bookstores and then spend an hour on Amazon evaluating the competitive books on the shelf. Find a way to talk about the niche that your book occupies between the existing work and what benefits your book offers to the reader. Polish a speech where you deliver this information in five seconds or less. Once you can do this in your sleep and you've practiced on a few people, master a 30-second follow up about the book in greater depth. Then write the outline of the entire book with the author.

Development is more important than editing because ultimately it's what makes your book get discovered by the kind of person who would enjoy it. It's easy to think of development as superficial, but the packaging of a book, not its content, is usually what makes or breaks it in the end. And even if you hire the best design team in the world, it's a worthless purchase if you can't give them proper direction.

A successful book is the result of many hours of research and critical thinking before it is written. Once you have a strong idea of what your book is, create a proper outline for how the book establishes the emotional payoff and benefits to the reader as well as what its niche is and what the audience looks like. Your research project should give you new ideas or even change your editorial approach entirely. That's *good* because it'll save you a basement of unsold books and a ton of heartache.

The book itself must fulfill the promises that the back cover makes while not repelling its readership. You have a tremendous advantage by doing your development before the book is written. Your books should each tap into a need or demand that other books in print are not addressing. Carefully look at the continuity of the cover designs between all of your competition. Look at the keywords used in the titles and subtitles. Look at how they emphasize the benefits to the reader. Pay close attention to the price per page of these books and price your book accordingly for books in the same subject, production values, and category. Many publishers think that by making their book very different from the successful comp titles that they will stand out. This is folly. Account buyers will ignore a book for this reason because they fear their customers won't "get" it.

While the classic pitch of "Nothing like this has ever been tried before!" sounds tantalizing, it is likely not true and, more important, it does not inspire confidence or sales. Publish a zine or a digital information product instead. These formats scale much better and have much lower costs involved.

On the other extreme, there are publishers who make their living by creating copycats of whatever the current best sellers are. They are trying to crowd a hot subject while readers are still flocking around it. These books shine bright and then burn out hard. If you're independently publishing for the long haul, it's a bad bargain. You're winning the battle to lose the war.

Never write or publish a book solely because of its commercial appeal. You will fail every time. You need the perfect mixture of passion, knowledge, and commitment alongside a vacant niche. If your book is autobiographical or contains elements of memoir in a nonfiction book, this can help the reader feel more invested in the author but the book shouldn't be marketed around this. The reader isn't invested in the author's life yet, so tell them how the book relates to them. Make a list of every sales handle that the book has from "offers a new perspective to teachers" to "a tale of one woman's abortion." Share this information with the author so they are involved in this thinking from the very beginning. You don't want them to be shocked by the final cover design or marketing language. Bring them along for the journey.

Sometimes the process of clearly differentiating and communicating your niche is immediate and obvious. Other times it takes months of back-and-forth and doubt. When you're sure that the world definitely needs a thousandth book about organic kombucha, create a profit and loss statement (see page 244) to determine the likely outcome of publishing that book. The end goal is to make sure that each book is described accurately and that it fills a wanted and empty niche in the world of books so that excited readers can happily discover it.

Even when you follow those rules exactly, there are still things that can go dreadfully wrong. There are long advance windows for publication and things move slowly. A larger publisher can introduce a competing title with a much bigger budget that commands the whole shelf. The author may not be able to write as well as they did in the accepted sample. The premise of the book may not be fulfilled accurately by its execution. The marketing copy and book development may not match the content. The author can be obstinate and a skilled reader can see where the author and editor are at war in the text revisions. Often it is better to delay or cancel publication than to create something that is less than you promised or is just unsellable.

Find Your Muse

Think about what drew you in to your favorite books; go find those books on your shelf or in a bookstore or library. Pick them up, open them, examine every part of them. Ask yourself: What is the cover like? How do the title and subtitle combine to tell a compelling story for why you want to read the book? If you were seeing the book for the first time, what would you think was inside it? Who would you buy it for as a gift?

Go back to your local bookstore. Identify and purchase a successful book that is a comp to your own with jaw-droppingly good development. If you're having trouble, ask an employee what books in your category are most popular. Let one of these books serve as your muse for each decision of your project. Keep it on your desk. Refer to it before making decisions. How did they handle things?

Read articles about your muse title. A book that has already proven successful is the best teacher that you can hope for.

Think of a five-second pitch for your muse book. Then write one for your book. You may have a few different pitches depending on whom you are talking to. Different people and groups have different interests and concerns, and you'll want to think of each of them. Again, one of the most important parts of publishing is to be able to give a clear, concise pitch for each book in five seconds or less with a 30-second follow-up on deck. These are the pitches that you'll use to sell the book on every level from readers at events to executives at wholesalers and distributors and rights sales to other publishers. Write the best ones down and be consistent from here forward when you talk about your book.

Development conventions are used to show where you fit in and how you are unique. When you're starting out, try to be 70% similar to your muse and 30% different to showcase your niche or unique take. As you become more established, be 60% similar and 40% different.

Firebrand, a workflow management company for publishers, partnered with six publishers and did a study where they tweaked keywords and studied how they impacted and propelled longterm book sales.[2] The study demonstrates that the books were not selling on their own merit but rather on readers' ability to find them. Keywords created a way for readers to sort the wheat from the chaff and find books of interest. Per Henningsgaard of Ooligan Press recommends studying your data and how changing keyword affects

2 https://firebrandtech.com/research/increasing-sales-visibility-keywords/

your sales—this practice "moves the publisher away from feelings-based decisions and anecdotes and helps to honestly assess the merits of a given title versus your own."

There are different development conventions for fiction and non. Fiction generally does not have a subtitle and, if any confusion is possible, includes the phrase "A novel" on the cover. I worked with an author who had written a novel about pirates who found this confusing and unnecessary until I showed him a different book with a near-identical cover about real-life pirates on a real-life hunt for gold. But even I was a bit confused when our distributor told us that we had to clarify that our book of short stories about bicycling zombies was fictional. Always look at the comps for guidance.

There is almost never a good reason to write a book longer than your muse but sometimes creating a shorter, cheaper book has advantages in gift stores. If you have a book on a subject that partners well with a store, like a book about wine or horses or a certain kind of lifestyle, approach a store that would be your best bet for sales and involve them in the process early on. Consider partnering with them or putting their logo on the cover—as long as that choice won't scare away other people that you want to work with.

Titles, Subtitles, and Cover Details

Your title should not be an emotional albatross around your neck that you are dead set on. The title should tell the reader what the book is about. This seems obvious but until you are a *New York Times* bestseller, a vague title or abstract noun or adjective isn't doing you any favors. You want to be visually and emotionally evocative. More importantly you want to be clear. Just like *Reefer Madness* would not lead you to think that it's a book about economics, a book called *A Better Tomorrow* could literally be about *anything*. Abstractions aren't doing you any favors. If Rebecca Solnit hadn't previously sold millions of books, *The Faraway Nearby* would have been a highly inadvisable title due to its inscrutable vagueness. Pick something coherent and clear but that contains a few cues to your audience that they are in the right place. *Diary of a Teenage Girl: An Account in Words and Pictures* is a good example. It tells you who it's for and what it is.

If your book is nonfiction, it should also have a subtitle that assures people that they are in the right place. Your subtitle should really distinguish your book from the comps and clarify your niche, such as *Hellstrip Gardening: Create a Paradise between the Sidewalk and the Curb*. The title is really cranking the emotional payoff of what the wrong reader will dismiss as an exhausting chore and the right reader will romanticize...even if they never actually get around to gardening. The book is clearly distinct from other gardening books and occupies a brilliant niche with unique content.

Smoke Gets in Your Eyes: And Other Lessons from the Crematory conveys a nice visual image and gives you an idea of the humorous tone of the book. *Images You Should Not Masturbate To* might be the most brilliant title of all time when coupled with the cover photograph of a nude, elderly man taking a hatchet to a frozen lake.

Once you've formed your perfect title, you'll create your metadata, which are the keywords about your book. If you've ever made a website, think about your keywords and metadata like search engine optimization (SEO). You want to find every reason for people to pick up your books. If your book is hyper specific and in a crowded subject like self-help, you'll want to create a tagline or "reading line" that further clarifies it and cements your sale. For example, *To Ruin & Redeem: How to Build a Constructive Mindset in Prison* shows that it contains advice for people whether they have been incarcerated or not with the tagline "How to change your behavior and seize control of a better life." In another example, *Juggalo Country: Inside the World of Insane Clown Posse and America's Weirdest Mainstream Music Scene* uses the tagline "A gonzo ethnology of the world's most hated clowns" on the back cover. It helps to clarify that it's a journalistic work from an outsider rather than coming from a devout fan. Are you offering insight into a particular kind of yoga or casino gambling? Name it. Is the book for an audience that wouldn't immediately recognize a specific detail? Does your book feature an autistic protagonist? Tell your potential readers. Is the book set in a certain city or state where it will have strong regional interest? Tell the reader. Incorporate all of these details into your website landing page and on the book's back cover. If you have relationships with celebrities or successful authors in your genre, ask them to write endorsements for your book to help show your relationships, focus, and niche.

Buyers are most swayed by interest in a book's subject. E.g. *We immediately sell every book on witchcraft that comes through here!* The next most important detail is credibility of the author on that subject. They rely third on supporting blurbs and authority that the book seems to possess. Focus on these aspects but don't mislead or be dishonest.

How to Choose Your Format, Size, and Release Date

Remember the 70% similar rule? You want your book to be the same size as the other books on the same shelf. If it's a children's picture book, it should be roughly 8x10". If it's a young adult novel it should be 5x8". If it's for babies you'll want a board book in 6x6" printed on thick cardboard with rounded corners. If it's a serious book about business management, you'll want a 5.5x8.5" hardcover format with a dust jacket. If it's a cookbook or a book about psychology, you'll want a 6x9" paperback. If it's a coloring book, you'll want an 8.5x11" format with a thin cover. I get a lot of pushback about trim and format from new publishers. "Isn't it better to stand out?" Actually, no. Standing out confuses buyers. They can't tell what you're up to. It makes you appear ignorant and not yet ready for shelving. Even if the stores ordered it, it would confuse their customers unless they were already familiar with your work. So *always* defer to the other books on the shelf regarding format.

If your comps are all spiral bound, there's a reason for that. If they aren't, yours shouldn't be either. If they are all hardcover with a dust jacket, make sure yours has a dust jacket too. Some genres, particularly in gift, use a printed-hardcover format where there is no dust jacket called paper over board. Make sure yours matches the comps, always, unless you're going for a cheaper price point that isn't yet taken.

Sometimes a certain shelf, such as memoir or literary fiction, features titles both in hardcover and paperback. How do you blend in these cases? Essentially, either is acceptable, so choose what is best for you! If your book is about appreciating golf or wine, your upscale audience is likely willing to pay $29.95 or more for your book; you should publish in hardcover, sell through that printing, and then issue it in paperback the season after it is sold out. This looks authoritative and is the best for your bottom line. However, a hardcover can sometimes cost you over $10,000 at the printer, you may have trouble finding a vendor you like that can print them, or you're just unsure if your audience can stomach the higher retail prices. These are real concerns, and you may be better off sticking with paperback.

One vital part of your planning is deciding when to publish your book. You want to publish during the same month that your muse and comps are published. People who have more money than you did the research and know that this is when buyers are seeking this type of book. For example, if you're publishing a first-time author without strong media commitments, it's best to publish in January as that is the slowest time of year, and thus it's easiest to get coverage and interest. If you're publishing a hot gift item that doesn't rely upon media, you'd publish in November, the busiest time of year. Joe Matthews, CEO of Independent Publishers Group, points out that the simple economics of too many books being published in November often makes it a poor time for a small press to publish. If your book relates to a specific holiday, the trick is your book should be in print two months before that date so stores have time to stock and familiarize themselves with it. So if you are publishing a book about Hanukkah, you'd send it to the printer in September, send it to your distributor and wholesalers in October, and have it be in stores throughout November so customers hear about it, find it in

Anatomy of a Book

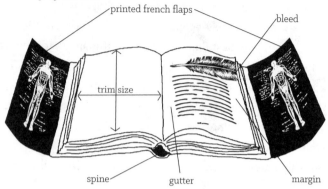

their local store, and purchase by December. There is a lot of data that goes into publication dates and the best wisdom is always to publish during the same month your comps came out.

Ebooks, Audiobooks, and Piracy

Make a decision about publishing an eBook edition on a case-by-case basis. The revenue from them is much less, but most of the work has already been finished when you've edited and developed a book. Some genres are, of course, exceptions to this. If you write science fiction, business, fantasy, self-help, "erotica," or vampire slash fiction, your odds of having much higher eBook sales figures are vastly improved, as these genres constitute the vast majority of eBook sales. But if you write other kinds of nonfiction, there's almost no point in releasing an eBook, and it may hurt your print book sales.

Digital piracy is another real concern for publishers. Novelist Maggie Stiefvater had hit the bestseller list for three books in a row and had suspicions that when sales waned on book three in her Raven Cycle series, it was because of bootlegging. She had more starred reviews of her Young Adult books than any other author in history but still

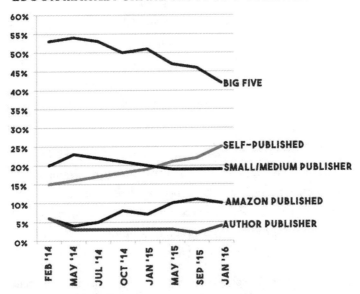

EBOOK MARKET SHARE (IN $) BY PUBLISHER TYPE

BIG FIVE

SELF-PUBLISHED

SMALL/MEDIUM PUBLISHER

AMAZON PUBLISHED

AUTHOR PUBLISHER

MARKET SHARE OF PRINT VERSUS DIGITAL

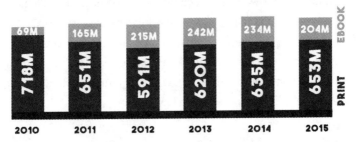

EBOOK

PRINT

	2010	2011	2012	2013	2014	2015
EBOOK	69M	165M	215M	242M	234M	204M
PRINT	718M	651M	591M	620M	635M	653M

her publisher believed that this critical reception wasn't translating to long-term sales. When her publisher told her of plans to halve the print run of book four, *The Raven King,* Stiefvater asked them not to release advanced readers of the eBook. Next, she asked her brother to create a PDF of the first four chapters repeating until the text was the same length as the real book, and to distribute it to every bootlegging site. For 48 hours, dozens of bewildered "fans" asked if anyone had "the real book" and failing to be able to steal it, fan after fan sucked it up and bought the book. The first printing sold out in two days. The bookstores couldn't get copies during her book tour and her publisher bought the rights to her next series. More important, Stiefvater had proven the damage that piracy does to authors, publishers, and bookstores.

If you're going to release an eBook, simultaneously publish it with with your paper book so that you get the most marketing for the least work. A general rule is to expect your digital sales to be about 5% of your paperback in nonfiction and less than 40% in fiction. If digital makes up a larger proportion of your total sales than this, it means your paper books are not available widely enough.

Because fiction is so competitive, many publishers, especially self-publishers, are intent on fighting their way all the way to the bottom. "I'll give away my eBook for free for 90 days, then I'll make it 99 cents for the next 90 days, and finally raise it to $2.99." This approach can be effective when proper marketing is being done alongside it. But it does not address the basic need of distinguishing the book from others like it. Instead, it's fostering a bidding war to see who is willing to work for the lowest pay.

If your comps don't have audio books, don't waste the time and money making one yourself until after your book is tremendously successful. Of course, if your audience is elderly, blind, or otherwise reading-impaired then audiobooks might be incredibly important for your list. Otherwise, unless your book has trouble finding distribution, it's probable that your audiobook will sell 10% or less of what the paperback does. I had never successfully made money from producing and distributing an audiobook...until the day that I sold the audio rights to seven of our titles for five figures (See page 276 to learn how to do this) and in talking to other publishers, the experience of every one of them was the same.

How to Price Your Book

There are three factors that go into your book's price.

1. What customers are willing to pay, which is based on perceived value, the volume of other options, and what other books are being sold for.

2. Your costs in producing the book, which might create greater perceived value or have costs that others don't have and so you can or must charge an extra dollar or two.

3. Where you are distributing: do you have better access or distribution to certain channels? Are you selling your book where none of your competitors are, like at a specific conference?

Since you probably read books like your own already, you should have a good idea of what to charge for your own. If you want to calculate it like the pros, divide the price of your comps by their page count. Then multiply the price per page by the number of pages in your book.

You may want to increase or decrease your price, depending on how vacant or crowded the shelf is. For instance, the market is oversaturated for Young Adult (YA) novels. As a result, you can't charge as much for a YA novel as you can for an adult one with the same page count and production values, which prices a lot of publishers out of that genre entirely.

When considering your book's value and total cost, a good rule of thumb is that your printing cost should be 10% of your list price. So if you're paying $1 a unit for printing, your cover price should be $10. There are two reasons for this. First, your expenses are higher than just printing. Even if you're photocopying zines and shipping them out of your living room, you still have other expenses whether you can see them yet or not: fees for having an online presence, mailing supplies and postage, any contractors you've hired, the computer you're using, shipping review copies, meetings, your own time, etc.

Second, in order to reach as many readers as you can, you'll sell most copies of your books for less than cover price. When you sell to bookstores or other retail stores, the standard wholesale discount is 40% off the cover price. So you're selling your $10 book for $6 each. Wholesalers and distributors need bigger cuts. You could be selling your $10 book for as little as $3 each. Which is fine, because you only paid $1 each to print them, right? Not if you used a print-on-demand digital printing service—and if you've ever wondered why so many self-published books are sold for $20 or $30 for a paperback, this is often why.

Perhaps you are aiming for a crowded shelf and your costs are substantially lower than those your competitors. In this case, it can be to your advantage to undercut prices a little. If you undercut prices drastically, your book will suffer because the perceived value will be too low. Alternately, if you have special expertise in a unique subject that cannot be Googled, or if you already have an enthusiastic following of hundreds or thousands of people ready to buy anything you produce, charge a little more.

At a comic convention, I met a man who fixes espresso machines and, due to a lack of documentation, he wrote a repair manual. He has direct access to his entire reader base and doesn't need to be sold in stores, so he can justify a high cover price of $70. If you Google "espresso machine repair," you find his book. He has no competition and has effectively cornered his market. Numerous publishers of business books use similar models and sell their books only at speaking events. Honestly, situations like these are the strongest arguments for self-publishing.

It's unlikely that your situation is as simple as Mr. Espresso Machine Repair. You will probably need to work with wholesalers and retailers to reach your audience. Consider how books are priced in the outlets where you'll be selling books. If you are producing high-end art books, a $40-50 cover price will not deter readers as it's par for the course. But if you're writing a memoir, you probably cannot convince your readers to pay that much. Sometimes your trip to the bookstore means increasing or reducing page count or even cutting your book into two smaller books to fit in better to the ecosphere.

Sometimes you'll be tempted to increase your print run to get the unit cost down. This is only a good idea if you are confident that you can actually sell more books. It is not a good idea if this is your first book or your marketing skills are untested. It's better to pay more per unit than it is to risk being stuck with a basement full of unsold books that you paid thousands for. Always evaluate your likelihood of selling them all and what the worst case scenario could look like.

What You Need in a Cover

You probably have a friend that you think is a phenomenal artist. Forget about them for a minute. The biggest mistake that publishers make with book covers is treating them like fine art rather than graphic design. Check out *Boneshaker Magazine*, a periodical in Bristol, England. While the publisher referred to it as a magazine, it was really more of a graphic design business card that has more in common with books. It was a cultural journal about bicycling. Each issue has very strong visuals, a consistent use of the title, and almost all of them feature a single element that really tells you "hey, this is an artistic journal about bicycling." That's what your book cover needs to do, too.

It's easy to overdo it. Many publishers attempt to do too much with a book cover, creating a dizzying array of elements, words, fonts, and emotions, leaving potential readers puzzled about what exactly is being offered. Brainstorm a list of things that the book offers and things that it makes you feel, focusing on the one idea that both appeals to the widest range of people and best summarizes the book in one concept. Make sure your cover is also authentic to your identity. If you're small and scrappy, make your cover have a little bit of that, too.

The only thing more competitive than fiction is memoir or poetry, so those three types of books really need to have covers that are not only emotional, evocative, clear, and concise but also drop-dead gorgeous. And fiction cover designers will charge a pretty penny for their services. You could easily spend $10,000 for a book cover that looks like it emerged from one of the Big Five houses. But you can't afford that. Instead, if you can, slash your design budget (see page 244).

There are many freelance cover designer services for hire these days that can create affordable work. Perhaps suggest that the designer might receive a percentage of the profits like the author would. This is good when you're starting out, but ultimately a bad idea in the long term as you will come to spend more and more on royalties than any other expense. In my early days, I paid designers and illustrators in copies of the book that they can sell at their own events.

The best advice I ever received about cover design was also the simplest: make the title the width of the entire cover. The second best advice I received was to evaluate the contrast on the cover by converting it from color to grayscale and see how distinguishable the elements look. In the 90s, you did this because this is how it would appear in magazine reviews, but now you do it merely to know that you have solid contrast and composition.

When you think you have a solid book cover that looks like your muse and the other comps, bring it to the clerks at your favorite bookstore and ask for feedback. Tell them to be straight with you. Padding your feelings here will cost you dearly later.

On average, a bookstore customer will give your front cover four seconds of their attention. So time yourself. What do you take away from your cover in four seconds? If that communicates what it needs to, they'll give your back cover seven seconds of their time. In gift shops it's a little better. The books are face-out towards the customer and there are fewer of them so your book cover gets five seconds of each person's time. You want to give each person a reason to keep looking because the longer they hold onto it and inspect it, the closer of an emotional attachment is developing and the closer you are to a sale.

Don't forget to make the spine visually compelling too. Consider how it'll look sandwiched between two gigantic books from major publishers. Will it stand out next to the Penguin signature orange? Is there adequate contrast in your type against the background? Will it be legible in both fluorescent and incandescent lighting?

Not only does your cover need to look great in the store, it needs to look great on blogs and online reviews and retailers. This means that your cover design also needs to look great as a thumbnail. So zoom out and view it at 1" width on your monitor while leaning back in your chair. Squint your eyes slightly. What detail does your brain zero in on first? Second? Third? Is this the order of significance of these items to the importance of your book and cover? If not, revise until they are.

The longer someone touches and holds one of your books, the more they will feel attached to it. So create something that the person can relate to in terms of language, colors, iconography, and emotional range. A non-scuff matte cover feels nice and creates a different kind of emotional appeal.

Let the final cover composition sit for a month and try not to look at it during that time. You'll see it with new eyes if you let it sit. Then look at it both as a thumbnail on your screen (100 pixels x 200 pixels or so), printed out at full size, and at about 3" wide or somewhere in between. Show dummy covers to stores that sell your books and ask for their advice. Get someone else to look at it, too, someone who's completely unfamiliar with the project. Ask them what they think it would be about.

Long-Tail Development

Sometimes you'll learn that you have brilliant and sought-after content but a book is not the right medium for it. Maybe the stores just won't put it on the shelves. Maybe your fans want a PDF download, audiobook, guided walking tour, blog, or seminar instead. Give your fans what they want in the medium that they want it instead of trying to force it to work as a book.

If you have a basement full of thousands of books, turn them into a giveaway premium with your other mediums. Find a way to make the book drive everything else that you do. If you have some real flop titles, give them away with your other orders. It's cheaper than pulping them and your fans will thank you.

On the other hand, if you have a book that is a runaway bestseller, congratulations! Now you have to figure out what's best for you. If you have the capacity to keep pace with printing and distributing the book, keep reprinting it. When sales start to wane, release a new edition and increase the price by 10%. The book is obviously successful and sought after. People want it and are willing to pay more. Once you have a book that surpasses 100,000 copies sold, you might consider creating a sequel. Bear in mind, that if the book looks too much like a sequel, it will sell 10% of what the previous book did. So try to make the book seem about a similar—but not identical—topic. Unless the book is the second in a fiction series, develop it to stand alone rather than as *Book 2*.

If you cannot keep up with demand or you are tiring out or discovering that you just don't like being a publisher, you can usually sell the publishing rights for a successful title to a publisher who produces similar work. If your book is successful, even if you want to keep publishing the English paperback edition, you can probably sell hardcover rights, foreign rights, Spanish language rights, or audiobook rights (see page 270).

Homework:

• What need does this book fulfill?

• What are the other books in the genre doing? What are they not doing?

• How can we distinguish from these other books and package the book clearly to show readers how it is different?

• As someone interested in this genre, what would you want to read about that hasn't already been done (or hasn't yet been done at this price)?

• What is your book's emotional payoff? Write and distill all of the details into a five-second pitch. Make sure that you can actually recite it in five seconds.

• Write the thirty-second follow-up pitch for when someone is interested in more information.

• Did you bake all your sales handles, details, and emotional appeals into every aspect of finalizing the title, subtitle, tagline, and cover design?

• What will the average reader take away from your book in four seconds? What about with the extra second in the gift market?

• Does the book cover appeal to the widest range of people and best summarize the book in one concept?

• Focus on evergreen titles. How will your book be selling in one year? Five years? Ten years?

• Does your book match the page count and trim size of your muse and comps? Is your price per page similar to your comps? Does your book match the format of the comps?

• What month of the year are books like yours typically published?

• Is there a store that you could partner with and develop the book around?

• Have you thoroughly researched successful comps as your best proposition for your own success?

3. PRINTING BOOKS

Making the Package Match the Product

Just as Amazon began pumping millions of dollars into convincing authors that they were the only sales platform that mattered and that self-publishing was the most profitable method for authors, Microcosm was vending at a home and garden show. A young man approached me and asked if we could print his book. When I explained that we don't own any printing equipment, he began shouting, "If you don't do any printing then there's no reason for a publisher to exist!"

He wasn't willing to have a conversation, but let's take a look at his "expert" stance. A book publisher's function is development and packaging expertise. Without proper development no one would ever find your book. The volume of daily publishing would render each book lost in the marketplace. A manufacturer specializes in the minutiae of printing.

What our "expert" is suggesting is vertical integration. Vertical integration is when a company handles an aspect of their business that would normally be handled by an outside company, like a publisher handling printing. You might have read about Delta Airlines buying an oil refinery in 2012 to make their own fuel. The difference in cost between crude oil and refined jet fuel fluctuates wildly, so the move made sense. Still, many experts were dubious because vertical integration is very hard to do well, and, in the end, the results varied for Delta. Direct sourcing is a good idea when a market is unstable, like oil can be from time to time. Printers, on the other hand, are remarkably stable. Printing prices barely fluctuate and there are hundreds of great printers all over the world, so it almost never makes sense for any publisher to finance and learn to operate printing equipment.

Deciding How to Print Your Book

You should learn how to work well with a few printers that you like. From there, you can understand best practices about getting what you need at the price you want. Let's take a look at the various options for publishing and what the associated costs are.

Traditional-format offset printing

Traditional-format offset books look the best and can be sold at a price that is attractive to readers while earning a margin that pays the bills. An offset printer uses a relief printing process where your book is digitally converted into a series of metal printing plates. Oil and water repel each other across the plates on a giant printing press, leaving ink on each page in a much higher image quality than any other printing method. Offset printers own hundreds of thousands of dollars of equipment and buy paper by the truckload to get the best pricing. They also own elaborate cutting and bindery equipment that creates four nice, square edges. The majority of an offset printer's time is spent converting your files to plates and getting the press set up to print your job. For this reason, it's easy for the printer to produce 10,000 copies in a few hours. Above that quantity, you'll notice that the majority of your cost is the actual paper. This kind of printer needs a month from the time that you submit your files to the time your finished job ships.

Offset also offers the most production options from varnishes to french flaps, unique trim sizes, limitless paper options, embossing, and metallic/fluorescent inks. Your finished book can be a beautiful object that stands out on the shelf.

To know if the printing cost works for your book, divide your total bill by the number of books printed to find your cost per book. The cost per book should be 10% of your cover price. For example, a standard offset run of a 128-page paperback book with a spine, a full-color cover and a one-color interior (e.g., black text) looks like this: 3,000 copies for $2,800, or roughly $1 per book when you include shipping from the printer. The cover price is $9.95 so the math works out.

Part of working with a printer is entering into a risky contract. Remember the story from the introduction where the printer used the wrong line screen (the amount of detail printed per inch) on 4,000 copies of our most expensive book ever, costing us $18,000? It took six years to fully resolve the situation by holding our ground through several different owners. We did get the money back in discounts eventually but this process was exhausting. For this reason, the publisher/printer relationship works best if you're making informed decisions and know your options and how to get the best speed, price, and quality.

Many publishers, looking solely for the best price, seek printing in Asia. But printers in the United States are bound by U.S. labor laws, meaning that minimum wage is enforced. If you print elsewhere in the world, especially in Asia, you don't know the labor conditions that your books are produced in. But you do know that these companies use the same offset printing and bindery equipment. So the only way that they can produce the same book and ship it across the globe all for a lower cost than an equally efficient U.S. company is through reduced labor conditions and lower wages. Perhaps this aspect of globalism isn't a concern to you, but let it, the cost of tariffs, and the time it takes to cross the world in a boat and rectify any mistakes inform your choices.

Digital printing / print on demand (POD)

Digital printing is the fastest method for making books and while the quality is improving, it is still inferior to offset. Worse, your production options are few and the cost is prohibitive. Some publishers prefer POD as their default method because the bills are small and they can print as few copies as they need each month. For most publishers, this is a fool's errand. If you're going to put the time into development, editorial, marketing, and distribution, I would hope that you also believe that each book could sell at least 2,000 offset copies, which will also save dramatically on unit costs. Plan your publishing goals realistically for the long term rather than out of fear or hesitation.

One notable exception to this rule is Eraserhead Press. Led by publisher Rose O'Keefe, Eraserhead is the leading bizarro fiction publisher and has published over 300 titles by 150 authors since 1999. Developing an early relationship with a digital printer and locking in low unit costs, O'Keefe has brilliantly built her company in parallel to the industry in a clearly defined genre with virtually no competition. Designers, editors, and authors are paid on a percentage system, more like the music industry than the conventional publishing royalty system, and her distribution is handled by online retailers. O'Keefe's model has a solid proof of concept, there are no shortage of would-be bizarro fiction authors, and there's no inventory to hold up cash flow. O'Keefe has begun teaching her model to other publishers—creating imprints Deadite Press, Fungasm Press, Lazy Fascist Press, and The New Bizarro Author Series—allowing her empire to grow beyond the limits of her own time. The company has grown exponentially over 20 years.

While digital printing doesn't make sense as a general default method for most publishers, there are times when it is your most practical choice. If you are printing a few hundred advanced reader copies (ARCs) for reviewers, or if you need to reprint a book that is selling fewer than 100 copies per year, POD is a good option. If you are creating a keepsake about your life or producing something solely for the enjoyment of your family or friends, POD is a great option. You don't need thousands of books and you never will. Technology is providing a great service for you. Similarly, if you are publishing high-priced technical niche books with a very limited audience, like the espresso machine repair manual, you will never need thousands of copies. It's worth paying the higher price per unit rather than losing money on a big print run.

Digital printing is similar in technology to a fancy photocopy machine, where it's just as easy to print and bind a single copy as it is to print 100. The labor is often performed by a book lover who does not receive a professional salary or have professional skills. POD will cost about $3-10 per copy for a 128 page paperback book. You may receive discounts based on volume, frequency, service, and quality. Some providers are Lightning Source (best price), Gorham (best quality), and Lulu (best interface).

Print-on-demand books are problematic in several ways. First, they are tough to sell, in part because they are lower-quality and lack the diversity of production values that offset offers. Most POD/digital printers offer roughly two options: gloss or "matte," white or cream paper, and choosing from the predetermined trim sizes. With very few options, almost all POD books tend to look very similar to each other.

POD is tough to work into most business models because of pricing. Let's say that your book's retail value is $10. If you used an offset printer, your costs would be around $1/book. If you used a digital/POD company, you likely paid at least $3, and often much more. I stumbled across a gentleman who was overjoyed to find that Amazon's CreateSpace program could print his book for "only" $16.40 each. For this reason, many trade publishers couldn't print using POD because they could not make these numbers work to sell to stores with a profit.

Why Printing Needs to Function as a Percentage of List Price

While other industries operate on a net pricing model (e.g. wholesale price is $5.35, sell for whatever you want) books have a "fixed" list (retail) price and publisher discounts are given based on account type and volume. A retailer can offer a discount to the customer but the list price is still acknowledged.

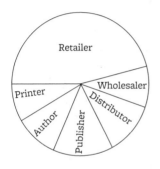

Typically, if you are selling directly to a bookstore, the retailer will take a 40-50% cut (leaving you with $10-12/copy on a $20 book). A wholesaler, such as Ingram, Baker & Taylor, Follett, New Leaf, Diamond Comics, Brodart, Bookazine, or Blackwell, takes a 50-60% cut (leaving you with $4-5/copy) and fulfills existing demand for your book. When you work with a distributor, they take a fee of 9-30% of each invoice. This works out to 5-18% of the cover price, leaving you with 32-45% of the cover price or $6.40-$9/copy on that $20 book. This means that if you use print on demand services, you must either charge $30 or more—that's more than most readers are willing to pay for a low-quality paperback book—or you just can't use these distribution options without losing money on each sale.

Ebooks

Even faster than POD, eBooks are published as fast as the files can be uploaded and propagated onto servers. Many bloggers argue that eBooks are "free" to produce, effectively cut out every middleman, and that Amazon is the only distributor they need. After all, Amazon controls 30-40% of the book market and over 60% of eBook sales. But this thinking is born of the same misunderstanding as that of the man at the home and garden show.

Many people are led to believe that the marketplace is changing rapidly, and think that eBooks eliminate production expenses and offer a level playing field against the majors. But in 2011, eBooks only constituted 8% of total book sales. In 2012, that number went down to about 6% of sales and has continued to drop since then. Microcosm's eBook sales dropped -41% from 2017 to 2018 which we are told is consistent for publishers of our size. It is getting harder and harder to find reputable numbers about eBook sales, but by all accounts eBooks have continued to shrink while print book sales grow. The problem is that eBooks were released during the U.S. recession and due to extreme price busting, they have low or no perceived value. The other clear trend is that Amazon has been mightily (and ineffectively) trying to find a way for eBooks to destroy print because it will assure their eventual market dominance. Naturally, once their monopoly is complete, they would certainly put more and more constraining terms on independent publishers.

In 2012, I was on a panel at a festival in Pendleton, Oregon, about the future of books. The opposing view from my own was presented by a woman who had sold 100,000 copies of her fantasy novel eBook. At that time I had sold a little over 1.3 million books, with about 100,000 copies of my bestseller. Naturally, the juice was in the details. The other panelist revealed that the first 30,000 copies of her book had been "sold" for free. She had then raised the price to 99 cents for the next 30,000 and that the remaining 40,000 copies had sold for $2.99, making her net profit less than **$15,000**. Still, she was the envy of the room. Everyone wanted to be her. She was the exception that proves the rule: if you followed your dreams and produced good work, you could be a "successful" author. But after expenses and paying the author, our company had netted over **$400,000** on 100,000 copies of one title alone.

In a 2014 interview with my business partner, Elly Blue, the interviewer made the case that once you reach certain sales echelons, eBooks just make more economic sense. But here's the thing: successful eBooks immediately become print books, because the profit always works out worse for the publisher of an eBook than for a print book. Because eBooks have a lower perceived value (30-80% less than paperbacks), your $20 paperback is likely only worth $5.99 or less in eBook. After distribution fees and formatting/encoding costs, you receive roughly $4.20 per copy sold, at best. Your offset paperback nets you $17.50 per copy sold of a $20 book after printing, fulfillment, and processing fees. Even if you get to the point that you have to hire someone to package and fulfill your mailorders, you are still making more than twice as much money on a traditional-format offset paperback.

Let's back up a bit. For proper formatting and book design, eBooks require hours spent perfecting a skill that is not transferable to print design. Most publishers find it easier to pay a "conversion" fee to an author services company for their eBook creation.

For this reason, eBooks work best as the icing on your cake. Once you've created proper book development, a cover, and editorial, you can earn an additional 1-70% net income by publishing a digital edition. Notice that wild variance? It's because romance eBooks are 70% of that market while genres like children's or comics can be as low as 1%.

Amazon pays a 70% royalty on eBook sales for books $2.99 or higher—so for each three buck eBook you sell, you earn $2.09. This marketing sounds enticing on the surface—but to make money, you need to sell quite a few books, and to sell books you need to direct people to find your books there, in the most crowded marketplace the world has ever seen. If you work economically and do much of the work yourself, you might end up paying $200 for good-quality conversion; this means you need to sell nearly 100 books just to break even.

Today, the average eBook earns under $100 because 300 new ones will be published *each hour*.

Even when we aggressively priced all eBooks at $5.99 or less, most Microcosm titles still sold 99% in paperback and 1% in eBook, if they sell any eBooks at all during a given month. This will likely change as paper becomes more expensive and the technology becomes more widespread, but how much and how quickly will it change? Even if our eBook sales double in the next year, they would still only make up 2% of our sales. The numbers aren't looking good. For this reason, major publishers have been increasing their eBook prices; sometimes slowly and sometimes dramatically. This is because when a book is new and available in hardcover for $27.95 or eBook for $9.99, you will only buy the hardcover if you want the keepsake. So publishers have raised prices to $14.99, partially as a gradual step towards moving consumers towards higher prices and partially to prevent the lower cost option from cannibalizing too many hardcover sales.

Still, if you have no international distribution or want to offer accessibility, creating eBooks might allow you to reach countries that you cannot reach with your physical books.

Printing Zines

An affordable option to consider is testing out interest slowly by publishing zines. Champions of the underground press since the 1920s, zines are the photocopied and stapled bastard children of pulp novels retaining more in common with a book about a passionate subject than a magazine. During the Great Depression, zines were published because readers believed they could write better stories than were appearing in pulps. Today, you can take this same low-cost, democratized medium and see how your readers respond to something a bit off the beaten path. Because books exist in a constrained, crowded field, doing a book well is slow, expensive, time-consuming, and complex. Zines, on the other hand are the perfect way to test interest in a new subject matter or author's voice. Zines offer a very economical way to publish with no bar to entry. They stand out more because of their unique, albeit lower-production-value look and are often easier to market and promote because they tend to have more character and it's easier to see their apparent passion. They can have a low cover price and low production costs with short lead times. Best of all, book stores have very limited shelf space and can only maintain stock of best sellers but a good zine about the right subject can be restocked on the shelves forever—with the cover face out towards customers. And amazingly every rigid problem created by the millions of books in print is miraculously waltzed around by a zine.

Jessica Mullen and Kelly Cree, publishers of School of Life Design, first discovered zines in 2008. Cree was enamored by publications created by artists for friends as well as the forms the zines took. Mullen earned a master's degree in 2010 and wanted to move her practice of teaching mindfulness and emotional literacy outside the bureaucracy of the academic system. They are both graphic designers so print was a given. Together, they created their own school and curriculum, publishing the *Monthly Manifestation Manual*. Their work was well received, and they were asked to teach workshops. They created five new zines based on their workshop exercises. Eight years later, they realize how the first zines they had read subconsciously influenced their own publishing. They've sold more than 5,000 books and continue to expand their practice.

Create a zine that is 20-60 pages to have at events and to offer to your local stores. See what the response is like. We print zines 40-200 at a time at a photocopy shop in walking distance of our office. I email them files and quantities and they deliver boxes of printed, folded, and stapled zines. You can probably find something comparable in your neighborhood. When sales exceed a few hundred copies, expand it into a paperback.

Determining Your Print Run

Many books have been unprofitable solely because their initial print run was too high. Not being able to manage this complex predictive math also can cause small publishers to collapse under the weight of managing their bestsellers.

So let's look at a healthy way to be smart and plan ahead.

The longtime conventional wisdom is that a third of a book's lifetime sales occur before its publication date. Another third of the sales happen over the first year of publication and the final third happens gradually over the rest of the book's lifetime. While advance sales are thinning in a crowded market and have been down a bit each year, making it increasingly difficult to predict in a changing bookselling climate, the wisdom underpinning it still makes sense: math is your friend.

The conventional wisdom is that for an independent book to make sense to publish, there should be at least 5,000 people who would want to read it that you can identify and reach. Of course, that does not mean that every initial print run should be at least 5,000. Indeed, we print as few as 3,000 or even 2,000 copies of some of our titles. It's not that we doubt that we *might* sell 5,000 copies in the book's lifetime. It's that it's safer to hedge our bets rather than to save 20 or 30 cents per copy. The average book store sells one copy of the average book during the average year. When you consider that the vast majority of these book sales are bestsellers, you realize that most books sell even fewer copies than that. It's healthy to be a little conservative. If you have to reprint, that's a great problem to have!

If you have a sales team, common wisdom in the past has been to print two to three times as many copies as you have preorders for. But if you're generating preorders with technology like Kickstarter, these orders may not indicate your ability to continue selling to this audience after the campaign ends or even that an unreached audience still exists. Similarly, development that is effective on Kickstarter is rarely as effective in the book trade or retail in general. Instead of assuming, do a little investigating. Inquire with stores how many copies they might purchase and try to estimate based on how many stores you can reach and how many other stores like them exist. From there, determine a realistic print run that will last one to two years.

Without research, we blindly printed 3,000 copies each of our first print runs of our first ten books. When I tell people this they respond that it seems bold, lucky, or outrageous that we have long ago sold all 30,000 of those books and that all of them have undergone reprints and new editions. But my point is the opposite: many of those proved much more expensive than they should have been because it's much cheaper to add 1,000 or 2,000 additional copies to a print run than it is to reprint when you run out in a few months. But it's even worse to have sales of a title dead stop, leaving you with thousands of copies to warehouse.

For my first ten years in publishing, I lacked the understanding of how to predict the difference in sales from one book to another. Focus on the size of each book's audience, the volume of competition, and your ability to reach readers. You won't sell a book to every person interested in it simply because you won't reach them all or some of them don't have time to read it or they think they know everything already or they don't have the money or they simply never run into it at their favorite book store. But look at who is out there and how you can reach them. How much competition is there? Draw up a plan. Then realistically think of how many of those people would buy the book.

The number one mistake I witness firsthand is people making print runs that are much too small—100-500 copies. When they inevitably run out of them, they need to print more. The amount of time and effort that goes into making a book is the same no matter how small your print run is. Look at your unit price and calculate a conservative estimate based on sales of similar titles. If you're serious about publishing, I'd suggest starting in the neighborhood of 2,000 copies. If that is too much to store or you cannot afford it, take a step back and start with a zine. While 2,000 sounds like a lot to a newbie, you'll need some for reviewers and samples. With a proper launch campaign, you should be able to sell 2,000 of any properly developed book. It's always better to err on the side of giving a free book to someone who could create a positive influence for it than to be forced into stinginess by a lack of copies. Besides, generosity creates more of the same.

When you have less than a two month's supply remaining and sales data is consistent and steady, plan a reprint. For reprints, a good rule of thumb is to look at your sales history and see what the patterns are. Is the book slowing down or speeding up year over year? Are you just reprinting because you're emotionally close to it? Are there busier times of year than others? Plan a two-year supply and find a good place to store them or switch to POD if it would take ten years to sell through an offset run. Sometimes sales completely taper off, and you'll have a lifetime supply. But at least you won't have to face the question of how many copies of that book to print ever again.

Working with the Printer

Once you've decided how you want to release your work, your next publishing decisions are going to be technical.

If you use a full service digital platform like Amazon's CreateSpace, your production setup will be mostly automated, and your options will be limited to a few choices. If you are printing offset, there's more to it. Here's a look at some of the nuts and bolts of offset printing production.

Asia Citro of The Innovation Press printed a new book and transferred some copies from her distributor's warehouse for a trade show. When the books arrived she discovered that ¾ of the books had the printing horribly misaligned on the spine. It was only a week before her publication date. Panicking, she arranged for the warehouse to return the books to the printer who sorted 7,000 books by hand over the next 24 hours so the books could be back in the warehouse in time for the release date. The printer gave her a sizeable credit, and she donated the misprinted copies to low-income schools.

While most printers today are highly invested in retaining publishers, resolving problems isn't always this easy. In most cases where a printer makes a mistake of this caliber, you'll at least have to put your foot down and withhold further work until they resolve to your satisfaction.

Pop open the covers of most hardcovers, board books, or full-color books, and you'll find that most of them are printed in Asia. Domestic labor may not be important to you, but it's important to understand that if you are seeking the best price you'll likely be working with a print broker for a printer in China, waiting six months between submitting the digital files and receiving the books to the U.S. warehouse, and navigating tax paperwork to import your books on a boat.

Citro published her first children's picture book with a printer in Asia for both paperback and hardcover. Sales took off immediately, especially in paperback. Because of the season, the wait for a reprint from the overseas printer was at 12-14 weeks. So she placed a reprint order just one week after the book released, with over 80% of the first printing already shipped. Three weeks before the reprint arrived, sales abruptly stopped. She still had around 100 copies of the previous printing when the new books arrived and sales had dwindled so much that it took six months to sell those last 100 copies and any returns.

And then every publisher's nightmare occurred: a customer reported that the new printing has six pages bound out of order. The misbound books had been sitting in a warehouse for six months without being inspected. Similar reports continued to come to her attention. She contacted the overseas printer seven months after the job was finished. It was too expensive to be practical to ship the books back to the printer for inspection and they concluded that it was cheaper to pulp all of the books rather than to inspect them all. The world will never know how many copies were defective and these decisions are one way that publishing is very strange. The printer credited her, but the experience taught her a vital lesson. Because of the delays, she now prefers a printer in the U.S. whenever possible. She's found that this is the difference between 12-14 weeks and 2-4 weeks for a reprint, which allows a publisher to wait longer to order the reprint and ensure that the sales are consistent and not being returned. In any event, she recommends vetting your printer beforehand so you know problems can be resolved painlessly.

Choosing your production values

Pick up your muse. What size is it? Is it a paperback or hardcover or spiral bound? Does it have a dust jacket? What kind of interior paper does it have? Is the paper coated/glossy? How thick is the paper? Can you feel the paper grain with your fingers or is it smooth? How thick is the cover stock? Do they have any full color sections? Are the interiors one or two colors? How much overall effort is going into design? Are the inside covers printed?

Essentially, you want to match all of the production standards of your muse and comps. For example, cookbooks are often 6x9" or 7x9" and have stunning and scrumptious full color photography inside with the best photo on the cover. Travel books tend to be smaller and use lighter paper because they get carried around in the bottom of a bag for a month when every ounce counts. Fiction books run the gamut of sizes but disappear on the shelf if the spine is too slim. Other genres, like local interest or seasonal books, will be displayed face out. If you are producing genre fiction with the goal of being sold in Target, you'll want to copy the trim sizes and production values exactly.

If you cut corners on production values or change the formula too much, there is a danger that people will see your book as lesser. But sometimes this can be a good thing—being seen as the underdog is the secret weapon of the independent publisher. Occupying that space in people's minds makes people feel kinship with you and want to help you because it feels like you need it and they can relate to that. Yours is a passion project, and people love passion!

Make informed choices that don't stray too far from the norms of your genre but also give your book a bit of character. Choose production values that help your book reflect who you are and what you're doing, but be wary of going overboard with either expensive add-ons or extreme budget cutting measures.

Choosing a printer

Once you've selected the format for your book, you need to find a printer. It's important to get at least two or three quotes to compare to each other to understand the pricing that you're getting. Further, not all printers are alike. You are specifically looking for a book printer. Other types of printers will have to outsource your job because they don't have in-house bindery equipment or don't have their equipment set up for this type of production. Book printers that have been operating for many decades can often offer better pricing because they have already paid off their equipment.

Many people want to find a local printer, believing this to be both cheaper and an ethical choice but the opposite is true. For most printers, it's quite time-intensive to assemble books without the correct equipment and they don't have access to the right vendors to properly price paper. Unless your region has established book printers with bindery equipment, the cost is likely to be quadruple what it would cost at a printer who is set up for it.

Sometimes changing printers or even changing your trim size can really save costs. We discovered that we could save $800 per book by reducing the width and height of one of our signature sizes by ¼". Then we found that we could save another $800 per book by changing printers and moving that ¼" from the width to the height. Over the course of a year, that's a *lot* of money.

For starters, I'd recommend getting quotes from printers of various sizes and see how comfortable each one feels for you:

1984 Printing in Oakland prints digitally only on post-consumer recycled papers. They are a friendly one-woman shop.

United Graphics is a larger printer in Illinois. We've worked with them during our entire career as a publisher. Great service and quality. It'll be a lot easier to work with them once you know the ropes and industry jargon a bit better than beginner level.

Versa Press offers some of the most competitive pricing in the United States as well as both paperback and glued hardcovers in-house with sewn binding coming soon. While sewn (smythe) binding is arguably "better," glue binding is fairly indistinguishable. In any event, Versa is friendly, surrounded by farmland in southern Illinois, and is run by engineers.

Kansas City Book Manufacturing is a fast and efficient printer that specializes in booklets, spiral binding, and textbooks. They can turn around a print job in only ten days which is 66% faster than their competitors for only 20% greater expense.

Impression 4P is in Montreal, which is fairly accessible to New York City. In my experiences there, the prices and quality are great and the sales people are helpful, but when they made a mistake, they were reluctant to resolve it. Sometimes that gamble is worth it.

Transcontinental is a big company, the fourth largest printer in North America. They used to refuse to return our phone calls but now they send salespeople to bother us every few months. They may not want to work with you right away but they might be a good fit when you have substantial business to offer. They are in Canada, which has subsidized printing prices, but if you are not located in eastern Canada, shipping costs may be a concern for you.

Requesting a printer quote

Because you're a relatively new publisher, it can be tough to get the time of day from some printers. Like all secret societies, printers and publishers use a lot of shorthand and jargon to communicate common subjects quickly. This is one reason it's important to have all your details dialed in and to be able to speak their language.

Printers have the responsibility to print your job according to the parameters you choose. They typically will not correct or even point out your typos or formatting mistakes, or consult with you extensively about your options. Any mistakes you make will be at your peril and may result in considerable extra expenses and delays.

You can avoid such mistakes by communicating well in printer speak, making sure your book is properly designed and formatted for print. We'll talk about that next.

Here's a sample quote request:

Bikenomics

192 pages

5×8"

1/1 on interior

bleeds

60# natural text

Quotes for 7,000 and 10,000 copies

14pt c1s matte 4/1 cover

Let's take a closer look at what each line means:

Bikenomics (The printer includes the title on the outside of your shipping boxes and uses it to organize multiple quotes for the same customer)

192 pages (This is the number of pages in the book. Often times it is most economical to plan your book so it's an exact number of signatures—the number of pages produced by one parent sheet of paper on the press—so there is less waste and you get everything you are paying for. Signatures are typically 16 or 32 pages each, unless it's a very small printer, in which case they can be four or eight pages. When in doubt, ask!)

5×8" (This is the finished trim size of the book, always using the format of width times height.)

1/1 on interior (This is the number of colored inks on the inside of the book. Meaning both sides of every signature will have one color of ink. This is usually black, but for this book we used a dark teal ink 'cause we're sassy.)

Bleeds (The image runs off the page, so the paper size quoted will need to be a ¼" larger)

60# natural (this is the type of paper stock you want on the interior of the book. You'll want to use something that the printer stocks on site as it will be vastly cheaper than ordering a special stock. The exception here is if you need something special to fit the kind of book you are doing. Since every printer uses different paper suppliers, ask for a sample or request how many pages per inch [PPI] their stock is.)

Quotes for 7,000 and 10,000 copies (printing quantities—sometimes it's good to request two options here to see how the unit price changes. We don't normally print so much for a new title, but the author had a large platform and our distributor had put this on page one of their catalog so we knew it would be a hit.)

14pt c1s matte 4/1 cover (The first number is the weight of the cover stock, in this case, fourteen point. This is a more exacting caliper-measurement system than paper "pounds," which relates to the weight of a case of that paper without really telling you much about its thickness. The second detail means "coated on one side with a matte varnish." The outside of the cover has a matte varnish and the inside remains uncoated. You could coat both sides if that is the look you were going for or leave both sides uncoated, which is appropriate for certain special cover papers that are "toothier" in texture. The last detail is the number of inks used on the cover. In this case, it's four colors (Cyan, Magenta, Yellow, and Black that are used to create CMYK or full color on the outside and one color, a metallic gold ink, on the inside cover. Most books are 4/0 but plenty are 2/0 as well, containing a black ink and a pantone color or two pantones, see page 122).

Here's another example, for a more complicated graphic novel:

Threadbare (title)
6×9" (finished trim size, width by height)
Bleeds (images run off the page)
60# white paper (because it's a graphic book white paper has a cleaner look and the illustration detail shows better)
224 pages (length of book)
2c interior (two different pantones, second pantone color changes every 32 pages)
5,000 copies (number in print run)

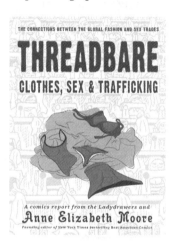

14pt C1S cover 3/1 cover matte with matte etch (three PMS colors printed on the cover so we can use metallic gold ink on the outside and inside cover and a more complicated finish, where an image is actually cut into the matte finish separate from the image printed in ink.)

Double-Wall Cartons (thicker boxes to prevent damage to books in transit during re-shipments)

Life Cycle of a Print Job

Once you've received your quotes, you can sign and return them to lock in the prices even if you aren't ready to submit your finished files yet. Your quotes will expire sometime between two weeks to three months after you receive them. The price might go up if the printer's costs for paper or boxes goes up. We've also had printers send quotes in error and then try to refuse to honor them after we've signed and returned them even though the specs were correct. To have the printer try to change the price after you've done a P&L (see page 244) for the book is obnoxious, so ask them to stick with the contract.

Your quote may not be the final amount that you pay—if a printer prints too few or too many books, aka "unders" or "overs," your price will be adjusted to suit (the quote will tell you how this is calculated), and your quote may or may not include an estimate for freight shipment of your finished books.

Once any questions are answered and adjustments are made to your quote, you will sign it and upload your print-ready files. You may have to pay a large deposit up front and the rest before your job ships; or you can submit credit check paperwork to see if the printer will allow you to open a line of credit and pay later.

The printer will give you the option of digital or printed proofs, which they will send you once they are done setting up your files and getting them ready to print. The proofs are not an opportunity for further copy editing, content changes, or editorial decisions; they are simply to make sure that what the printer is printing matches the page layout, colors, fonts, and alignment you submitted. Digital proofs are cheaper and faster, but if precise colors or close checking is more important, request overnighted prints. If you do see any major bloopers, like a low-resolution image, a spelling error on the cover, or a mistake with the spine alignment, this is your last chance to fix them. But keep in mind that each page you change will cost you a nontrivial amount of money. It's essential to make sure you've completely finished your editing and formatting before sending your files to print.

It is very important to return your proofs within 24 hours. Printers operate with a tight schedule, and a one day delay on your end might result in a ten day delay on their end.

Once the book is printed, it will be shipped to you. If it's a small job, like 1,500 zines, it'll probably come via UPS or something similar. If it's a larger job, you'll have a pallet of boxes delivered to your door by freight truck or carrier. Once you have credit terms with your printer, you won't have to pay the final bill for 30-60 days after your job is delivered and your printer's sales rep will start calling to ask when the next job is coming.

If the final print job does not match your expectations, check the quote to see if the specs match. Then check that the printed books match the final proof. If both match, then the error was not the printer's fault and the results may have been your fault. However, if there is a discrepancy, you're going to want to bring this to the printer's attention immediately. While this can be crushing, it's ideal to present a resolution plan rather than a rushing river of feelings. For example, "I'm going to need you to reprint this job" or "I'd like an $800 credit for this error" or "I'd like you to reprint all of the unusable copies." Due to fierce competition printers are incredibly motivated to resolve issues as long as you are reasonable.

Formatting for Print

The gold standard of book design of the past fifteen years has been Adobe Indesign. If you're feeling stingy, there's also a freeware alternative called Scribus.

The biggest rookie mistake on small press books is assuming that layout and design are not professional skills. Like any other skill, you can learn book layout with a few hours of watching YouTube instructional videos and a few hundred hours of practice, so if you're under pressure and focused elsewhere, it may make sense to bring in an actual professional.

When creating your files for print, create a new document at the proper trim size and page count. You want to use design grids to guide the eye and make the page stress-free and manageable to navigate. Aim for an ideal of 66 characters on each line and increasing the leading (the space between lines of text) to about 1.5 the default for the most pleasant reader experience and so reading the book feels fast. If you're unfamiliar with design grids, open a magazine and then compare to a few different kinds of books. In your mind draw an "X" over the portions of the page with ink on them. Be mindful of where the gutters and margins are and what these decisions do for the reading experience.

One mistake I have made repeatedly across my career is not properly formatting the ISBN barcode on the back cover. There is a specific science for printing readable barcodes correctly. You'll take your ISBN and the price for your book and visit a website that turns these numbers into barcodes[3]. Just paste your thirteen-digit ISBN in the ISBN field. For the price, if your book is $14.95 and the book will sell primarily in the U.S., enter 51495. The "5" indicates to the computer that this is the U.S. price and the $14.95 tells the cash register how to ring up the book. Take a look at your muse and how their barcode looks. Place this barcode file on the bottom of your back cover. Still, there are a number of expensive things that can go wrong after this stage. You want your barcode printed in 100% black, not as a CMYK image. If the colors don't align, the barcode won't scan. If there's no black in your cover printing, use the darkest color available. If you print the wrong ISBN on the book or it does not scan, you'll probably have to pay someone to resticker the whole print run with the correct one.

When your design is finished, you simply export a print-ready PDF of the file with all of your images, text, colors, fonts, and layouts as they will look in print. For designing a zine, Indesign has a nice "print booklet" feature where you can export a PDF formatted for a photocopier.

How Many Pages?

Your book should be as long or as short as it needs to be in terms of content. But figuring out the right page count and designing your work to fit is an art form you can spend many years perfecting.

---

3 Such as https://www.bookow.com/resources.php

Building for the correct page count is partly a development issue and partly a production issue.

Once you've decided on a printer, ask them how many pages fit on each signature for a book with your trim size. The signature is the number of book pages that can be cut from one of the giant sheets of paper the printer feeds through their press. This is typically four, sixteen, 24, or 32 pages, depending on how big the printer's equipment and size of your page are. Then you'll want to design the book to be a multiple of that number of pages. For example, if your book will print with 32 page signatures, you'll want it to be exactly 64, 96, 128, 160, 192, 224 pages, or so on. If it has 24 page signatures, you would likely save money by having a 240 page book over a 232 page book, for example. We once created a book with 20 pages of blank pages for notes so it would reach the finished signature size.

Paper

Consider how you want your book to look. White paper? Unbleached acid-free natural paper? Colored paper? Textured paper? Coated paper for a cookbook, children's picture book, or art book? How thick? How many pages? You can simplify this decision (and lower your price considerably) by just asking your printer what their stock interior paper options are.

If you decide to order a special paper, there is a dizzying array of options. Paper is always classified by its "weight," which used to mean something universal, but modern paper weights have virtually no meaning except in relation to other paper from the same supplier. So the question you want to ask is "what is the pages per inch (PPI) of this paper?" That will tell you how thick your finished book will be and give you a better idea of how its perceived value on the shelf will stack up against the price you want to sell it for, though it won't help its perceived value in a catalog.

Bleeds and Margins

Another fundamental question to answer while you are setting up your document is: "Will the book have bleeds?" This means: "Will the printing extend all the way to the edge of the page?"

The alternative to bleeds is margins. Most text-based books have a margin around the edge of the page, which is usually at least .75" on all sides with a little extra space in the gutter. This allows for a pleasant and painless reading experience. Bleeds allow you to do a number of interesting things in print that are more artistic in nature, like inverting your colors, printing patterns behind your content, simulating colored paper when it's not available, or making a visual point when your art wanders off the edge of the page. A printer's trimming equipment cuts thousands of books per hour and is accordingly imprecise. This is why your art needs to extend beyond the edge of the page or the printing needs to have an unprinted margin.

But like all things, there are consequences. Adding bleeds requires roughly an extra .25" of paper on all three exterior edges. The printer trims this extra paper off after the book is bound so you have four nice, clean edges. Your book will be printed on large sheets of paper and then cut to size, so even this much extra can require the printer to use more paper and raise the cost of your book. Experiment by asking for a variety of quotes!

If you are printing with bleeds, you'll need to set up your cover and interior files to include a (usually .125" or .25") bleed when you export your PDF. The printer will then trim this off to create the desired look. Your book formatting program should have a bleed setting within its preferences. Look up documentation instructions about how to do this properly.

If you want to draw attention to a certain page, you can print a "flood." This means that the ink prints everything on your page *except* your text and image, which remain the color of your paper.

Colors

The most costly part of pre-press is proofing and plating your book. This is because before they hit the big green button, the printer needs to thoroughly check to make sure that what you have ordered from them is the same thing as what they are providing for you.

Most books are printed in one color, usually black, and that ink comes from a single plate used to print the whole book on the printing press. Each plate is a piece of metal where oil and water repel each other to put an image onto paper. They wear out after tens of thousands of uses and you'll start to see detail disappear. If you add a second color (known as a "spot color"), that would be done most economically as a second set of plates for the whole book. The printer would be set up to make a second pass over every page to print your second color.

If you're printing with spot colors, you'll need to identify these colors by the Pantone Matching System (PMS). PMS is a code; each color number is the key. The PMS number instructs the printer how to create that color from the inks they have in their shop. You can purchase a Pantone book which shows you what the ink will look like on the paper at 100% opacity. You can look up these colors online, but what you see on your screen is unlikely to be the same as what you see in print. The only way to verify that you are choosing the exact colors you want and to compare ones that you are considering using together is by matching up your numbers with Pantone's proprietary (about $100 new) color booklets.

Adding colors to your book's cover often doesn't raise the price very much because it's only one printing plate. Even if you print your cover in full color, the printer can do that with only four plates (Cyan, Magenta, Yellow, and Black or CMYK) to create every color. But adding a second color to the book's interior increases the work of printing so much that it can add 10-40% onto the cost of a project. On the other hand, it can also give your book a notable flair and value and make it more fun as a designer. Sometimes designers can get carried away and want to use a lot of colors; or they get confused and forget that black is another color and use black ink plus two pantone colors, which requires three sets of printing plates and yet more cost.

What about full-color printing? There are only four colors involved. Just like your home laser printer, CMYK can effectively create purples, oranges, greens, greys, and most colors that you can imagine. Using four colors this way is called "full color" and makes sense for photo books, cookbooks, and art books. But as you might have guessed, it is even more expensive to use four-color offset printing on the interior and costs at least double what the same book would cost with one color of ink. The good news is that unless your designer has really taken over your project with wild ideas, you can reliably create almost any (non-neon and non-metallic) color with four sets of plates.

If you are only printing in one, two, or three colors though, there are a number of interesting tricks you can still pull off. You can play with white space and use your paper as an extra color. You can lower the opacity of the ink to create lighter shades of the same color in portions of your design, just like grey is created from using less black. You can overprint one color on top of another to achieve a blend. Some printers will do more experimental things like putting a variety of unmixed colors of ink into the press to produce different colors on different parts of the page, for instance so that half of the page is printed in blue and the other half is pink. This is called a split fountain.

When working with Pantones, make sure that every color in your final document (including black!) is set up as a Pantone that you are printing. Adobe Acrobat has a print production feature where you can ensure that all of your colors have exported correctly. Otherwise, correcting this mistake later can be extremely time-consuming and costly, often delaying your book at the printer. If you are working in full color (CMYK), the computer knows how to create the separations on its own and you don't need to set up colors in Pantone.

Another simpler option, often used in travel books and biographies, is to create one signature in full color to print photography or art while the rest of the book is only one or two colors. This color section can be printed on a coated paper to make the visual pages look nicer.

Images

If your book is made of images instead of or in addition to text (e.g. a graphic novel, photo book, or children's picture book), assuming it's all one color, your printing cost will be the same as if the book only contained text. Check your muse for things like additional colors, varnish, or heavier paper. The major difference with a graphic book is that your pre-press work will be quite a bit more complicated and time-consuming.

Any full-color or image containing grays (such as a black and white photographs) in your book should be at least 300 dots per inch (DPI) at the size that it's printed. If your original is less detailed than this, it will print as grainy and washed out. A computer isn't smart enough to add missing detail to low-quality images so you will have to recreate missing data yourself or print the image at the size you have.

If you have images that are only black and contain no grays such as line art without shading, you'll need to scan or convert them to black and white/bitmapped images at 1200 DPI for best printing quality. If you want them printed in a Pantone color, it's best to start with a black image and then format the colors in Indesign.

If the book is in full color, the computer knows how to automatically separate the CMYK plates. Computers will separate the colors at the printer. You'll just need to make sure that your files have sufficient resolution.

If your book includes photographs or halftones, a series of dots that simulates a continuous tone used to ensure that the final image prints correctly, ask the printer for guidelines regarding shadows, midtones, and highlights before you begin design and production. They will know what reproduces best on their press and setting it up correctly in the first place will save you both time and energy and create the best-looking book!

Cover Stocks & Varnishes

When working on your cover, go to the bookstore again. Look at the multitude of coatings on covers there. Look at the variety of thicknesses and textures of paperback covers and all of the neat tricks that can be employed. If you're going to use a textured paper, you likely would not want a varnish put on top of it, potentially defeating the effect on the outside of the book.

Frequently your cover will be printed in glorious full color, but sometimes the best results and most visible covers can be created by doing interesting things with two Pantone colors. When you are setting up your cover file in Pantones, be sure to use the appropriate kind of Pantone to match your varnish—uncoated, coated, or matte.

Matte covers are a generally accepted standard for any book that is remotely artistic. Coated covers have a glossy look, that while it may make your book feel special or professional, can also convey an outdated aesthetic. That's not to say that you cannot or should not choose it, but understand the implications when you do. They make your cover colors appear more contrasted.

When you look at textbooks or novels with painted covers, you'll see a lot of glossy finishes. Aqueous gloss is the thinnest and cheapest way to protect a book throughout its life but it looks painfully cheap as well.

If you use a textured cover stock, you will probably want the paper to remain uncoated. This can create a nice effect and look very "natural" if that is a suitable aesthetic for your work. Be warned that these books are the most likely to be damaged in shipping, as the varnish's other job is to protect your book from harm. Books with a gloss varnish and black ink floods tend to have the opposite result, where they are often damaged in transit and you can see every fingerprint.

Another option is a matte etch, which is an image cut into the gloss coating on the cover that is visible when you hold it up against the light. Most big publisher mass-market paperbacks use this method to make the title of the book stand out on the cover. An interesting variation on this is to create non-corresponding artwork on the matte etch that creates a hidden image on the cover for those inspecting it up close.

Don't Cut Corners!

Know your priorities and put as much time into the details of the layout as makes sense for your project. While generally you shouldn't cut corners, sometimes literally cutting the corners gives a nice look. The printer could give a rounded or angled cut. It's a nice way to add a little more production value and take advantage of using offset instead of digital printing.

When you are all finished and ready to go, export two finished PDFs, one for the cover (and inside cover if you're printing on it) and one for the interior. Check all of your export settings and make sure that you are putting out print-quality files and that you aren't compressing line art under 1200 DPI or putting JPEG compression on illustrated pages (so they don't look choppy). Sometimes it is safest to turn off all image downsampling or compression. Export two large files and send to your printer. Carefully review every page at least once for layout errors or typos. Fixing one thing might break another. Review until you cannot find more corrections. If you're unsure of how your printer would like to receive some aspect of the book, ask them. Some printers who are particularly helpful will also go over near-finished versions of your book and double check that there are no errors before press time. This can relieve your stress as well as save time during the eleventh hour! Good luck.

Homework:

- What is a reasonable first print run for your book?

- Does it make sense to issue an eBook edition?

- Does a zine edition of your content make sense?

- What kind of production features do your comps have?

- What kind of interior paper do your comps have? How thick is the cover stock?

- Do the comps have any full color sections? Are the interiors one or two colors?

- How much overall effort is going into their production? Are the inside covers printed?

- Is the paper thin or thick? Coated or uncoated?

- Do they include photography or illustration? Color or black and white?

- What printers will you request quotes from?

4. WHERE TO SELL BOOKS

Putting Your Work in Readers' Hands

Once all of your ducks are in a row and your development decisions are locked in, you'll be selling your vision as well as the ideas and mission behind it. Remember, when your development is good, your books act as a passive sales force for themselves. Otherwise, you would be stuck explaining and handselling every copy into the world because, without proper development, your audience cannot deduce the value, emotional payoff, or purpose of each book on their own.

Behind marketing and development, sales is the next most important part of publishing. It's rarely what people romanticize when they get excited about publishing, but it's fundamental.

Books are sold in many different environments, known as sales channels:

- The book trade: Barnes & Noble; Books-A-Million; Hastings; Indigo; independent bookstores; Amazon; wholesalers; libraries

- Mass Market: Target; Costco; WalMart; airport stores

- Specialty Market: national parks; FedEx Office; hardware stores; sporting goods stores; pet stores; gardening shops; clothing stores; grocery stores; record stores; anywhere that uses books as a way to express the story of their mission to their customers

- Gift Sales: Urban Outfitters; Bath & Body Works; museum stores; hospital gift shops; boutiques; anywhere that the books don't serve to tell a composite story about the organization but are there as impulse buys

- Institutional Sales: hotel chains; city governments; inter-corporate use; anywhere that isn't selling the book but buying in large quantities

- Educational Market: Textbooks; professional reference; teaching aids; secondary education retailers; as reference materials in special collections libraries

- Often the most neglected sales channel for publishers is selling directly to fans and readers—on your own website, at events, and in person

Books are an industry where the recognizability of your brand name barely matters—unless your primary goal is to bring all sales traffic to your own front door. The author is the brand that readers shop. Most readers won't be too concerned about the brand of your publishing company. They will buy your book because it fulfills a need.

There are exceptions. With children's, comics, and travel, the publisher is sometimes more important than the author. If you take a look at the travel shelf, you'll see that the author's name often doesn't appear on the cover, and the publisher's name and the series name are on the covers instead, giving them a consistent look and feel. Fodor's, Avalon, Lonely Planet, or Not For Tourists brand names are organized into neat little rows with the brand visible on the spines and front covers. Comics operate similarly, where the DC or Marvel logo is almost always the most recognizable focal point on the cover. As far as children's, remember Little Golden Books?

Big Five publishers earn 95% of their revenue from 5% of their releases. They use huge marketing and advertising budgets to achieve this and have adequate financing as well as huge back catalogs to pay for it. Their systems are designed to create bestsellers and everything else is garbage. I mean, literally, they pulp books that have stopped selling at the end of each year if the author doesn't want to buy up the remaining copies. So your sales focus should be on being nimble and relying on middling successes. Per Henningsgaard, former Director of Publishing at Portland State University, told me "The late 1970s 'Golden Age' of publishing is exaggerated by the industry. As a small publisher it's harder to have the large, public breakthroughs. A small publisher can do a lot in niches that were never possible before and leverage a niche into a large book that sells well." Treat all of your books as equals, at least for the first few years until you have a clear sales pattern.

The 5%/95% rule is why most publishers expend so many resources trying to make hits, hyping their latest key titles and authors while building series and lists around bestsellers. It's a logical approach, but it's tremendously expensive. They cannot give this treatment to all titles and rely solely on the author for marketing in 95% of cases.

And the bookstore marketplaces are horribly competitive. If you want a taste of this, visit Book Expo America (BEA) or the

American Library Association (ALA) conference. Both events are near the heart of the Literary Industrial Complex. They are huge annual gatherings of publishers hyping their forthcoming titles. You can wait in line to get an autograph with a celebrity author or receive promotional items of all stripes about new books. There are certainly companies there who spend five figures on their booth and giveaways. When you're ready to get your feet wet in the industry, there are also regional trade shows that are more affordable and focus on marketing new titles to bookstores in local and neighboring states. While publisher recognition is largely inconsequential to readers, brand and reputation are important *inside* the professional trade. You'll want to have a name for yourself or at least a strong key title with name recognition before you begin developing your presence at trade shows and with trade publications.

We are an exception. Microcosm has ignored the conventional wisdom and promoted around our brand. We have always directed our sales towards our own mail order and website, as well as convincing retailers to order from us directly. We try to tie our publishing together in a manner that makes our customers lifelong ones. We offer subscription programs where we mail a book to you each month at a reduced rate. We produce an annual comics poster to hang on your wall that tells our story or offers ideas about personal growth or talks about how we landed on our values. We don't have budgets for a booth at BEA or ALA, and, even if we did, I would be willing to bet that what we are doing offers a greater return.

Prior to 2010, Amazon was talked about like the boon of the publishing industry; free money for publishers as the icing on your cake in the form of 10-30% additional sales. Then Amazon gradually began demanding deeper and deeper discounts and dictating terms. Then they began putting other customers out of business. Within a few years, Amazon was paying less per book than wholesalers and began to aggressively negotiate on eBook pricing limits with publishers. While Amazon contractually prohibits us from telling you just how big of a discount we are forced to give them, I can tell you that it's the largest discount of any retailer by a wide margin. If Amazon could cap eBooks at $9.99 for new titles, they could use their advantage in the digital market to undermine their competition and seize an even larger piece of the book market. Fortunately, publishers fought back, remembering that hard covers are more profitable and that monopolies are bad for business. The publishers renegotiated their contracts furiously in 2012 and Amazon had to take a few steps back. Simultaneously, Amazon was launching a marketing campaign to brand publishers as greedy and unnecessary while announcing their self-publishing platform, touting 70% royalties. The feelings of years of rejected manuscripts led many authors to chase this carrot but over time it remains apparent that Amazon's arrangements are only in the best interest of Amazon.

Our sales reps from the post office asked why we don't just use the big-A as our retailer, and I was speechless for a minute. Because to me, giving away our sales to a ruthless monopoly makes no sense. Amazon only comprises 1% of Microcosm's total sales. We've created loyalty over the years and send overstock books with orders. In this way we build a relationship with our customers who are concerned with more than just the lowest price, though if that's what they care about we offer that, too. Our customers can change the price of our books on our website as much as 30% lower (or higher) than the cover price.

While our methods are fairly unheard of in publishing—most publishers don't have a retail website, let alone a physical store—and I wouldn't recommend discounting books deeper if they aren't selling, the sliding scale system has been a tremendously popular innovation for Microcosm. Since we implemented it in 2009, we turn away fewer customers over price. More surprisingly, the average sale ends up being the cover price because just as many customers turn the price *up* as people turn it down. So in effect, more sales at the same price is the final outcome. This once offended some economists who were upset because they wanted to believe that consumers were rationally self-interested. But books are an emotional purchase and our customers are invested in our long-term success. Even if *every* customer turned the price *all the way down*, we would still be making more money than if they bought the same books on Amazon. We keep the whole pie, and the next person will probably turn up the price to pay more than retail because our customers are adorable, loving, and loyal.

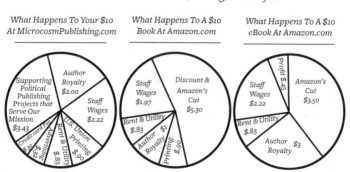

What Happens To Your $10 At MicrocosmPublishing.com

What Happens To A $10 Book At Amazon.com

What Happens To A $10 eBook At Amazon.com

Once you have generated interest in your books, you'll begin to get frequent inquiries from accounts about how to "set up an account" with your company. We receive weekly phone calls and emails asking for us to fax over new account application paperwork. This is because, even in 2018, the Literary Industrial Complex communicates solely via faxes to their legal department and has extensive paperwork to purchase books, complete with credit references and bank account information. My earliest innovation in establishing Microcosm was that from the very beginning, I made the account establishment process simultaneous to a customer placing their first order. Literally when they enter their billing and shipping information our database creates an account for them. Honestly, this is to make it as easy as possible to buy books from Microcosm and because it just makes sense to me as a customer.

Get Your Mind Around Selling

Kelly Cree of School of Life Design offers vital advice:

> "One of the most important lessons we've learned is 'just try.' When we first submitted our work to stores and distros, we had no idea what we were doing. We had no idea if our books would sell or if they were even viable in any market, but we applied everywhere we could find. One of the first stores we were stocked in was Quimby's in Chicago because they have an open consignment policy. We were honestly shocked when we heard back from them that we made $50 or so. We walked in to every store in Austin that we thought would be a good fit and asked them to stock our

books on consignment. At first, we were terrified. Afraid of rejection, afraid of stuttering when trying to explain what the work was about, afraid of failure. Some people said no, but a lot of them said yes. Slowly, we built up confidence in our work and its ability to sell. Slowly, we started selling more and more. Most independently owned bookstores and boutiques are happy to try to help, especially on consignment, and while the sales may be small at first, they will give you the confidence and stamina to press on and keep creating."

Selling books always goes right back to fulfilling a need. When you're in selling mode, consider which of your titles a store would be interested in and why. Deliver the five-second pitch for each title with a smile and let the buyer hold the book. They won't always buy every book, but you'll practice your schtick and with time you'll find the right customers for each title. It should bear without being said, but you never want to sell books at a loss unless it's dead inventory.

Selling books from behind a table at a public event is great practice for learning to sell as you'll have hundreds of opportunities to pitch different books to different people with different needs and different interests. Try to hone in on the need that the book fulfills for the reader and explaining details that are not apparent in the title and cover development. The store buyers are a bit savvier than readers and aren't shopping for themselves but based on the known interests of their customers. As a result of this practice, you'll move through details a bit faster.

For my first ten years in the industry, I thought like most publishers that I meet today: by making good books and making them available on our website, that the right people would find them and order. They did. But some people are just too inundated and busy to notice. So we began designing and mailing brochures. That helped but there were still some accounts that I felt we should be landing who just kept persistently ignoring Microcosm.

In 2016, we hired Jeri Rossi who had just spent the previous ten years hustling at Last Gasp of San Francisco. The first day that Jeri sat down at her desk, she picked up the phone and began calling. And she kept calling. She calls about 100 accounts per day. Sometimes they don't answer. Sometimes the buyer isn't in. Sometimes the person that answers the phone tries to steer you away. Sometimes they are rude or tell you that your books are terrible and the terms don't work for them. And sometimes you land a big sale. Sometimes you have to try calling the same account ten times before you land that big sale. But so long as you keep calling, you're either refining your list down to only the places that you should be contacting and removing the chaff that will never buy your books or you're inching closer to another sale.

Jeri changed my perspective about the industry. I learned more about how disconnected retailers are from publishers and how busy the buyers often are by listening and watching for her first two weeks on the job than I did in my first ten years. Actively calling new accounts daily increased our total sales 27% in her first year and an additional 52% in her second year. Stew on those numbers for a few minutes. That's enough of a sales spike that we had to refine systems and get our warehouse in perfect working order.

Who to Sell to

A fundamental part of your publishing strategy is finding the right balance between direct sales and sales to stores. There are essentially four different strategies:

- **Direct to consumer**: Selling books to readers at events and shipping from your office to the reader's home.

- **Direct to retailer**: Walking into a store and convincing them to sell your books or negotiating this relationship on the phone.

- **Direct to wholesaler**: Once you're an established press with demand for your titles, most bookstores will not want to phone in a restock order from you. They would work with a wholesaler that they order many different publishers' titles from each week. This is for convenience as well as receiving practically free next-day shipping. Once there is demonstrated interest, you would fulfill orders from these wholesalers so they always have stock of your active titles.

- **Sales/warehousing managed by trade distributor**: You also have the option of delegating your entire sales, fulfillment, and warehousing operation to a company that specializes in these publishing functions. Generally a trade distributor manages a publisher's debt collection, customer service, and returns as well.

It's healthy to diversify among these for a number of reasons. For one, direct sales are paid for immediately, while wholesalers need 60-90 days to pay. For another, direct sales pay 100% of the cover price while wholesalers pay 45%. The bigger margin will help to balance out slow months or when people are late to pay.

Still, you cannot do everything or be everywhere. You have to find the right balance for your list. If you're a textbook publisher, you won't be doing much business with gift shops, but you have a choice of managing sales directly to students or working with college bookstores. If you publish children's picture books, gift shops could be the bulk of your sales, but bookstores might be important, too. It's easy to get so busy and caught up in managing your accounts that you forget to sell directly to your readers.

Most publishers diversify for reasons that go beyond making the sale. For example, IT Revolution Press, a small, innovative Portland house for business speakers, sells many of their books directly to readers at conferences and on their website. They sell to bookstores via their trade distributor National Book Network but know how to market and sell to their entire audience. According to Per Henningsgaard of Ooligan Press, "IT Revolution Press isn't only interested in putting out the books and selling them to the attendees of conferences and sessions. They are really attuned to using their presence at events and immersed in those communities to gather data for optimizing future books and other products that their readers might be looking for."

Selling Directly to Readers

The most sustainable way to both build an audience and sell directly to them is to have a retail website. It should tell the world everything you want people to know about your publishing operation and it should offer a way to order your books. Print that website's URL on a postcard, brochure, or catalog that you have on-hand to give someone whenever they express interest in your books or publishing, especially at events.

Tabling at the right events is the best sales and marketing for your money. Even if you pay $1,000 for travel and a table at an event and only sell $1,000 worth of books, your presence will slowly create residual, passive sales as people learn about your books and order more in the future. Passive sales are the best kind because you only have to fill the orders. Your book development is doing most of the work.

Similarly, industry events are important for many publishers, but these are part of the slow, long game of marketing in the general direction of retailers. You need to appear, first and foremost, at consumer-facing events. If you publish books about music, have a booth at music festivals. If you publish books about crafting, bring them to crafters at conventions. If you publish comic books, bring them to comic cons.

In 1997, I began organizing tours, selling books through them. First, I would tour with bands and set up a table of books for sale every night. Then I began creating packaged author tours where we would charge admission to pay the talent and the costs of the tour while also having a table set up to sell our catalog of books every night. In 2010, we took this package tour idea to new heights and created Dinner & Bikes. Punk rock chef Joshua Ploeg, with seven cookbooks under his belt and a strong background in music touring, was eagerly cooking for dinner parties and benefit events for everything from nonprofits to political parties. We put together presentations based on our bicycling books and films for a presentation that the audience could experience while eating Joshua's seven-course meal. And then everyone could purchase books afterwards. Every night we would partner with a different bicycle advocacy organization who would promote the event to their membership and be able to use the event as a fundraiser for themselves, as well. The organization would offer us their credibility and the word of mouth spread. They used their mailing list to promote the event, draw their network, and share their credibility. Best of all, we sold about $10,000 worth of books on each tour—not just books from featured authors on the tour, but from our whole catalog, curated for the audience's interests. This concept was very successful because we were targeting towns that did not have local bookstores. Not content to leave it at that, we also offered a coupon that attendees could use on our website. Repeat customers continued to return, and we distributed many catalogs at coffee shops along the way. Even if attendees didn't purchase books that night, many audience members would order them from our website or buy them from local gift stores that we sold to along the way. It created a perfect cycle.

The common business vernacular refers to this behavior as a "sales funnel." Through handing out our catalogs at events and while traveling, we are introducing tens of thousands of prospective readers to the wide end of the funnel every year. But Microcosm isn't right for some people. They aren't interested and keep looking elsewhere. Still, they remember what we offer and the kind of

PEOPLE LEARNING ABOUT YOU

Awareness

Interest

Consideration

Action!

people that it might be for, and they tell those people. The successful dissemination of this information is called the "Awareness" stage.

Some people are immediately captivated by at least our mission and some of our titles. This is the called the "Interest" stage. They may not be a reader, though they might buy our books as presents for others.

If they linger at our table or on our website long enough, they are hovering at the "Consideration" stage. They may need some questions answered or need a discount or it may take them a bit longer to understand the payoff of our books and how they might benefit their own lives.

Finally, a select few make the decision that our books are worth the money at the "Action" stage.

The people who reach these final two stages are those that you want to focus your effort around because they are the most likely to keep coming back for more books. Give them reasons to.

People who have ordered from you in the past should be told about new, similar books that you are offering. The ideal time to announce a new title is when you have final data and cover and when the book is available for preorder. The industry needs about nine months between your announcement of publication and the book's release. But the timing of your announcement to the public isn't the most important thing. What matters is that you tell the world about a book that is available for preorders. Above and beyond the sales themselves, what you're doing is moving new people into your funnel and giving your fans a reason to spread around the link to your website.

Amazon heavily employs "loss leaders," products sold that lose money but bring in customers to buy other products that Amazon can make money on. Amazon's loss leader model has convinced many publishers to deep discount their brand new books during preordering. This is a losing proposition, since you don't have the resources that Amazon does (if you do, please get in touch). Loss leaders support the notion that people don't buy your books because they want them but only because they are *cheap*. You want your book to compete on the merit of the work rather than because yours is the most discounted.

If you are going to go through all of the trouble to make a great book and find an audience for it, you owe it to yourself to understand the mathematics of what you are doing. Take a look at the chart to the right. It outlines how many copies of your book you'd need to sell each month using different publishing and distribution models to pay yourself minimum wage. Some of the results surprised me a little, but overall I think it makes the best case for starting out by setting up a website and doing your own mail order of your book. Consider the work that goes into each one and what your core competencies are. According to Haymarket's Julie Fain,

3,000 copies of an Offset printed paperback
Self-distributed (website or events)
$9.95 Retail, Publisher's Unit Cost: $1
Distribution Cost: 5%, Net Income $8.45

179

3,000 copies of an Offset printed paperback
Sold direct to bookstores
$9.95 Retail, Publisher's Unit Cost: $1
Distribution Cost: 40%, Net Income: $5

302.4

3,000 copies of an Offset printed paperback
Distributed by Amazon
$9.95 retail, Publisher's Unit cost: $1
Distribution cost: 50%, Net Income: $4
(though Amazon makes you sign non-disclosure agreements and we are aware that many people receive less)

378

3,000 copies of an Offset printed paperback
Sold direct to Distributors
$9.95 Retail, Publisher's Unit Cost: $1
Distribution Cost: 50%, Net Income: $4

378

Publishing through a service like AuthorHouse
(spreading expenses from a $999 package across twelve months)
$9.95 Retail, Publisher's Unit Cost: $3
Distribution Cost: 30%, Net Income: $3.79

399

eBook
Sold through various eBook distributors
$6.99 Retail (eBooks are perceived as 30-70% less valuable than paper books)
Publisher's Unit Cost: $1.50 (These numbers assume market rate conversion costs of producing ePub, Kindle, and PDF formats across twelve months)
Distribution Cost: 30%
Net Income: $3.39

446

3,000 copies of an Offset printed paperback
Sold to a Trade Distributor
$9.95 Retail
Publisher's Unit Cost: $1
Distribution Cost: 60%
Net Income: $3

504

"Print on Demand" digital printing
through a vendor like Lightning Source or similar
Sold through vendor's direct sales channels
$9.95 Retail
Publisher's Unit Cost: $5 (which we know is low)
Distribution Cost: 70%
Net Income: $2

756

(To support one person at minimum wage, of $1,512.)
Based on a minimum wage of $8.40 per hour, for 40 hours per week with 45 weeks per month

"A significant part of our strong non-trade program is direct-to-consumer sales. As a niche press with a clear mission, it's been possible for us to find a committed audience who comes back and buys our books direct from us time and again, building and expanding the readership for our books and ideas more broadly."

Selling to Bookstores

Many publishers have a direct audience that understands their book development intimately. The audience is familiar enough with the authors and publisher that they hunt out information about new titles. Unfortunately, this is not true of a general audience or most bookstore customers. To develop your book for bookstores, make it abundantly clear what the book is, what benefits it offers, and what similarities it has with other books to so that when it's sitting on the shelf, it both blends in and is distinguished.

Mark Suchomel, with over 30 years of industry experience, sees independent bookstores as the biggest sales growth channel for publishers. "General retail, chain stores, and big box stores are having a tough time while the independents have a chance to be special." And these accounts are growing. According to *Planet Money*, the number of independent bookstores increased 40% between 2009 and 2018 and sales were up 40% for these accounts, too.

The biggest problem with bookstores is that competition is fierce. While paper book sales have been steadily climbing for six years, the amount of new publishing and competition from other entertainment options is growing hundreds of times faster, and bookstores are increasingly forced to be hyper-selective about their shelving space.

The average bookstore sells a single copy of the average book during the average year. Fortunately, for them, there are tens of millions of books in print. Unfortunately for you, this means that without marketing there is a 1% chance that the average bookstore will stock your books, much less actually sell them. If bookstore sales are a priority, begin to cook up sales, marketing, and publicity incentives, like appearing on local radio and telling listeners where the book is available. It also means that you need to pay for books to sit in stores that can be returned later and ask many bookstores to carry your titles. Mailing postcards, following up with a phone call, and letting them know how to order your books (and that they can return unsold stock) is shockingly effective. Successful publishers are rejected more often than unsuccessful publishers, so take risks.

When I founded Microcosm in 1996, the company consisted of myself, a computer, and several boxes of zines and books in a closet. It was an interesting time in the industry's history, but I did not expect distributors to come knocking and was rejected by even the smallest, least reputable operations. Still, I walked into local bookstores with my titles and showed them to the buyers. I didn't have International Standard Bookstore Numbers (ISBNs), which further irritated the places that believed in the bureaucracy of the Literary Industrial Complex while the edgier places saw me as a weird underdog to champion.

For the most part, if you're serious about selling in bookstores, you'll need to purchase some ISBNs from Bowker, register them to your books, and print a barcode of the ISBN on the back cover. An ISBN identifies each format and edition of your book as unique to the universe so they know that when they key in those thirteen digits that they will receive the correct title. If you, like teenage me, neglect to do this, it will be the first of many annoyances, and buyers have the right to be much choosier today.

A bookstore will typically want a 40% discount—or sometimes more. Initially, they will probably want to stock your books on consignment, meaning that you will still own the inventory and they will pay you for them after they sell. Even after you've convinced a store to purchase your books outright, they'll probably purchase your books on net-30 terms. Meaning, they will pay what they owe you 30 days after receiving the books. Bookstores typically reserve the right to return unsold books for up to a year. So essentially, you are always floating a line of credit to the store to purchase your books even after they have paid you. This might feel unreasonable at first, but it's the standard. Many publishers want to sell non-returnable books but most stores will either not stock your titles or ask for a bigger discount. Approach this topic as a negotiation conversation rather than a unilateral imposition.

There are good reasons for this system. Half of each bookstore's customers march into the establishment knowing exactly what they want to buy already. They are responding to author branding, identity, advertising, or effective marketing. Increasingly, these customers are shopping at online retailers instead. The other half of bookstore customers are book addicts and are fiending on the hunt for new loves. These people are easier to land, and your underdog selections satisfy their human foraging instinct. A bookstore's sales rely upon their staff being familiar with your titles so they can recommend them to the later customer. As a result, these customers are the reason indie bookstores are growing. However, marketing to these stores and customers is expensive for publishers outside of their region. For this reason and more, bookstores can be a shifty proposition. You likely can't compete because even if you can tell them that you have scheduled publicity for the book, the store can still return the books four months later if they do not sell. You can cultivate a relationship with store management, but honestly, in most cases, your odds of winning the lottery are better than building fruitful enough relationships with enough bookstores to carry your bottom line. Fortunately, there are places to sell your books where you don't have to compete so fervently.

Libraries

New publishers tend to forget about libraries, or at least not understand that they represent a huge sales opportunity. Combined, libraries spend over *one billion dollars* annually. There are many different kinds of libraries from special collections archiving unique, strange publications to technical libraries with books for a certain profession to city and county public libraries (23% of library book unit purchases) to college libraries (27%) to school libraries (33%).

Typically, a discount structure for an invoiced library sale looks like this:

1-4 copies, 0% discount
5-10 copies, 10% discount
20+ copies, 20% discount

Due to these small discounts and the fact that libraries are fairly obvious sales territory for most established publishers, they can afford to be choosy. If you aren't a local author and you've published a YA novel without a clear sales handle, they will probably not have a reason to purchase it. However, libraries search out subject matter based on the scarcity of the subject. So if you are publishing books about a specific kind of carpentry or gambling or regional history, the right libraries will purchase it without thinking. They just need to know it exists.

So create a postcard mailing campaign with your book cover and ordering information. Cataloging your work with the Library of Congress will make it easier for librarians to learn about and integrate into a collection. If you have a strong reason, call or email a library's purchasing department directly.

Libraries are essentially recommending books to their communities, so in order to add a book to their catalog they need to point to reviews for your books in trade publications that the library sciences consider credible, like *Library Journal, Booklist, Publisher's Weekly,* or *Kirkus Reviews*. This way when parents complain that your book contains frank conversation about abortion, the library can pass off the liability by pointing out the glowing review from a professional peer, who are often librarians or retired archivists themselves. To develop for library sales and reviews in relevant publications, create subject matter that libraries are lacking with clear sales handles and local/regional sales hooks. The simplest way to do this is to develop around category holes where the comps have gone out of print but the subject remains topical.

Non-Bookstore Sales Channels

Jack Canfield and Mark Hansen, two motivational speakers, were repeatedly asked by their audiences if their stories were included in a book. After rejections from 133 different publishers, Canfield and Hansen signed in 1992 with Health Communications Inc (HCI), a tiny, failing wellness specialty publisher focusing on drug and alcohol recovery titles. Publisher Peter Vegso wasn't even interested in reading the manuscript before signing. Even though Vegso knew that anthologies are almost always risky flops, he recognized the passion of the authors and the value of the package in front of him. The stories had potential because they had been tested hundreds of times by real audiences.

The book, *Chicken Soup for the Soul*, launched a series that sold over 110 million books by focusing on selling in restaurants, pet stores, women's catalogs, dentists' offices, gift shops, and grocery stores. The authors and publisher worked together to grow this into a recognized brand of over $2 billion worldwide, including many licensed products and translations in 43 languages. More importantly, *Chicken Soup* invented the entire genre of spiritual uplift, creating a new market for all publishers. The books were essential to growing the special sales and gift markets. HCI is now one of the largest publishers outside of New York with revenues over $100 million/year. And the company holds onto its quirk. When Vegso's own skills fail him, such as when all employees in one part of the building aren't "having fun" for ten years, he hires a mystic or a feng shui expert.

For obvious reasons, Vegso told *Forbes* that he relies on his gut more than ever. You should rely on your gut while also having your brain invested in the data, such as knowing the genres that sell well outside of the bookstore: exercise, weight loss/diet, relationships/dating, parenting, health, sex, self-help/mental health, business, cats, financial planning, and management.

The first rule of bookselling is that, because the market is so clogged, obvious outlets just don't work. Everyone has thought of them. They are overflowing with books. Absurd outlets, however, do work. Joe Matthews, CEO of Independent Publishers Group, is feeling the pinch of a trade that isn't growing while competition continues to balloon. "We're continuing to see growth outside of traditional bookstores. We're trying to find new places to sell books. We're worried about the long-term health of Barnes & Noble. And what it might mean if they go under. So we're now putting books into convenience stores, 7-11, and Rite Aid." Microcosm also recognizes the importance of selling to diverse outlets, including a taco stand in Tokyo, clothing shops, record stores, grocery stores, and gift boutiques.

Books that are heavily based on regional interest can be sold at your local gas station or hardware store. Developing a sufficient number of similar titles that can be sold in venues outside of bookstores and won't go out of topical trend is the most tried-and-true way of creating consistent monthly revenue (see page 355).

With success in one sales channel comes trade-offs in another. If you are publishing genre fiction thriller novels that do well in Target and airport stores, you probably wouldn't have much luck in boutique gift shops. For each title—and ideally your whole list—pick a few key areas and focus on them.

If you're finding that stores aren't willing to purchase books directly from you because you don't have enough titles, you can offer to sell books from other publishers in your anchor subject matter. You can sell them both on your website and to retailers. This cements your authority on a subject, suggests you as an information center, and gives you a "wider bag," selling more books on one subject for retailers to use as a one-stop shop. You can even trade boxes of books with similar, friendly publishers, and everyone wins!

Special sales

Special sales are one arm of non-trade sales, meaning those outside of bookstore accounts. Non-trade sales are often easier, more fun, and more lucrative. They are not as focused on jargon nor on increasingly difficult standards as bookstores. And selling to speciality accounts doesn't exclude bookstores—it just expands your options.

Per of Ooligan Press relates, "When I was teaching in Wisconsin and running a press, the gift and specialty stores always outsold the bookstores. You'll have so much visibility. Get books into places where those titles have limited competition. We sold 200 copies of *The Portland Red Guide* to the Portland shipyard union gathering."

Similarly, when bookstores weren't receptive to Microcosm titles, I visited nearby record stores, newsstands, candy stores, clothing shops, and anywhere that I could deliver a compelling argument about why they should have our books. I went on tour with bands and would show the books to store buyers in other cities. Within a few years I had stores coming to me to make orders. I was sending out boxes to stores daily and needed to hire other people to ship these orders out. I didn't need a distributor. I had effectively created interest and demand for what I was doing, or, as the sales director for one distributor put it, I had created an alternate specialty market.

My sales strategy was extremely fringe in 1996 because the Literary Industrial Complex still focused primarily on bookstore chains. Now this strategy is called "Special Sales," meaning that stores buy certain books as a way to communicate their mission to an audience. A hardware store would sell books about building a deck or exterminating bugs. A record store would sell books about music. A tea shop would sell books about tea. Grocery stores sell cookbooks. Sporting goods stores sell books about sports history and trivia. Gardening and homesteading shops sell DIY books. Travel agencies sell guidebooks. Even chain stores like Whole Foods, Michael's, and Crate & Barrel sell books. And often they buy a book simply because it occupies a niche topic that they know their customers are interested in.

The distinction between speciality and gift is often confusing to publishers, and these two markets are often clumped together as one though they are quite distinct. Specialty is using books to communicate the mission of the business, which means there's strong thematic messaging in the book selection. A hardware store wouldn't sell a cake decorating book unless the owners knew the author personally or had another clear reason why it belonged in the store. Gift, on the other hand, would sell a book about cake decorating next to a book about golf next to one about making a living as an artist. Gift focuses more on impulse items with clear messaging and audience. For example, someone in your life might enjoy a golfing coffee table book, or some friends that just had a child and are moving to Boston might enjoy *Goodnight Boston* as a parting gift. These books are always communicating their value, their audience, and what they have to offer them.

Sometimes these accounts will want displays for your books—cardboard stands to make the book cover point at the eyeline of the customer. These are, for some obnoxious reason, called "dumps." We've produced them both for displaying six copies of a single title and for displaying four different titles. The latter has been much more popular, especially for grocery and record stores. Unfortunately, the manufacturing costs for them have skyrocketed.

Gift and specialty are great but in order to work, you have to develop for them years in advance, not try to sell into these stores after the books are published. While a bookstore relies upon recommendations and their staff being familiar with their inventory, gift and specialty accounts rotate stock frequently and keep their book offerings minimal so you have to develop each book's reward into the title and cover. Your development needs to immediately show how the books work together as a set. This is why it's powerful to develop a number of books as a series. For example, in the *Storey Basics Books for Self Reliance* series, Rosemary Gladstar has half a dozen books about implementing herbs for various daily purposes. It's clear and easy for a store to buy six copies of each to display together, increasing sales for everyone.

Gift accounts

If a retailer isn't primarily a bookstore but their selection of books is not about a single topic or related to their overall theme or mission statement, they are likely a "gift account." Again, the distinction between specialty and gift is a thin but important one. The gift subject matter offering is much more diverse, but browsers want less technical books. For example, a hardware store (specialty) might stock a book about caring for a very complicated kind of plant while a gift shop would be more likely to sell a photo book of plants of the world. A law resource center might offer a case law book on Ruth Bader Ginsberg, while a gift shop would stock a photo book of inspirational phrases from her. Gift shops primarily stock impulsive items or books with really clear development so you can see the benefits to the reader and understand who it's for even if the subject matter is outside your interests. The most sought after gift account is Urban Outfitters because they purchase at least 1,000 copies of every book that they stock. More importantly, having your books sold in gift shops, even if they aren't national chains, is better advertising than you could buy anywhere. The books are always displayed face-out to the customer and displays are normally on tables for maximum visibility and browsability.

When most people think of gift, they think of boutique stores in walkable tourist neighborhoods. For example, Hawthorne Blvd, Alberta St, and Mississippi Ave in Portland all play host to numerous gift shops featuring a wide variety of books being sold next to shirts with puns on them and tote bags proclaiming "A Woman's Place is in the Resistance." These accounts can be your bread and butter if you are likeable and your books have impulse appeal. Museum gift shops stock impulsive purchases and, if you have the right book selection, will be a much bigger customer than other channels combined. If you have books about teenage boy pop celebrities, a mall jewelry store would be a good account as it fits the interests of their customers. The sky's the limit in regards to gift, and often considering why a store would stock your book and delivering a persuasive argument will get it on the shelf—even if there aren't any other books in the store.

To be fair and clear, some retailers don't know what they are doing when they order books. Sometimes an herb shop will stock our books about train hopping and punk rock when we have some herbal medicine titles that would probably sell quite a bit better. Sometimes the owner or buyer purchases books that they would read themselves even if it's not appropriate for the store. Sometimes this is okay. If a specialty account really loves you, they will hand sell your books like a bookstore does. But you don't want a retailer to buy too many copies of the wrong titles and be left with the impression that your books "don't sell." You want to be thinking about the the second order while you're leveraging the first.

Gift can be incredibly bountiful. Gift stores tend to need a 50% discount and free shipping, but they almost always buy non-returnable copies. If you want to connect with dozens or hundreds of gift stores trying to find new books at once, visit the New York Now show in August in NYC.

Adam Gamble, publisher of Good Night books, switched from regional travel titles to his company's namesake children's line in 2005. He graduated from selling books out of the trunk of his car to building a group of in-house gift sales reps. "By selling to a wide variety of markets, both geographically and sales channel-wise, we have remarkably predictable sales with overall steady growth but few serious fluxuations." Gamble has gone on to sell millions of books, primarily through the gift channel.

Mass markets

Stores that offer deep discounts like WalMart, Hudson News (typically in airports and subways), Costco, and Target often seem like a ripe retail market for publishers. Indeed, some of these accounts tend to buy up to 10,000 copies of a book at a time. In 2018, there are 741 Costco stores, so that's planning on 15 copies sold per store. And your books compete for dollars/inch against every other product in the store. These retailers are also competing with Amazon for loss leaders, which is essentially a race to the bottom on the publisher's dime. The easiest way to approach these accounts is through a distributor who has pre-existing relationships, but, if you have a title with suitable interest and adequate justification for them to purchase, you can close the sale yourself. Sometimes these stores purchase at up to a 70% discount and often request a custom edition of the book, as well.

Laura Stanfill's *City of Weird* was picked up by Costco. She told me this story: "I spotted Pennie, the main buyer, at [large publishing trade show] Book Expo America. She appeared formidable, sweeping through the aisles, with several assistants trailing her—and when I glanced at her nametag, I gushed, 'Pennie! I'm such a fan of yours.' She pulled a business card out of thin air and dropped it into my palm. I felt like I had been anointed by royalty. I followed up by mailing *City of Weird* to Pennie's attention. She emailed back personally, telling me she had staff considering it for regional Northwest placement. I followed up by sending that information to my distributor's sales rep, and, voila, we got our Costco placement."

Stanfill then brilliantly pointed out something that I hadn't considered about what the placement did for her book. "We had people posting social media photos of finding our book in Costco, and all the authors felt special that they had this opportunity, so they told their communities about it. Some people went to Costco just to buy the book. Others saw it on social media and then recognized it at Costco and sent us photos of putting it in their shopping carts among oversized packages of paper towels and the like. *City of Weird* had our lowest return rate of all our titles to-date, and the added visibility definitely helped. If I were to sit down and add up the cost of flight, hotel, conference admission, meals, on-the-ground transportation, I'm sure we didn't earn enough direct sales at Costco to support what it took to get my book into Costco. But looking at it from a business growth perspective, we've been on a ride in the last few years, escalating our national visibility, earning more buzz, appearing in more industry journals, and receiving an explosive increase in submissions and interest from literary agents. Getting into Costco didn't cause all that, but it's a social marker of success that counts for a lot especially in the small press literary world. That placement didn't just make *City of Weird* more accessible and discoverable to target market readers in the Northwest; it made my press more discoverable and—maybe—even more legitimate. All thirty authors were able to tell their friends and family that their book had made it to Costco. Plus, I have Pennie's business card now, which is like having the most coveted baseball card."

Granted, the first ten publishers that I talked to about mass market accounts did not have as much success as Laura did. Each of them had a book adopted for national placement, and they received an order for around 10,000 copies at deep discounts. In most cases around 9,000 copies were returned sporadically over the next year in various states of damage. When you take return fees into account, the costs and losses are staggering.

If you are intent on a mass market strategy and you have the cash flow to support it, go to mass market stores like Costco look at the other books they are stocking and develop yours to resemble them. Many of these major retailers only buy through wholesalers like Readerlink or TNG. Do your diligence and take a look at their selection before researching how to pitch your titles. If you have a book with strong local or gift appeal where you can stomach some risk, research the buying guidelines and schedules for these stores and send them a sample with a post-it note making your case.

Institutional / corporate sales

One day our phone rang. It was a corporate purchaser for a major hotel chain. They wanted to buy 1,000 copies of one of our books with the indicia (often incorrectly called "copyright") page replaced by a letter from their CEO. Their plan was to give the books as gifts to their entire staff for the holidays. A few years later we landed an even bigger sale—10,000 copies of *Everyday Bicycling* to the metro government of a large urban area to be used for commuter incentive programs. They merely wanted to add a chapter written by one of their staff. It was really easy work, and it financed quite a bit of growth for us that year. Institutional and corporate sales are not always for a custom edition, and we've had some wonderful days where we simply ship 1,000 finished books out of our warehouse.

Haymarket has a unique but common sense strategy for institutional sales. "We sell in bulk to nonprofit organizations, who use our books with their staff, as premiums for donations, for local reading groups, or to resell at events. We also have dedicated authors who will often buy their books in bulk to sell at events, and occasionally we have teachers buy their own sets of our books individually."

Unlike mass market sales, institutional sales are non-returnable, and the publisher sets the terms rather than the customer. But they can be elusive. Naturally, whenever we've had similar "brilliant" ideas they haven't panned out. The other party isn't interested, or they have very specific purchasing guidelines that make books an impossible incentive. Some publishers have specialized departments to handle these kinds of sales, but we've found that answering the phone is the most effective method of executing these sales.

Trade Distribution

As your publishing grows, you'll slowly start to see the limitations of only doing direct sales on your website or at events. It's hard to sell even 100 copies of a book in a month, let alone every month. Eventually, you'll have enough titles that carting them around to stores and events is a hassle. Stores will give you the runaround of why they can't stock your book because of such and such ordering policy. If you don't have five new titles on the same subject each month, the section buyer at Barnes & Noble won't even meet with you. If a book is not published with advance notice and it's by an unknown author and an unknown publisher, that's three strikes for most major accounts and you're not even considered. I cannot tell you how many new publishers have expressed to me that gaining access to trade distribution would be the holy grail of their publishing quest. But like all things that we think we want, the results are not exactly what many have built it to be.

A trade distributor is a partner company who takes over the tasks and responsibilities of selling your books to trade accounts like bookstores and wholesalers. Because of their size and scope, trade distributors often have better leveraging power to sell books, get good placement for the books they represent, and, last but not least, get paid for books that have been sold. A trade distributor typically takes 27% of each invoice as their compensation. In this way, they are never losing money on a sale—though you may be. Compare some numbers of what you are currently paying for these services versus what outsourcing them will cost.

Independent Publishers Group (IPG) invented the concept of a trade distributor for independent presses in 1971. The explosion of independent publishers at that time created a problem because stores were reluctant to set up accounts with every new publisher due to the extra work that it creates. A trade distributor brought credibility and stability to new publishers, and stores were more comfortable working with a familiar entity. IPG was bought in 1987 by Chicago Review Press, and today they employ 150 commissioned sales reps with the most boots on the ground of any distributor, including 100 gift reps, 20 commissioned education reps, and a special sales force that was up 14% in 2016.

There are smaller trade distributors like Midpoint, SCB, and National Book Network. There is the family of larger trade distributors owned by Ingram: Consortium, Publishers Group West, Two Rivers, and Ingram Publisher Services. Other large trade distributors include Baker & Taylor Publisher Services, Diamond Book Distributors, Hachette, and Penguin Random House Publisher Services.

The two greatest functions of a distributor are helping you with title development—they are experts in making it easy to understand what a book offers—and getting you into all of the stores that would love to have your books but just "can't" purchase directly from you. A good distributor allows a bedroom publisher to operate competitively with major houses. Distributors create demand for books by contacting account buyers. Wholesalers fulfill that demand and keep stores stocked quickly after the initial push has caught on.

Once you have a book that has sold at least 5,000 copies and at least three titles that are selling consistently month over month, it's a good time to begin shopping for a trade distributor. These stats show that you have an audience who will buy your work and is hungry for more.

Shopping for a distributor is like seeking any other kind of relationship, business or personal. You want to shop around and go with the one that seems to really get you and your books the most. You also will want to negotiate your terms, and continue to work on improving the relationship so that you can both succeed. It is vital to stress that it works best when it's symbiotic and you are working together.

According to Mark Suchomel, Senior Vice President of Baker & Taylor Publisher Services, a publisher should approach a distributor "when they have plans for a good, ongoing publishing program. I've taken on publishers who have just a few titles where I saw that they could take that into a program and make it work. The distributor has to invest a bit of time and resources in order to make a publisher successful. Most distributors should have some room to make those investments. I've watched publishers go from a few books in a few years to a few million dollars in annual sales." Mark Suchomel has been a veteran in book distribution for decades and has long helped to build many small presses into formidable category powerhouses. "The reward I get is seeing good books get into the hands of readers. That and the growth of my clients' businesses is a lovely way to measure success. I am in a position where I am constantly learning. The range of subjects and topics that I have been introduced to in my career is astounding. I am hopelessly curious and through my work am constantly finding out about things of which I was never before aware. At the same time, I have the pleasure of working with people from all kinds of backgrounds who find publishing to be a good fit for them for all kinds of reasons. To be able to help my clients, who oftentimes become my friends as well, is incredibly rewarding. Building a business and keeping that business growing and healthy is tough to do. If I can play a part in something like that which helps people accomplish something they have dreamed about and at the same time educates and entertains others, I'm having a good time."

Because of competition from new distribution models like those pioneered by Lightning Source and Amazon, it is becoming easier than ever to sign a traditional trade distribution deal. The perception of many new and would-be publishers is that this is great, that having a trade distributor allows you to cease focusing your efforts on selling and marketing so that you can settle in to work on the artistic aspects of publishing: editorial, design, and even writing.

Even working with a distributor, you'll still be able to sell your books directly to readers and to some sorts of stores (depending on what is in your contract), but your distributor will take over sales to bookstores and large accounts. Keep in mind that any terms you are offered will seem harsh at first, especially if you are used to doing all your sales directly and even more so if you are no longer able to sell to many of the stores you have built relationships with and are now paid less for the same books. But this is part of the math of this relationship. It's also important to remember that the staff at your distributor is doing work that you either can't or don't want to do yourself. The work is often not nearly as glamorous as the artistic side and involves a lot of paperwork and rejection. Appreciate trade distributors for what they do and don't approach them until you are ready and can't move forward on your own.

A word of warning: distribution is not a substitute for building an audience. It's tempting to assume that once your books are widely available via trade distribution, readers will organically discover them. It makes sense in your mind and it harkens back to those emotional moments of our own childhood when we discovered our favorite books by simply browsing our favorite subject or section at our favorite bookstore. For many, this is the dream that trade distribution (or its cousins at Amazon and Lightning Source) represents: that the existence and intrinsic value of your work will attract readers.

But having a trade distributor isn't quite that simple. It's more like having a new partner that you work with to reach new places rather than a new person to do part of your work for you. Signing with a trade distributor means you are changing your distribution model, and it's not necessarily a better one than staying small. The things that are profitable for your distributor are not necessarily in your best interest.

Working with a trade distributor is a risk. There are many other publishers competing for the same shelf space; meanwhile that space is shrinking. Of the millions of books published last year, Barnes & Noble stocked only 15,000 of them—and returned many copies of each of those. A trade distributor takes a much bigger cut than retailers or wholesalers—you normally only get paid 40% of your book's cover price or less on the books that do sell through— and there are many little costs and fees that can add up quickly.

What's more, your distributor may sell 500 copies of your new book in advance—which is a great number—only to see 475 of them returned eleven months later. It works like this: a store orders five copies of a new book, puts them on display, but only sells one and returns the other four copies after a year. Your distributor will charge you a 10% processing fee for reshelving the returns. The fees might add up to more than what you get paid for the 25 books that sold through. It's easy to quickly get in over your head and even end up owing money to your distributor. The best way to make this relationship successful for you is to already have a growing audience that is eager to get its hands on your books from all kinds of outlets.

Just World Books, a leftist publisher of global affairs distributed by IPG, has created an effective strategy for convincing stores to stock its titles. They consistently and effectively encourage their fans that support their political mission to march into independent bookstores to buy their books. This direct influence to drive customers to stores gives stores a great reason to stock their books.

Laura Stanfill bootstrapped her press after an enthusiastic conversation with Gigi Little, who became her graphic designer. "When I founded my press, I printed short runs through a great regional digital printer, Gorham Printing, and drove them around to bookstores. Out-of-area stores could order direct from me or through Lightning Source, Ingram's print-on-demand service. The Lightning Source channel fed our title metadata to other commercial bookselling sites, though I've always urged our readers to buy local as much as they can, so online sales have always been secondary for us. We started as a regional press, publishing only Oregon authors, and that's why such a hands-on, grassroots distribution system of lugging boxes and making sales calls worked for us. And that's why we could create a business model that didn't rely on Amazon. But as we grew, I realized that we were spending so much time and money on marketing our titles that having them available regionally wasn't sustainable. We needed to make our books more available nationally—and not just by print-on-demand, which has high overhead, low economy of scale, and doesn't really convince random booksellers to order copies unless there was some sort of local connection we could bring to their attention.

"When we accepted Ellen Urbani's novel, *Landfall*, set during Hurricane Katrina, I knew we would need southern bookseller buy-in, and, for that, we needed a distributor with a sales team that could reach the South. I began looking, soon realizing I didn't print the five or so titles per year required to qualify for most trade distributors. Then I discovered a newer boutique distributor, Legato Publishers Group, a sister company to Publishers Group West (PGW). I sent some books to the president, he liked what he saw, we met for breakfast when he was on a business trip, and then his sales team watched me interact with booksellers at a local trade show a few weeks later. I've been with that team ever since."

Eventually Adam Gamble, founder of Good Night Books, went to a distributor to keep up with his own success. "I just don't see how a small press can afford to do all that a traditional trade distributor does, without it being even more expensive. Really, I don't see much choice for publishers, unless they want to spend huge amounts of time and money dealing with issues of billing, collections, fulfillment and sales." Good Night signed with Independent Publishers Group (IPG) and handed over their lucrative gift sales accounts to IPG's sales team, who continued to grow these relationships and sales.

Similarly to Microcosm, the publishers of Haymarket Books began to take the press more seriously when they landed a distributor. Co-founder Julie Fain says, "In 2005 we started trade distribution with Consortium, publishing five titles our first season. At that point it felt real, like we were starting to find an audience."

From 2002 to 2010, Haymarket sold books from other publishers to complement their early list. According to Fain, "We did the fulfillment by ourselves, but over time, the volume has grown to the point where we're now moving to do as much of this out of our distributor's warehouse as we can. Our consumer orders are now fulfilled by our trade distributor. Our office space just isn't scalable as the volume increases, and we think the costs are outweighed by being freed up to do the work of publishing and promoting the books, which is what we're good at."

Still, distribution is not everything. Laura Stanfill learned many lessons along the way. "Distribution definitely has surprised me in terms of the inability to predict returns; that may get better as I have more titles out, and a better set of numbers to help me project, but with fiction it's always variable. But I do know, for sure, every time we publish a book, our reps are selling it into stores across the U.S.—and a lot of small-press publishers and micro publishers don't have that kind of reach. I have found that one of my top obligations as a publisher of a distributed press is to constantly ask myself how readers in a certain city or town will hear about our book and want to order it. With nonfiction, that's subject-based, but with fiction, it's a mix of getting the right reviews, creating events, making the book available in galleys to churn up interest, having eye-catching covers, picking the right sales descriptions and phrases, and building a brand that is recognizable by readers."

To reach an audience:

- You need to be clever—more clever than the other people who are doing what you do.

- You need to spell out exactly what the book is.

- You need to have an online presence that appeals to your reader base.

- You need to work hard to promote your book through traditional media as well as more creative channels.

- You need to find ways to interact with your readers and keep them invested in your output and success.

You don't need a trade distributor to do any of these things—good ones that are a good match for your work will do them, but not as well as you can and not in a way that replaces your own efforts. A trade distributor can expand your reach, but if you haven't yet built up a way to connect with your audience, that expanded reach may not stick or be sustainable.

For many publishers, signing a distribution deal feels like the Holy Grail. But there are many pitfalls if the relationship isn't working for all parties. Rob Broder, President of Ripple Grove Press, who focuses on timeless children's picture books that stress narratives over morals, sent a copy of *Mae & The Moon*, about a child searching for the new moon after the old one disappears, to Barnes & Noble's small press buyer. Barnes & Noble ordered 350 copies, which Broder excitedly communicated to their distributor. Their distributor responded to tell Broder not to contact Barnes & Noble directly in the future, citing that the distributor would manage the relationship on Ripple Grove's behalf. Broder followed directions but subsequent books that they published were not picked up by B&N in a similar fashion. Broder was left not knowing whether

Barnes & Noble was no longer interested in their other titles or if they were simply not seeing them. Trusting these responsibilities to their distributor was hurting Ripple Grove's sales.

Two years after his experience with Barnes & Noble, Broder read an article from title development manager Mary Rowles citing how IPG gave small presses a chance to succeed. Broder immediately sent over copies of his books and Ripple Grove left his distributor for IPG, a larger company that helped them continue to grow. Broder was "ready for my titles to have further reach. I felt like that was the next step for growing our publishing. I was disappointed about how frequently Midpoint would ignore my emails while I was trying to build a relationship together."

A distributor doesn't always have congruent goals with a publisher due to their economy of scale. It's a physical impossibility to show every book to every buyer or even to put every book in every catalog. It's impossible to answer every email, and, in the end, corners must be cut and decisions must be made. Again, a distributor's goal is not always your goal. Your distributor can make money through storing your books, shipping and processing returns of your books, and the various aspects of managing data and inventory that goes into publishing—without ever actually selling any books. You have to evaluate when your goals are in sync and when they are not. Someday maybe you'll outgrow your first trade distributor and collaborate with someone else. Or maybe you'll find that you preferred (or have a better bottom line) being smaller and getting more personal mail and doing fulfillment for some stores selectively.

Asia Citro of The Innovation Press reinforces the value of this relationship. "I can't overstate the importance of choosing well when it comes to your distribution. My first distributor was bought by a (large) company and once the takeover was complete it was clear that the new management neither understood my books nor valued them. Though it was costly and scary to switch distributors, I felt that it was time. I moved my books to Baker & Taylor Publisher Services, and I couldn't be happier that I did. I have such a dedicated team now that is excited about my books. Dan Verdick, Jeff Tegge, and Mark Suchomel are such huge champions of them, in fact, that my sales have doubled in the last two months!"

BTPS serves Citro's books about kids doing science projects because they specialize in access to libraries and schools. Baker & Taylor Publisher Services, which merged with Follett in 2016, provides superior access to libraries. According to Mark Suchomel, "Follett School Solutions services about 85% of the K-12 school and library market, and is heading full steam into school book fairs. Follett Higher Ed runs more than 1,200 retail stores on college and university campuses around the country. B&T wholesale has about 65% of the public library market, and is the largest exporter of English language books in the world. Not only can we get specific titles in front of the eyes of those people that make decisions on what gets stock and purchased in those outlets, we have the volume and infrastructure that allows us to ship books quicker and more economically than anyone else."

However, outgrowing your distributor doesn't always benefit the publisher or turn out how you would expect. Adam Gamble eventually outgrew IPG and followed their former President to his new distribution company, Legato. "We really went 'with Mark Suchomel' to Legato, because he sided with us when another IPG publisher created a copycat series to our Good Night titles. We eventually shut them down with our lawyers, but during the process I asked IPG to stand with us against them. Mark agreed and took immediate action on our behalf. [When Mark founded Legato Publishers Group in 2013] I felt loyal to Mark while IPG was raising our fees in a way that rubbed us wrong. In the short term, [leaving IPG for Legato] was a bad decision for us. Since then, I've come to recognize IPG as an excellent partner and to gain even more respect for IPG's ownership and top management."

Legato, then owned by Perseus Books Group, was in constant transition during their partnership with Good Night. "We lost many accounts during the difficult transition to Legato, and our growth rate declined substantially. We also had a very difficult time adjusting to the Legato model from the IPG model we had been so successful with."

Gamble eventually changed distributors again to sign a deal with Penguin Random House Publisher Services [PRHPS], the largest distribution option for an independent publisher. "PRHPS appears to be a more stable company to us than Legato was during our tenure there. So far, PRHPS have exceeded our expectations, and we feel very comfortable with their staff and management. PRH fulfillment is fast and their reporting systems are more robust than anything I've ever seen. They have reinitiated some relationships with accounts that have dropped us in the past. They have monthly scheduled phone calls with us to review expectations and performance. They have us give them power point presentations for the six sales conference meetings per year (two for each of three seasons) as opposed to the two sales conferences with the other companies—one for each of two seasons."

The largest companies aren't necessarily the best fit for your publishing. Oddly, the bigger the company, the simpler they need your publishing program. Good Night Books fits in well at PRHPS largely because they are very strong in a single category so it's easy for the sales team to integrate into existing infrastructure.

Even if you cannot land a distribution deal with PRHPS, Baker, or another distributor, who are highly selective about publishers who are very strong in any one category, you may be able to create other kinds of interesting deals. You can divide production expenses and sales territory, partnering for co-publication with a larger publisher that isn't as personally in touch with the audience as you are. A larger publisher will have booktrade distribution on lockdown because they have better staff and relationships, but you could handle direct sales as well as specialty, gift, and appropriate conference sales. In this way you can grow the audience and sales without hurting each other's reach.

Microcosm terminated our distribution agreement with PGW in 2018. Within three months of self-distributing, our sales immediately grew by 64% and that growth remained consistent throughout the first year. Similarly to Microcosm, in 2016 Bazillion Points, who publishes coffee table books about music, also left PGW, a different division of Ingram Books Group. According to Ian Christe, "We were satisfied with PGW, but in the end [receiving all of our payments in a single monthly check] just put a chokehold on cash flow. Having checks arrive daily instead of monthly is just a breath of fresh air. Surprisingly, very little else has changed. Even during our five years with PGW, we were handling all direct sales to readers, record stores, and music distributors ourselves. So we would break down shipments from a printer into three blocks, with the majority heading to the [now Ingram] warehouse in Tennessee; a few pallets to Turnaround in London; and then a thousand books or so to our office in Greenpoint, Brooklyn. Once we had enough books in print, we needed a short-term storage space in Long Island City, Queens. For a few years, we were playing this time-consuming tile puzzle game with shuffling pallets of books around New York City. We were probably the most muscular publisher in America, but after ten years it just became ridiculous. Sitting in a rented car in the rain in Queens drinking coffee in Styrofoam cups waiting for book delivery was awesome; we called it being on stakeout, but in the end we've been able to add a book a year to the schedule and save a ton on shipping by letting somebody else throw the boxes around." Bazillion Points went independent—doing their own distribution. They turned over their fulfillment operation to Ware-Pak in University Park, Illinois, a warehousing and fulfillment company.

Similarly, Per of Ooligan Press pointed out that "Pomegranate Communications, a high-end gift publisher, handles their own sales, fulfillment, and warehousing from Portland. Their warehouse employees are part of conversations about new titles, taking advantage of all of their institutional knowledge."

No matter what, the bottom line is that your job as a publisher is first and foremost connecting readers to reading—not books to a marketplace. Evaluate if and when a distributor makes sense towards those goals for you or how to best reach your most important customer, the readers.

Homework:

• What stores and libraries can you sell your books to on your own?

• What are some relevant specialty and gift accounts for your books?

• Is there a reason to push for mass market sales?

• Do you have books that would work well in chain stores or are you more suited for independents?

• Are you prepared to collect on money owed to you?

• Can you afford to do consignment?

• What kind of institutional accounts might find your books to be great premiums?

• What conferences can you sell books at that your fans attend?

• Have you set up a website to sell books directly to readers?

• Are you the kind of personality that can be a team player within the push-pull relationship of a distributor?

• When you've sold 5,000 books and are hitting walls, approach a distributor for your next stage of growth.

• Constantly keep tabs on which accounts are growing your reach and which might be holding you back.

HOW TO SELL BOOKS

Fulfillment at Every Level

The best advice I've heard for bookselling for new publishers comes from Russell Nohelty, author of *Sell Your Soul: How to Build Your Creative Career* and founder of Sell More Cool Things, an online school that teaches creatives about commerce. Russell distills the fundamentals of finding, knowing, and focusing on your best customers based on their other interests and it boils down to repeatedly putting your books in front of the kind of people that would be interested in what you're making. His is the kind of chutzpah and bringing in ideas from other industries that new publishers need to succeed, running online "builder" campaigns to help numerous small publishers combine resources to develop relevant mailing lists.

This chapter will help you to hone in on things we've discussed previously and offer the opportunity to think about marketing your press as a whole rather than each individual title. Your marketing strategy will, in turn, determine how you build your audience and feed your sales funnel. This will determine your fulfillment strategy. For this reason this chapter will focus on how these three aspects of your publishing intertwine.

Once you've built up an audience, they want to interact with you. They want signed books and little bonuses and lovingly handwritten letters and postcards and a relationship. And then you can meet them at events and learn about their lives and what attracts them to your work and probably relate to them as human beings. This will create circular investment, and, when they see your books in a store, they will buy them. Maybe they'll become your next author; they'll almost certainly share their feelings about your work with their friends. Along the way, you'll also find some stores that like the cut of your jib and want to put your books outfacing on their prime real estate, and your friends will tell you how excited they were to see your book at such and such place and how proud of you they are.

Fulfillment at Every Level

The phone rang this morning. It was a customer in New York who had bought some of our books from our website but wanted to inquire about gift wrapping, overnight shipping, and adding a few things to their order. In our office we have shipping software, a gift wrapping area, daily postal pickup service, and we can walk into our warehouse to grab the books we need. So in the span of a few minutes, I was able to take her payment and get her order out into the mail stream to travel across the country within 24 hours. I included a handwritten note, a comic poster about Microcosm's history, and a promotional t-shirt. It is likely that when she and

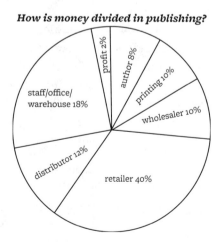

How is money divided in publishing?

profit 2%
author 8%
printing 10%
staff/office/warehouse 18%
wholesaler 10%
distributor 12%
retailer 40%

her husband celebrate his birthday, they'll have positive feelings about Microcosm.

Most independent publishers don't offer services like these. They rely on fulfillment companies or distributors to handle things like warehousing, sales, and order fulfillment. But the monopolization of the industry makes it more vital than ever to build your ground game, creating interest and awareness for your books by bringing them to where their audiences naturally congregate. The easiest way to do this is through purchasing a booth at events where you want your books to establish an entrenched presence. Microcosm does this through bicycle conferences, mental health counseling symposiums, gardening shows, and vegan festivals. These type of events plus adequate publicity (see page 311) and web promotion are the only way for a small publisher like yourself to shine in a specific category. You can't always rely upon your authors, so treat your press like it's worth telling the world about.

Once you've got a firm understanding of who your audience is and what they like, you're in an ideal position. You can develop your books around their interests and even ask them directly for feedback. You can understand what books they want and commision them to be written. But most importantly, you'll understand where, how, and why your audience buys books. Do they *ever* go to Barnes & Noble? If so, do they ever actually purchase anything? If not, why not?

Talking to most people it seems that books are purchased most often from gift stores with killer merchandising. While they might have gone in as a joke, they left with a copy of *Soccernomics*. The same thing might be true of your audience, but it might not. Asia Citro's audience consists of very busy moms that never have time for a trip to the bookstore so they defer to ordering from online retailers. Lone Pine Press does killer business selling to hardware stores because that's where their customers are. If you are publishing literary fiction, most of your fans probably hang out in bookstores. Microcosm's audience is cultivated at lots of specialized consumer events and through direct mailings and then encouraged to order directly from our website.

You probably didn't get into publishing to ship books. That's okay but it's important to understand the place that delivering books to your reader serves in your future publishing empire and what managing some aspects of that in-house can do for you.

If your books have a *very* niche audience, as in "my grandfather's war stories" or a business or technology book about a very specific piece of software or science and you know how to reach your entire audience directly, there is no need to sell your books through a distributor or even stores. If your readers all come to speaking events or conferences or your website, why give someone else part of your pie?

The Ground Game

Handling warehousing and fulfillment in-house is another kind of vertical integration. Just like it doesn't make sense for a publisher to purchase printing equipment, it makes perfect sense for some publishers to handle warehousing and shipping. Distribution, unlike printing, has been changing rapidly over the past 50 years. If, as the joke goes, publishing companies were started so people would have something to talk about at cocktail parties, fulfillment quickly disappears into a theoretical warehouse in the midwest. Book distributors were created to represent the large volume of small presses that did not have significant enough sway or a big enough catalog to bend an ear at major retailers or wholesalers. A distributor could offer a sales staff, warehouse, and access to new sales channels. But today, the publishing industry is ruled by a handful of monopolies that dictate terms onto publishers and make grievances difficult to resolve. Fortunately, that's not as much of a problem as it sounds like. While this problem is much worse today, let's take a look at some cases where people have overcome the stranglehold of monopolies in the past.

In 1901, Encyclopedia Britannica was experiencing financial difficulties as the allure for their sophisticated product was fading. To resolve this, they created the first fleet of door-to-door book salespeople for their encyclopedia sets, also introducing vertical integration to the book business with direct-to-consumer sales. This newfound ground game saved Britannica and these operations became so tremendously successful that the Mid-American Bible Company followed suit, leading to a cultural touchstone in the 1969 Maysles brothers documentary film *Salesman*.

The Internet has largely replaced knocking on doors because it sorts the customers out of your funnel who wouldn't be interested. Still, it's important to learn the power of a conversation in reaching your audience.

In 1966, Stewart Brand picked up a similar torch. A biologist educated at Stanford, Brand demanded that NASA release their image of the "whole earth," believing that it could become a powerful symbol of shared destiny. Championing powerful beliefs in ecology and social justice, Stewart and his wife, Lois, loaded up their Dodge truck with tools and books to embark on a communal teaching tour. The Brands demonstrated how to use homesteading tools but found that audiences were more interested in purchasing their publication, the *Whole Earth Catalog*, a book featuring extensive rants and write-ups about tools too big to fit into the Dodge. The Brands came home and focused on their publishing operation by mailing books to readers via mail order so they could find their own inspiration and be empowered to shape their own environment and adventure.

What Whole Earth lacked in business or financial planning, it made up for in passion and vision, offering a turnkey option to a whole new lifestyle. Brand was at the center of every emerging cultural trend for its first five minutes. He coined the term "personal computer" and was part of the entourage of *One Flew Over the Cuckoo's Nest* author Ken Kesey. Brand published work about everything from welding to female masturbation to mountain bicycling to managing drug busts to building your own geodesic dome inspired by their hero, Buckminster Fuller. In a 1972 article for *Rolling Stone*, Brand predicted the existence and power of the Internet.

Brand's hot button access to culture put him in the perfect position to sell books and his preferred method was through vertically integrated mail order to his readers. Whole Earth burned bright and disappeared but left an indelible mark. *Whole Earth Catalog* won a National Book Award in 1971 (and sold over two million copies) and in 2005, Steve Jobs referred to Whole Earth as a predecessor to Google. Former "shelter editor" for Whole Earth, Lloyd Kahn became the champion of the tiny house movement and is now the publisher of his own press, Shelter Publications. A former Whole Earth editor went on to found *Wired* magazine and Cool-Tools.org.

Brand literally brought his books to his readers until they could see why he was so excited about them. He perfectly demonstrates how you don't want to sell your books door-to-door but rather need to demonstrate your own infectious glee about them to a set of carefully selected audiences so the right people can see how great they are.

Zine publisher Aaron Cometbus took the ground game a step further in 1990, traveling from city to city with bands that he was friends with. He brought along copies of his zine, *Cometbus,* and convinced newsstands and record stores to purchase copies from him. When he returned home to Berkeley, he kept the stores stocked, mailing out new issues as they were released. Within ten years, Cometbus had created a veritable distribution network that many other publishers continue to use.

And while it's changed, there is still a thriving model of door-to-door sales. You might know Educational Development Corporation (EDC), which publishes under the Usborne and Kane/Miller imprints, by their signature title *Everybody Poops*. It was a Japanese book that they licensed in 1993 and went on to sell over a million copies of in the U.S. In a 2014 interview with *Tulsa World*, CEO Randall White said "Two years ago we made the decision to cut Amazon out because they were taking too big of a cut of our sales." That year, EDC sold twelve million books.

How did EDC do it? They sell their children's books direct to parents through "the party plan," in-home parties similar to Tupperware or makeup parties. They have thousands of independent sales consultants and an annual sales training conference that focuses on selling the 1,500 backlist titles at home parties, book fairs, and events. They employ stay-at-home moms and other people invested in parenting books about science that want extra income. The company trains the sales force on how to manage a business and approach schools. They found that their customers were buying the books cheaper from Amazon during the sales presentations, cutting out their reps. So EDC dropped Amazon and grew their company's sales by 20% to $10.8 million in total sales.

Make Your Memorable Mark

Starting in 1975, countercultural rebels Loompanics Unlimited carried a similar torch of vertical integration. Loompanics expanded and refined the ideas of Whole Earth through the editorial vision of its publisher, Mike Hoy. Focused on questioning authority and just as critical of corporatist libertarians as he was of Democrats and Republicans, Loompanics published about fifteen titles a year for 31 years. If Whole Earth made you feel like you could contemplate quantum physics while hoeing potatoes on your commune, Loompanics wanted you to think about why that was an attractive life for you and who was trying to limit those freedoms. These identities and emotional relationships were vital to the bookselling success of both operations and demonstrate just how vital building a movement is. Hoy published books about picking locks, manufacturing methamphetamines, conspiracy theories, creating fake IDs, and *How to Start Your Own Country*. His political views are controversial enough that his ads have been refused from eBay, Amazon, and Google. He was once hung up on in the middle of an interview with NPR for making fun of the War on Terrorism. The common logic among publishers is that you want to play nice and fit in, but Hoy cemented his editorial vision and built his ground game upon his defiance and opposition to fitting in. Hoy was very aware that his clear views would repel the wrong people and attract the right ones. He made jokes that anarchists had too many leaders and rules for him—though he was also quite serious. And indeed, just like Microcosm, his customers became his authors and the right readers flocked to him.

In a 2005 interview with Sky Cosby on the Last Word website, Hoy said "When you're in business at the level we're at, there is really no such thing as bad publicity. I'm not looking for people who are afraid to question what their television sets tell them. If I wasn't pissing off assholes like that NPR guy, I wouldn't have much to offer anyone with brains." And Hoy clarified that he isn't pro-drugs but rather wants to challenge the popular narrative. "'Just say no' makes exactly as much sense as 'Just say yes.' My position is 'Just say know.'" Whether or not you agree with that as a justification for publishing books about how to open a meth lab is immaterial, it merely decides whether you are inside or outside of Loompanics' customer base. Loompanics primarily sold itself as a brand and to widen its selling bag. It distributed 800 titles from other publishers and handled a substantial direct mail order catalog to readers.

Similar to Whole Earth, Loompanics' catalog contained articles alongside books to purchase. This deepened the reader's understanding of the topics and interest while defining Loompanics as the definitive expert on the material. And once the catalogs were out of print, Loompanics would publish books containing these articles about things like government spying and current events. Readers felt like they were a part of the mission and the culture alongside Hoy's adapted version of "Our Men Want Books," the government's propaganda design for troop support during World

War II. Loompanics shuttered their doors for good in 2006, saying that earning the same level of income from publishing had become too difficult for the amount of work it now required.

Getting the Books to the Reader

Publishers get into publishing to make books and spend hours tearing our hair out in unlit offices, sweating over a typewriter or arguing on the phone with a zealous author. That work is never done. But mail order work begins and ends each day, creating a satisfying feeling of accomplishment. You can gaze upon the mountain of outgoing packages as it awaits the delivery carriers in the morning.

At first, outsourcing distribution and fulfillment to Amazon, a trade distributor, or a pick-and-pack company makes sense on paper. It feels like you're taking work off your plate. But there are even more downsides to this than I mentioned in the last chapter. The books from one large indie's fulfillment company always arrive in a condition that leads you to believe that the staff must actively *hate* books. When a book arrives damaged, it requires more work from the store—calling in a report in order not to pay for the book. But this company also requires photographing each damaged book in order to receive credit. This is because the fulfillment company is not honest with the publisher. In one case, the warehouse insisted that UPS had re-packed the box. So we sent a photo showing that the books were packed in a thin factory box from the publisher with no packing material so that they could slide around loose until every one of them was destroyed. We eventually stopped ordering from this publisher. Keeping fulfillment in-house gives you more control of your inventory and your customers' happiness.

Still, there are only so many hours in a day and publishers are heavily resistant to overseeing fulfillment. Asia Citro is nervous at events, sells most of her books through major accounts, and is resistant and uninclined to grow her ground game. "We have many times considered selling books through our own platform, but realized that it won't actually work for major reasons. The first reason is that we wouldn't be able to get great shipping rates on our own—we wouldn't have the volume initially—so we'd have to charge a shipping fee on top of the cost of the book, making us less competitive price-wise. The cost of creating a shipping system on our end, time and money-wise, is a bit intimidating. And finally, most of our customers are busy and tired parents and/or teachers. Our customer demographic utilizes Amazon to purchase books, so having to visit an unfamiliar site and enter their address and payment in would be a deterrent to purchase. When it comes down to it, fast, easy, and discounted is their ideal path for book purchases—we simply couldn't compete with Amazon. So we don't try!" For this reason, Citro prefers to give Amazon the much larger discount. Unlike the indie bookstore market, Citro does not need to put in the time or expense of familiarizing the book market with the emotional payoff of each of her titles. Instead, Amazon's sales are built on metrics and data. However, the problem with reliance on monopolies like Amazon for fulfillment is that they are very good at understanding and using the same data to extort publishers—which they refer to derogatorily as "gazelles"—to give Amazon better and better terms every year.

While it's not right for everyone, Rob Broder of Ripple Grove Press—another children's picture book press—intends to launch a direct-to-consumer approach. "I'm interested in offering a more personal touch, to show that we are a family press, and to send a note with the book. This would create more investment in us from our fans and put more money in our pocket." And while it's certainly an opportunity cost trade-off, he's right about all of these things.

The key to successfully selling directly to the reader is to have a focused list and an easily identifiable and reachable customer base, so you are a destination for more than a single item. You want to make your audience think of you as the go-to source for those kinds of books.

From there you need to make the right people aware of your website and titles with a clear and easy way to order. Your customers will talk about you and attract like-minded consumers that tend to gather and communicate with each other. Publishers F&W have an Interweave imprint for their craft titles where customers gather socially to perform the projects in the books, trade patterns and techniques, and compare notes. Interweave has magazines, books, DVDs, tools, kits, etc. that they sell online, at their own craft shows, and at conventions. This is powerful because it creates an honest social network. Customers can share feedback with each other and promote the books organically. Ideas can brew and fester and be communicated to the publisher. It creates and grows a market around an existing audience.

Microcosm has reached readers very effectively through our package author tours (see page 311). By organizing our authors with new books to spend a month on tour in a car together, crammed between boxes of our books, we sell hundreds of books from our entire catalog along the way. Over the years, the tours, along with conferences and leaving a trail of promotional materials in our wake, have proven to be our most effective strategy for selling books.

Maintaining this proximity to your customers will help you to develop better books and ensure that they are more successful on every level. Many publishers make the mistake of developing books for certain retailers rather than for the readers who buy and love their books. By managing things like sales, fulfillment, and warehousing in-house you can get feedback directly. Often you'll find that no one else will have as much comprehension and passion for your books as you do.

Laura Stanfill of Forest Avenue Press continues to dabble in the ground game as well. Like Asia, Laura is a one-woman company who has to be protective of her time. "When I first started my press, I did occasional sales from my house, usually larger orders from indie bookstores who preferred buying direct from me. That involved stocking packaging materials and tape, plus waiting in line at the post office."

Within a year, Stanfill had signed the distribution deal with Legato but still wanted to maintain contact with her core fanbase. "To make my titles available to the marketplace, since I didn't have a commercial shopping cart program, I started off using Gumroad, which at that time was more for digital products than physical ones. I had a billing dispute issue, where the customer didn't recognize "Gumroad" on his credit card bill, canceled the sale, then realized what it was a few hours later, tried to reinstate the charge, and even tried to pay a second time. Gumroad flagged it and never let the sale go through, even though the customer swore he made a mistake and swore he received the product and owed me money. It was very frustrating for both of us, because he genuinely wanted to support Forest Avenue, but he couldn't get Gumroad to accept his money. So I was out the time, the hassle, and the cost of the book, shipping, and the royalty payment." Haggling with a mail order customer for $20 isn't a great use of any CEO's time and experiences like this can feel like such a flop that it's hard to get back up and try again. Sure, she could pursue payment another way but just about any other task is a more efficient use of her time. For very small publishers, outsourcing collections and customer service are a major selling point for working with a trade distributor.

Laura, like any good publisher, is not one to give up easily. "Soon after that experience I gave up on Gumroad and installed PayPal on my site. That was successful for autographed preorders especially, but ultimately I realized using my time to create and market books made more sense than fulfilling orders, which takes a lot of steps and at this small scale wasn't really worth the hassle."

Stanfill went back to the drawing board. "For years after that, I didn't have any way for customers to buy direct from Forest Ave. Then I went to a training in Berkeley about Aerio, the shopping cart system [that Ingram had recently purchased], which allows anyone to create an instant bookstore on their website. I filled mine with our titles and titles by authors and presses I admire, and started getting sales. Ingram fulfills the orders from its warehouses; if a product isn't in stock with Ingram, then I can't offer it on my site. But a lot of books are available. And if there are any customer issues, or damaged books, the customers are asked to contact Ingram directly. So now I just go to the post office for mailing review copies. And any sales I make from my website earn Forest Avenue some money—even if they were published by another press. I get a percentage of the cost of the book that would otherwise go to a wholesaler or another business. For Forest Avenue books that I sell direct, I get my usual cut from the distributor, same as if Ingram had sold it to an indie bookstore, but I also get a percentage of the sale, so if someone wants to buy one of our titles online, doing it through our website gives us the most dollars with no added hassle."

Determining if and when it makes sense to sell directly relies heavily upon your list, the natural habits of your customers, what best benefits your bottom line, and the infrastructure and staff that you have available. For many publishers it's about experimenting periodically and testing out a few different points of sale and fulfillment options until you find the one that suits you.

How to Decide Your Fulfillment Structure

For very select impulse genres, like romance, you will develop occasional passive "incidental sales" through online retailers like Amazon because readers devour these books mercilessly and are always looking for new stories. For everyone else, you will see little to no effect of listing your books for sale on these sites unless you are actively marketing and driving traffic there because they are the most overcrowded marketplaces on Planet Earth.

For most independent publishers the goal is to cement the idea of your authority and reputation on your subject and drive your readers to the place where similar books are typically purchased. Our fans often send us enthusiastic photos of our books in their local bookstore, mostly because they are surprised and excited to find them there. Often Microcosm will be at a conference where someone will buy a book from us because they previously read a review and saw it for sale at a local retailer. Marketing operates in a rule of threes: the third time that you see a book, it feels like it's *everywhere* and you reach the end of the sales funnel. If it's right for you, you buy it.

Because of this, you want to immerse your readers in your books. One way that this is done is by "showrooming," or using retailers as a way for your books to be discovered. For example, one of the biggest problems for stores like Costco, Barnes & Noble, and even gift or grocery stores is that their customers merely browse and order later on Amazon. While showrooming can help publishers, it can hurt retailers, and some gift and boutique stores won't stock books at all that are sold on Amazon. This is is another reason why you must fundamentally understand your customers, their behavior, and ideally have a way to communicate with them.

Who are your customers? Where do they shop? Where are they most likely to buy your books? If your books are truly unique and unlike any other books in the market, like books about repairing espresso machines, coping with alcoholism or photos of obscure sexual fetishes, then you can likely reach 95% of your audience effectively through Google and a website, trade shows and conferences, and direct marketing to your targeted readers. Sure, you could give Amazon part of your pie, but there isn't a whole lot to gain by doing so and you hold the power.

For every other kind of publishing, there are a number strategies to choose between:

- **Niche seeking:** If you are publishing underserved but sought-after topics, like *The Five-Gallon Bucket Book: 105 Uses and Abuses for the Ultimate Recyclable,* you'll want to service all sales channels since you will have virtually no competition. Start with your most loyal audience purchasing from you and sharing their passion for your work. Then leverage this into specialty, gift, library, trade, mass market, and any accounts that sell books—in that order. Other good examples of this type of publication include *Difficult Personalities: A Practical Guide to Managing the Hurtful Behavior of Others (and Maybe Your Own)* and *Damn! Why Didn't I Write That?: How Ordinary People Are Raking in $100,000.00 or More Writing Nonfiction Books & How You Can Too.* No customer cares who wrote *The Five-Gallon Bucket Book*, mostly because no credentials are involved and no one would write such a book without ample experience and passion. Similarly, you'd want the author of *Damn! Why Didn't I Write That?* To have some successes under their belt but ultimately there are no credentials involved (and, well, that's exactly what that book is about. Highly recommended.). But for a book like *Difficult Personalities* you're going to have readers and account buyers looking for either some degrees, certifications, or at least a tremendous mediation track record. With that in hand, you can march in and get the sale anywhere. These titles are very easy to maintain as evergreen backlist strong sellers.

- **Controlling your shelf:** If you are carving out authority on a niche subject and you have access to a core audience that you know is interested in reading and buying your books, you start inside your network. Unlike the book about repairing espresso machines, this model has an audience of tens of thousands. Still, you don't need to aim for the trade market even though that potential is there. For example, if you publish children's books about science projects, a few key writeups on the right blogs will drive traffic and sales to your own website. Those customers will talk about your books. Reviewers will wonder why they never saw your books and talk about how great they are. From there, invade libraries with force and aim for appropriate gift accounts. Specialty and trade are your final destinations. You'll probably want to ignore chains and mass market. Continue to focus on appropriate consumer events where your audience congregates naturally.

Jessica Kingsley Publishers (JKP) is a great example of this model succeeding. Founded in 1987, they publish both trade and technical books about neurodiversity, transgender healthcare, and queer sex, as well as comics about understanding anxiety, forgiveness, and pain. Slowly expanding into the U.S. in 2004, they have around 25 titles that have sold over 100,000 copies. JKP has 3,000 unique titles in print that sell an average of 1,500 copies per title and they publish about 250 new titles per year. David Corey, Vice President of Sales and Marketing, explained why this model works so well. "Jessica Kingsley started JKP at her kitchen table. She oversaw its growth into a multi-million dollar global company by sticking close to her original mission of publishing books that make a difference in people's lives. She also understood early on that an enthusiastic reading audience is also the best source of determining 'what's next?' and is an important partner in guiding editorial direction. Readers are the eyes and ears of what we do. For example, early success in publishing on the subject of autism opened pathways into covering other developmental disabilities. And publishing around developmental disabilities led to publishing books on counseling and mental health. And publishing in mental health led us to social work, and social work led to the topic of therapeutic parenting, including adoption and foster care. Audiences have diverse yet connected interests and life situations. Indeed it was one of our longtime autism authors who highlighted the research around the relationship between autism and gender diversity and sexuality. The gender spectrum is one of our newest and most successful publishing topics." JKP now sells more than 600,000 books per year with around 75% of those being backlist. After 30 years of dominating these shelves they were purchased by Hachette in 2017. The success and model of JKP is similar to that of Microcosm and is a great model to explore independent publishing being done exceptionally.

- **Cult of personality:** If you are publishing fiction or developing and selling on the worldview and buzz of your authors, look to the careers of Malcolm Gladwell or Lidia Yuknavitch. Both are stand-out authors in crowded categories. Yuknavitch writes memoir, arguably the most competitive category of all. But an early collaboration with Ken Kesey and her passion for sharing her story of how writing kept her alive has created respect and support. Gladwell made a career of writing oppositional business thinkpieces with surprising conclusions that draw as much criticism as praise. It's the conversation that propels his career even more than the support for his ideas.

Launching an author—let alone a publishing house—on this kind of author recognition is difficult. This strategy also applies if you are trying to create unique, distinct, and/or superior niche work within a crowded subject. Start with a model of associating with your successful friends and colleagues and appearing at conference/festival/trade show appearances in the appropriate area of interest where the author can connect to their audiences directly. Point to what is distinct about your book and niche. You'll need strong trade reviews and critical acclaim. Bookstores will be your bread and butter for sales. Indies will influence chains as the buzz reaches the suburbs. The same strategy applies if you have a "current events book," such as offering new information on the President or a new perspective on vaccinations. These type of books are hard to maintain unless the author is churning out a new one every year or two. You'll need lots of publicity and enthusiasm from all participants. Still, most burn bright and die abruptly—if they catch fire at all. But there are successful stories. Eight years after publication, Lidia Yuknavitch's *Chronology of Water* was optioned to be adapted for a Hollywood movie.

While you can change your strategy later, it's best not to sit on the fence between two of these strategies as doing so will confuse your audience and ultimately hurt your sales.

Fulfillment

Handling your own order fulfillment results in better control and count of your inventory, fewer errors, fewer damages, faster shipping, the ability to add insertions to your orders like advertising, free books, or special offers. While outsourcing your order fulfillment scales the cost to your sales, handling it in-house ties your costs to fixed figures like rent and hourly wages. Working with a distributor or fulfillment company offers a variable cost; you only have to pay when work is being performed. Do the math and see which makes more sense for you when you are in a position to make a choice.

When someone has placed an order directly from your website, they are the most invested customer in your operation that you will ever encounter. Sending them ads for future projects will pay off. Shipping promotional things directly to your readers is the most targeted marketing that you could ever hope for.

To set up your home fulfillment station, you'll need tape, a postal scale, padded envelopes that conform to the sizes of your books, and a way to print your postage. For many years Microcosm used Pitney Bowes, once your only option for printing postage in your office. But in 2006, we switched to Endicia.com, who offered built-in tracking for packages as well as discounted mailing rates. Perhaps more importantly, Endicia (now owned by Stamps.com, but without a decline or change in services) allowed the ability not only to print postage from the computer, but to click the tracking on their website and automatically email that information to the customer. For $16 per month, we save a dozen hours on the phone and in line at the post office each week. Endicia also sells the proper postal scales and label printers that work best with their software. Compare prices though, especially when buying more labels. Buying several thousand labels at a time through third-party specialty vendors like LabelCity.com is cheaper.

You'll need a sufficiently large table or desk to pull, pack, and organize your orders on. Double check everything twice before sealing the envelope and write the name of the customer on it in marker so you don't adhere the wrong label to it.

Your inclination will be to pull, pack, and ship an order as you receive it. You'll be surprised and excited as the first few orders come in to see that your system is working. You'll want to reciprocate and expedite shipment. But hold your horses.

Pack your orders on a regular schedule; perhaps every few days at first and then at an appointed time each day. This will economize the use of your time and your efficiency. It's easier and more streamlined to assemble ten orders than one. For our first sixteen years, the entire Microcosm staff used to spend our first hour or two of each workday pulling, packing, and shipping the orders. It was like a barn raising. While the money Microcosm received for performing this work was always far more than the cost of the salaries to do this work, we came to realize that operating this way was detracting from other tasks and that having certain people specialize and enjoy the work was better than dividing it.

How to Pack Books

Many years ago, Canada's then-independent Doormouse Distribution sent us a brilliant guide on how to pack a box. It was well-designed and fit conveniently on a single sheet of paper. We hung it on the office wall. You would not believe how many times we referenced that sheet over the years for best practices of how to put books inside of cardboard. Eventually these methods were committed to institutional memory, forever securing happy, healthy books arriving in their new homes.

The irony, of course, is that the largest distributors and wholesalers we work with don't follow these very basic and effective best practices. When a company becomes large enough, it's cheaper to replace books, especially if they belong to a client, than it is to purchase proper packing material and train the staff to pack the boxes correctly every time. If you are the publisher, then you should be concerned about your books arriving in good condition rather than having the hassle of sending replacements. To ensure this,

HOW TO PACK YOUR BOX

Stack the books flat on the bottom of the box

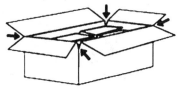

If the box is not completely full, use a boxcutter to cut down the corners to the stack of books

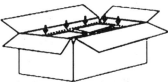

Starting with the end flaps, fold over the sides of box down to meet the pile of books.

Fill any vacant space in the box with peanuts, packing material, or crushed paper. Fold down the box and shake it. Does anything move? If so, add more packing material.

Tape each side at least four times, length-wise placing the tape slightly overlapping.

you're going to want to ship in double-wall boxes. These are just what they sound like: boxes with two sets of corrugation for extra thick protection against damage in transit. If you ask your printer to ship to you in them you'll always have some on-hand to re-ship in.

First, stack the books face-up in the box from largest to smallest. For most shipments, you can simply reuse your printer's cartons that they used to ship you the books. Never pack a book sitting on its spine unless it's okay for it to become damaged in transit. Fill the box completely with crumpled paper, bubble wrap, or recycled packing material that comes in your books' factory cases. If the box is larger than the number of books that you are shipping, you can either:

1) Cut along the four edges of the box and fold them over to make the box smaller. If there is excess material preventing the box from being folded shut, cut it off.

Or 2) Completely fill the remainder of the box with packaging material. If you do add packing material, move the valuable content into the center of the box and put the packing material on all sides and above it to cushion it from impact.

If you use an inadequate amount of packing material on the top of the box, the contents will rattle around, damaging your books. The end goal is to make all books flat, snug, and immobile. Pack the box tighter until they are. If there is an adequate amount of packing material, the box will appear a little bit bulbous once it has been taped. This packing material adds further resistance against any potential abuse that the box will undergo at the hands of the shipping company.

If you use an insufficient amount of tape, the loose contents will burst the top or bottom of the box open in transit. A properly taped box will appear shiny and appear to be excessively taped. But tape is cheap, much cheaper than replacing your books. Properly packing and taping a box also allows it to be reused on the receiving end.

When shipping too few books for a box to be practical, use a padded envelope. Similarly, the books should not be able to shift inside the envelope. If they do, add some packing material.

You have many options when shipping boxes. There's a certain loyalty in the publishing industry to UPS but it seems to be shifting gradually to FedEx, especially among larger companies that can bargain for bulk discounts. But for the little people like us, it's really best to ship via the U.S. Post Office, using media mail. It can take a week longer to arrive and take a bit more of a beating during that time, but, if you pack it properly, this should not be an issue.

If speed is a concern, the U.S. post office also offers flat rate priority mail and express mail flat rate envelopes and boxes. These are priced competitively against UPS or FedEx and, while priority mail is not guaranteed, it almost always arrives in two to three days and offers a competitive price for international shipping. Priority envelopes and boxes are available for free from the Post Office or usps.com but they are also quite thin. Getting there on time does no good if the books aren't in good condition. Stacking two vertical piles of books side-by-side to fill the box or envelope does a good job of preventing the books from shifting in transit. Putting styrofoam or cardboard around them should sufficiently protect them as well. The time saved by not having to replace damaged books will quickly create new efficiency! If the books are damaged in transit, ask the customers if they prefer for you to send replacements, remove them from the invoice, or offer the customer a further discount. Giving them the option will keep them happy and make the most of a bad situation.

Warehousing, Inventory, and Software

The ideal warehouse is easy to access, well-organized, and serves the ultimate goal efficiently: getting the books to the readers. Few things are as maddening as discovering that you have another box of a book that you thought was long sold out and reprinted...because you didn't put it in the right place.

From day one you'll need a system for storing books, even if it's that you load all of the boxes of books into your basement and bring up a case at a time to unload and fill orders with. Eventually you'll reach the limits of this system, either because you'll completely fill your basement or you won't be able to find what you need when you need it. Renting a storage unit is one option, but ultimately you'll need to create a five-year plan. Figure out what your strategy is to get books to customers, how fast they will accumulate and thus how much you'll have to store at one time, and if any of your inventory will be stored by a distributor. Compare the costs of renting a warehouse or storage unit where you live compared to what you would spend each month working with a fulfillment company or distributor. Compare costs at various volumes and see what makes sense.

Once you've got your warehouse plan in order, you'll need software to manage it from. This software takes your orders, subtracts them from your inventory, and gives you a system with which to pull and process your orders. There are quite a few options here and a lot of versatility. By dumb luck alone, Microcosm happened to hire a web developer in 2001 who foresaw the need for this solution. He coded custom warehouse management software, WorkingLit, that we still use today. Over the years we added more and more features, including invoicing and collections, author royalties, predictive systems for how many books we should reprint, any title's sales history and profitability, and accounting and payroll. As a result, I've never purchased a commercial product for warehouse management. For your first few years, a clipboard and a pencil will solve your problems and address your needs, but eventually you'll outgrow each system as you master it. One free software that is incredibly handy is Google Sheets, a mobile spreadsheet that can manage your operation with complicated formulas until you need to upgrade to a database. Haymarket Books uses the multi-site inventory feature in Quickbooks Enterprise. Julie Fain, co-founder of Haymarket, explained, "The workhorse accounting program for most small businesses is Quickbooks. I don't think it's earth-shatteringly amazing, but it got the job done for most things we needed as a small publisher. It will handle general accounting, payables and receivables, and has acceptable inventory and cost tracking, with one important caveat. If you are a publisher that has a trade distributor but you also do a lot of your own in-house fulfillment for special sales, web sales, and the like, the regular version of Quickbooks doesn't do multi-site inventory. We had to get the Enterprise version for that, which is expensive and isn't cloud-based. Boo! We've grown out of Quickbooks at this point, and as a nonprofit we can get the more powerful software Netsuite (from Oracle) for almost no cost—although we've hired a consultant to migrate us, which is expensive." When you're just starting out you can typically monitor inventory by looking at it. As you outgrow this stage, you can migrate to a clipboard and then a spreadsheet. You don't need to account for every copy given away or sold but you'll need to know at least a month or two before it's time to reprint. Running out of something will sneak up on you as you develop more and more titles and the best way to deal with that is to be prepared for it.

Homework:

• How do you plan to reach your audience where they are at?
• How can you learn from the stories of Whole Earth, Loompanics, and EDC and implement your own, similar ideas?
• How can you repel the wrong people away from your books?
• How can you passively attract the right audience to your books?
• What part of your audience can you reach via events, conferences, and direct mail order?
• What part of your audience will you only reach via stores?
• What kind of warehousing makes the most sense for your publishing?
• How will you handle fulfillment at first? Indefinitely?
• What books by other publishers could you sell to widen your bag?
• How can you tell the story of your publishing and mission to your fans?

6. DOING THE LABOR

Who Is Your Staff?

Years before you hire the first person to work for your press that isn't yourself, you're going to need to fundamentally understand how labor is divided and what jobs are involved and how work moves from one department to another. You're not going to want to immediately dive in and quit your job unless you are financially independent or have considerable savings on top of the costs of launching the press. As you're starting out, compartmentalize your brain to think about these various departments. Understanding how you align with, defy, ignore, and interface with industry standards will be helpful in talking to other publishers to find the staffing solution that works best for you.

Job Duties:

- **Publisher/Acquisitions**: The publisher has the final say on what comes out of the press and is accountable for the impacts of their actions and choices. They should be the one to approve a project and be able to explain how it fits into the press' mission and builds the backlist in the correct direction. The publisher sets the expectations with the author about what working together looks like and how success is best achieved. In a small

JOB DUTY

ACQUISITIONS OBTAINS NEW TITLES
BASED ON P&L AND COMP ANALYSIS

EDITORIAL DEVELOPS THEM INTO AWESOME BOOKS

PRODUCTION DESIGNS + SCHEDULES PRINTING + UPDATES STAFF

MARKETING CREATES PLANS + STRATEGY + MATERIALS

FLOW CHART

MANAGEMENT UPDATES P&LS TO DETERMINE SUCCESSES
+ FUTURE PLANS + BEST PRACTICES

COLLECTIONS ASKS FOR PAYMENTS

CUSTOMER SERVICES RESOLVES PROBLEMS

WAREHOUSE PACKS + SHIPS ORDERS
+ IDENTIFIES SHORTAGES

SALES CREATES STRATEGY + OBTAINS ORDERS

AUTHOR + PUBLICITY SECURES REVIEWS + ARTICLES + BUZZ

firm, the publisher also typically handles acquisitions and onboarding of new authors. But in a larger house, these duties are broken out between people and then between divisions who independently acquire titles.

- **Contracts/Legal**: Once a project has been selected as appropriate for the press to publish, that author needs a contract to create a firm understanding of what is involved, expectations, benefits, costs, and best/worst case scenarios and possibilities. In a smaller firm, the legal work is outsourced initially until the publisher has a strong understanding of standard protocols and terms and handles this work themselves.

- **Marketing**: The marketing department performs the vital work of identifying the big picture strategy as well as how each book will be brought to readers effectively. Marketing identifies how to get the book in front of its audiences, what events it should be present at, the creation of book trailers, and how to talk about the book. Done well, this job is just as creative as the publisher's and is just as important to the company's chances for success. Marketing is responsible for researching, identifying, and selecting comp titles for each book as well as researching how these comp titles were successful and how to imitate translatable parts of that success. Ideally, marketing should develop title/subtitle/cover design ideas with the publisher and the author and have those ideas reviewed by sales before they are committed to.

- **Editors**: The **developmental editor** focuses on the biggest picture and story, shaping the content cohesively. The developmental editor manages the relationship with the author and communicates desired changes, timelines, and expectations. When the big picture developments of the manuscript are finished, the **line editor** evaluates style and begins looking at each sentence to see if it coherently explains what it needs to and, well, if it belongs at all. Before layout, the **copy editor** checks consistency, grammar, spelling, word use, and that the publisher's **style guide** (see page 391) is followed. A thorough copy editor may double check the work of the line editor as well. Once the book is typeset and designed, the **proofreader** prints out a copy of the book so that they can very closely look for and correct different details than they would notice on-screen.

- **Art Director/Production/Design**: The design department, under the oversight of the art director, will create a book cover based on the guidelines laid out by the marketing department. The cover proposals will ideally be reviewed and critiqued by marketing, sales, the author, and the publisher. The author should *never* have final say over the cover but should review it, since they are more familiar with the intricacies of the subject matter and may notice something important that the professionals miss. When the manuscript is thoroughly edited within an inch of its life, it is moved into layout by the production department. In a smaller house, these jobs are done by one person. In the smallest house, they are handled by the publisher if they have these visual skills or by freelancers if not.

- **Fact Checker**: If you are publishing a book that relies on the credibility of its arguments or dubious legal gray area or is a guidebook or other reference, you'll need someone to verify every detail. Sometimes this is a matter of calling up your sources, and sometimes it's a matter of digging for facts in source materials.

- **Publicity Director**: Once the book has a cover, the publicist will begin to shop it around to magazines, blogs, YouTubers, TV shows, radio programs, and anyone else that would promote the book to its audience. Publicity follows up with these channels, sends out or oversees the sending out of copies of the book to reviewers, and actively brainstorms and researches how to reach marketing's identified audiences. Publicity may also be responsible for securing any paid advertising spots such as ads, billboards, or commercials.

- **Sales Director**: The sales department is involved at every stage of development to ensure that the final book that is published is saleable. Sometimes they will show prototypes or dummy covers to key account buyers. Sometimes they'll ask a buyer if they would be interested in a title before the house has acquired it. Often they'll begin selling a title up to twelve months before publication to major wholesalers and national accounts, especially for specific holidays. Becoming this organized requires years and isn't essential for your earliest books, but as you develop your strategy, it's important to understand that it's an industry norm.

- **Operations/Production Manager**: Operations reviews procedural steps and processes to find inefficiencies, stopgaps in material flow, and to see if additional (or fewer) staff or software would benefit the press. Things will go wrong. Books don't always arrive on time and "guaranteed" publicity or sales don't always happen. The Operations Manager solves these problems as they come up and asks questions when someone misses a deadline in order to both apply pressure and correct the problem in the future. If the problem was unavoidable, operations should see if expectations were unreasonable and how to make things smoother in the future. They may also handle negotiations with business partners and schedule production deadlines.

- **Finance/Accounting**: Finance creates profit and loss statements and manages the day-to-day financial health of the press. They process and calculate author royalties, send checks, manage payroll, and pay all of your vendors on schedule. They review the actual costs of a book and what actually happens sales-wise with that book a year later to see how close projections were to reality and share that in editorial meetings with the rest of the staff, or, if you're a single person operation, crying, alone, in your office.

- **Mail Order/Warehouse Manager**: When the orders have come in, someone has to pull/pack/ship them. Someone has to ensure that you have enough supplies on-hand and predict what to order before a new title arrives with hundreds or thousands of preorders. They also need to keep track of inventory and be able to predict months before you run out of something. Having a great warehouse manager will cut down on mistakes every step down the chain because they will honestly level with the publisher about their needs.

- **Customer Service Associate**: When something goes wrong, you need someone to fix it. Did someone not receive what they ordered? Did someone end up with someone else's order? You need someone to right these wrongs and show your dedicated readers that you care about them more than anyone else ever has in the history of the planet. Many publishers skip this step, but it's a vital one.

- **Collections**: When someone owes you money and doesn't pay on time, collections starts making noise, emailing the customer, and picking up the phone. While it seems logical for this task to be handled by sales—as they are talking to these accounts anyway—you ultimately want to separate these tasks so that sales can always maintain a positive relationship while collections may need to be a bit more pushy. It's sort of your classic good/bad cop routine.

In a larger house or as a company grows, each department is handled by a director who has a manager working beneath them and associates working doing the actual grunt work to carry out the strategy that the director creates.

Being Your Own Worker and Boss

Unless you started the company with quite a bit of financialization and have a pre-built audience, it will likely take some time before you are able to pay yourself enough of a wage to live on. When this time comes, some publishers hire people to perform the job duties that they don't want to do themselves, but better advice is to hire people who specialize in your weakest areas. Sometimes you can be quite adept at something even if you don't enjoy it. Other times you enjoy doing something but are quite terrible at it, whether that means that it takes you much longer than most people or the end result isn't professional quality.

You're probably ready to start paying someone, most likely yourself, when you're consistently selling at least 250 books per month for at least two quarters in a row. If you start sooner and you don't have a steady supply of cash flow coming from somewhere else, you'll be fighting a daily battle for having money in the bank. At first, reinvest any income beyond expenses into future printings and acquiring new books. Once you've made it through a year with enough additional income beyond production expenses that you can pay yourself, consider quitting your day job. Within another year, you'll see the limitations of doing the work yourself.

If your press is run well, its greatest limitations should be planning and managing growth. If your growth has been consistent but is now limited by the amount of work that you can do in one day, consider hiring someone to take over a portion of that work. If you're consistently spending more than two hours each day filling orders, hire someone else to do it part time. Otherwise, you are ultimately limiting your press's growth.

At a certain point you'll find that you're too busy, always behind, and trying to work more hours to get caught up. This will exhaust you and lead to poor decisions. Instead, identify all of your activities where you can train someone else to do the work so that the quality of their work would be almost as good or better than yours. As your press continues to grow and you are having trouble managing your time and other people's work, evaluate what work needs to be done and what to outsource based on this criteria:

- Start with activities where the stakes and context are low as it will take less training and mistakes won't be disastrous.

- Always focus first on tasks that are both urgent and important.

- Then focus on tasks that no one else could perform.

- Then work on your tasks within your specialized skills.

- Even for specialized tasks, you can hire other people to perform aspects of them.

- You won't want a stranger to complete your financial plan, but they could input numbers into your ledger or debt schedule.

The more that you trust other people to handle aspects of the press, the more you can focus on the things that bring you joy and connect back to your meaning and purpose. At this point you can see the forest through the trees, which allows you to have time and capacity to envision how to grow the press.

Interns

Internships in publishing are common. It's a competitive industry where there are many more applicants than jobs. Internships can be a mutually beneficial way to train someone, educate them about the standards of the industry and work involved, and have extra hands to complete work all at the same time. An intern typically sticks around temporarily for 200 hours of work across three months and is often done to fulfill educational requirements or sought out of personal interest.

Internships, when handled properly, should be a path to selecting employees or giving job referrals to other publishers. An intern should not be treated the same way that you would treat an employee or a freelancer. They are learning, so with every assignment, emphasize the goal of the task and reinforce the larger goals of the house and how each individual task fits into them. This can be helpful for you as a manager to focus on these individual tasks, create priorities, and rethink strategy.

Typically a publishing house will take on three interns at a time. Hours tend to be based on intern availability and school schedules. Of course, taking on interns will require scheduled office hours and preparing workloads for them. Interns are often coming to you from a place of theory, so it's often a leap to begin working on things that have a real impact and will be used in the world. This often creates nervous tension and fear of making mistakes. Begin with tasks that you can delegate, things that you've been too busy to do on your own, and tasks that do not require so much cognitive load, like data entry or entering proof corrections. After a few weeks, you'll start to see people's individual strengths and skills. From this point, focus on these tasks and avoid areas where they struggle or are prone to mistakes. Build a path of intentional growth to challenge them during the course of the internship, asking for a little more each day.

It's important to be conscious that you aren't offering predatory internships. Is there a possibility that you would be able to offer these interns jobs or referrals to other publishers at a later date?

Are the tasks that they are performing teaching them job skills and experience in the industry? Publishing as an industry does not have much capital but young interns are in a particularly delicate financial place so try to be thoughtful that you are giving more than you are taking.

In the appendix, I have included a sample interview (see page 389) with screening questions for interns or employees that should help cut through resumes and talking points to the substance of people's character and what they are looking for in life and work.

Freelancers

Asia Citro of The Innovation Press manages her entire workload with freelancers that she locates through word of mouth. "I read first as the developmental editor, then the manuscript is sent to a team of two other developmental editors. Once they're happy with the manuscript it goes to our educational consultant. Once she signs off on it, it goes to our copyeditor. Then to the illustrator. After the rough illustrations are turned in, we generally do a full layout to make sure we don't need to shift or move any illustrations to make room for the words. Then back to the illustrator—when the finals come through we pop those in the rough layout, back to the copyeditor plus ideally two to three volunteers who have not seen the manuscript yet, and from there to the printer."

Asia is thoughtful about creating jobs for those who might benefit from them. "I prefer to work with stay-at-home moms because society shits on them and contractors were the only way that I could possibly go without going in the red off the bat. Some moms have editing backgrounds, but some were just former English majors who had really insightful commentary on a test manuscript." She then gives each contractor a test job to start out. "One of my graphic designers is a former architect with a great eye who's been home with her kids for the past several years. I proposed that she teach herself InDesign and now she handles half of our layout work."

If you need to hire a freelancer that performs a specific task, ask on a publishing forum where experts and people that you trust socialize and share information. They can tell you what is an appropriate fee as well as which freelancers they prefer and why. There are many people who offer these services but not everyone will be right for you. In order to screen them, ask what kind of tasks they have worked on in the past. If you publish nonfiction books about trains, you don't want a developmental editor who only works on literary fiction. You'll want someone with some knowledge about trains themselves. This shouldn't be too hard to find though, because if you've built your movement correctly you're already part of numerous communities and forums about trains. Surely, some regulars there also have the editing or production skills that you need.

When you've found the right person, create a system where there is a certain amount of freedom and a certain amount of oversight. You don't want to find out that someone can't perform the job until it's too late so check in periodically about progress. Often people hire freelance publicists. This tends to be very expensive and never meets the expectations of the publisher. For a publicist to do a job well, they need months or years to really understand your list. Since a freelance publicist costs more than an employee, you're almost always hiring someone as an employee or just renting a publicist's contact list. Please don't enter into a monthly agreement with a freelancer until you've seen the quality of their performance.

Within a few years you'll see the limitations of hiring freelancers and should consider replacing them with in-house staff. Once you need the services of a freelancer every single month, hire someone to do that work for you directly. Staff should require less of your time as their manager as you are trusting them to do the job independently rather than every task being overseen by you directly. Replace freelancers one by one, so that you aren't overwhelming yourself by training multiple people at once and also so that you can gauge the financial responsibilities of having to pay a staff. Once you have more than one staff person, you're going to want to look into finding an office outside of your home. Relative to the costs of paying staff, renting an office is minimal, and it will restore part of your work/life balance and allow you to compartmentalize your life as your press grows.

Staff

The president of our European distributor, who employs about 70 people and has been in business over 40 years, says that hiring the right people and managing staff has proven to be the most difficult aspect of publishing. Most publishers focus on hiring skilled workers who have impressive college degrees and have performed the work previously. The logic is that these workers know their craft and require less training. But I've found that it's harder to retrain people who "know" how publishing works and who sometimes aren't interested in learning new methods, theories, or approaches. More often you'll find that unskilled workers who are smart have good attention to detail and are hardworking, critical thinkers are almost always better hires. I've found that degrees from prestigious colleges often inflate a job seeker's expectation of their net worth beyond what anyone in publishing would pay. And most importantly, the people who have grit but no college degree know the value of hard work and are happier to do it in an industry that they care passionately about. I've found that they enjoy the challenge of learning a new trade and mastering the problems they encounter along the way. There are great hires who graduated from impressive schools, but it's important to screen them for publishing skills and grit, as well.

Finding staff is never going to be a problem. There are so many people that want to work in publishing that you can afford to be choosy. Like all things in life, the most important thing here is to clearly state what you want. If you want to hire someone with five years of production experience who can deal with your rough-and-tumble work environment and wear ten different hats on ten different days, write a job posting for that on your website. If that isn't attracting the right people, post it on social media or Craigslist. Colleges love to have listings for internships as well as job postings. Look at colleges that have the kind of students and reputation that you seek. Look outside of your own social circle and talk to people in your networks. Who do they know that has the job skills that you are seeking? Is that person a good fit for you? If you don't want to hire more people that look, talk, and have similar experience as yourself, then aim for publications and networks where different kinds of people congregate. Even in the most myopic cities, there are hard-working people who are quite competent but just outside of your thinking and field of vision. If you properly put up the right flags, those people will already be paying attention to your work and eagerly apply when you have job postings.

In 2018, the staff of the publishing industry was 82% white, which was, believe it or not, an improvement over 88% in 2015[4]. Perhaps it's a painful result of the fact that publishing companies are started so that rich people have something to talk about at cocktail parties, or perhaps it's the values of Rupert Murdoch's Literary Industrial Complex. Either way, the employees of the industry at large bear little resemblance to the global population. Many publishers are clamoring to respond to this crisis but don't know how to proceed respectfully. Of course there are exceptions, especially in niche, midlist, and specialty publishers. At Microcosm we constantly ask the question, "How can we remove barriers to success for marginalized people in our industry?" This is partially about encouraging people of color to apply and know that they will receive equal consideration, and it's also about considering and understanding the impacts of other kinds of marginalization.

As publishers, we have a responsibility to represent the viewpoint of our own marginalization and lived experiences. Consider the views and experiences of the people that you are talking to, especially ones that extend beyond your own. Often the most interesting publishers succeed *because* they do not come from a myopic class of people. Publishers from outside of the "norm" show the importance

4   Publishersweekly.com/pw/by-topic/industry-news/publisher-news/article/75298-the-pw-publishing-industry-salary-survey-2017.html

of representation in both output and staff so others feel like they belong in publishing.

For example, Writers and Readers Publishing Cooperative was founded in London in 1974. They launched the *For Beginners* series based on two Spanish-language comics they liked, *Cuba para principiantes* and *Marx para principiantes*. The notion was to create entertaining and humorous content with a serious political message and the publishers did just that in 1976 with *Marx for Beginners,* which was much more successful than their inspirations had been. The group disbanded in 1984 when some owners sold publishing rights to a larger press without everyone's approval. In 1987, co-founder Glenn Thompson, a Black former street kid who hadn't learned to read until he was twelve and dropped out of school, moved the press to his hometown of Harlem, New York. He added children's publishing and poetry, creating amazing midlist publishing lines that spoke to the experience of inner-city Black youth. Thompson successfully shared his love of reading and comics to inspire a new generation of ignored, ill-educated kids to care about reading and politics and become publishers, including me.

Involving the kind of people that you want to see in publishing is an important part of the process. After 40 years in the industry, Shane Kennedy of Lone Pine Publishing spends months each year immersed with his fellow First Nations people, where he teaches them his publishing trade craft.

C. Spike Trotman of Iron Circus Comics told *Publisher's Weekly* that she started her own press because "I don't trust the intentions and motivations of a lot of large publishers. I think a lot of people at the top especially are extremely resistant to change. They have to be dragged kicking and screaming to expand the scope of their publishing even slightly."

Similarly to education or social work, cisgender women represent 78% of the staff in the Literary Industrial Complex. Still, they, on average, earn 36% less than men and hold lower positions in the hierarchy. Men are still the ones in charge and setting the financial priorities[5]. Aside from editorial and financial pressures, this is another reason why women have gravitated towards independent publishing, where they hold higher positions and generally have more freedom. Seal Press, once a strong, independent, feminist publisher of women's interest books, was acquired by Perseus Book Group in 2007, and the priorities shifted from mission-driven feminism to commerce as determined by male management. Hachette since acquired Seal Press from Perseus in 2016 and layed off the remaining female publisher in order for it to be run by the male publisher who runs the larger division. And the proof is in the pudding: their books aren't nearly as interesting or exciting as they used to be.

In short, we can't trust people without these lived experiences to speak about them. We have to represent the viewpoint of our own marginalization. And this reverberates down to our choices of who works at our companies. If you're curious, Microcosm has roughly three times the industry average of people of color staffers and, on average, women earn more than men.

---

5   Publishersweekly.com/pw/by-topic/industry-news/publisher-news/article/73469-the-indie-publishing-feminist-revolution.html

Once you've hired someone, the important step is to put your money where your mouth is. Plan adequate time to train them so they can do the job better than you could. Look at your own internal biases and create an environment where people can bring up and address problems or concerns. Have a policy of open communication. Marginalized folks may be the least likely to speak up, otherwise, because they have historically been punished for doing so. Hear the criticisms and let them make your press a better place to work and purchase books from.

Leadership

Even the best staff is only as good as the leadership. The best leadership allows your entire staff to consistently perform work that is greater than the sum of their parts, to believe in themselves, and to work as a unified team. It protects your staff from having to deal with things outside of their job duties. If the house is mismanaged, or worse, unmanaged, the results will be predictable. Failing to plan will generally result in failure, except in a few lucky cases.

As the leader of your company, set and maintain expectations. Without a lot of time and patience invested, your staff will not understand the ultimate goal of your operation or all of the details. Your job is to continually redirect and refocus your staff towards the big picture goals. These goals are best identified together as a team so that they are reasonable and within everyone's individual, personal goals. Creating attainable metrics for each staff person collaboratively and writing them down together will make them feel invested in those goals as well as feeling accountable for their performance. For each staff position: clearly define who their boss is, who their underlings are, what their responsibilities are, what they are accountable for, what their goals and objectives are, and create/review their budgets with them. Ensure that the collective goals of all staff, taken together, work towards the house's goals. Check in on how it's all working out in reality on at least a quarterly basis.

Ultimately, good leadership is about inspiring everyone around you through your model, enthusiasm, behavior, and example. Laura Stanfill is the only staffer of Forest Avenue and makes the hard decisions, but she frequently leans on others. "Gigi, my designer, has been on board since the first day, lending her expertise not only as an artist but as a literary fiction author and a Powell's employee. She's always designed for the bookshelf, which fits with our mission of urging people to buy our books locally at local indie bookstores. She's also shaped our brand and aesthetic by offering original, not-like-anyone-else's covers that are gender neutral and stunning. They look like Forest Ave while also matching the prevailing mainstream enough to sell alongside Big Five titles at the bookstore. Moreover, I wouldn't have started Forest Ave if Gigi hadn't offered to design my logo and first cover. A lot of early decisions about growing the business were made in consultation with her, and I still run things by her now, whether they're acquisitions ideas, tagline changes, or specific questions about interior layout, which I handle."

It's similarly important for you to have an extended mentorship you can reach out to. Laura continues, "There are so many people who have helped me grow my business, solidify my brand, and get really clear on why I have chosen this path as a publisher. Some of those are other publishers who I have met through [peer membership organizations such as] PubWest, or IBPA, or Women in Portland Publishing. Others are literary agents I've met at conferences. Still others are readers and writers who get connected with one of our titles and want to talk about it, and those perspectives have helped me grow to the next level. My business strategist Nikole Potulsky and I began working together in November 2016 to help me get even clearer about my mission, my goals, and how to incorporate my identity as an author into my everyday workflow. Out of the collaborative process she led me through, I created the Main Street Writers Movement, which encourages writers to connect with each other locally and to support their local bookstores."

Meetings

Once you have a staff of more than yourself, it's important to have meetings to work through problems, help make decisions, and ensure that everyone understands the materials. There are typically four kinds of meetings: administrative, editorial, management, and sales conferences. While it's typical to only include management, editorial, publicity, sales, and marketing in group meetings, I would encourage you to include *everyone*, especially interns, as you want the most ideas and discussion possible to form creative solutions. Here's the function of each kind of meeting:

Administrative Meetings

You will need to inform your staff of policy changes, review workflows, share information, set expectations, and resolve problems together as a group. It's vital for your staff to continuously and consistently hear the priorities and agenda from you in a variety of ways so that it sticks in their brain. I've had so many employees who said "I didn't realize that was a policy. I thought it was just a suggestion" even after I've written and verbalized the policy to them several times. Sometimes people have a hard time understanding the financialization of their job or that their job functions have to create at least as much income as their salary plus the other expenses. This can be very difficult for people who come from a creative mindset. It's important to set benchmarks and goals together as a group and to celebrate successes, lament failures, and process transitions. Administrative meetings give everyone a chance to express hesitation or concern and to talk about problems and create policies in a fashion that works for everyone. We have these every other month.

Editorial Meetings

Often an editor is disconnected from the actual book market and is developing books in a proverbial cave. The sales force often has the most experience and predictive feedback for the editors, which should be used to refine and develop works in progress. Publicity, customer service, and especially fulfillment staff often have the most valuable developmental feedback.

It's absolutely vital to create a culture, space, and expectation that your staff will speak up to voice opinions in editorial meetings. If they are afraid to contradict you or you are not receptive to feedback, they will stop speaking up. While this creates shorter meetings, it undermines their purpose, which is to take everyone's privatized knowledge and experience and incorporate it into making the best, most marketable book possible. It's most important to go around the room and hear feedback from your sales team about what they think is the weakness and deficiency in each title. The sooner each title is reviewed and changes are made after acquisition, the sooner corrections and redevelopments can be made. It's ideal to put these things on the table before final covers or even subtitles are in place so that you don't need to revise after announcing publication.

Management Meetings

When you have a staff of more than two people you're going to find that communication is increasingly vital so no one is spreading misinformation or ever saying "I don't know" to a buyer on the phone or someone who wants to interact with your books. For this reason it's important to meet one-on-one with each staff person every month or two for an hour. Talk about the same things that you talked about during their hiring interview as well as news and where they are excelling, improving, and struggling. Mostly give them the trail of breadcrumbs to figure out where you are going and let them feel like it's their idea. Then provide clear metrics and goals for them to achieve raises and promotions. This will motivate them to work harder and feel more invested in the organization.

Sales Conference

When you have "finished" covers, data, and development for each season, you will want to present each title again to the sales staff with bulleted marketing points and expectations for media coverage. The marketing director or developmental editor pitches the title, subtitle, author, and every marketing handle for each title. The presenter must be open to feedback and be willing to be interrupted by the sales staff who predictively respond with what they expect to hear from their accounts about each title. Sometimes major mistakes are caught and corrected. Sometimes a title must be delayed because it is fundamentally missing a vital component. The most important thing is always to wait until a title is ready, as releasing something prematurely or with misleading/bad data will confuse buyers and tank your chances of success.

Homework:

- What tasks will you perform yourself?

- When do you anticipate to be able to begin hiring?

- Who will be your staff?

- What aspects will you hire freelancers for?

- Will you accept interns?

- Who can you hire based on motivation, willingness to work hard, and critical thinking rather than experience or skills?

- What deficiencies does each title have? Vent these as a group in editorial meetings.

⓻ ACQUISITIONS & EDITORIAL

Connecting with the Right Authors & Making Their Books Worth Reading

Almost every upstart publisher, intern applicant, and would-be publishing employee that I meet is most excited to work as an editor. I have lost count how many times an idealistic person recounts their childhood love of reading and upon realizing that being an author is not a viable career, they imagine themselves as an editor for their favorite subject and create an idealized future where they work under candlelight, identifying and negotiating the creation of great literature.

Of course, that's all a farce. Editorial work is primarily telling an author what they don't want to hear and a substantial cost center in publishing. With so many thousands of new books being published each day, editing is expensive and complicated. Worse, the most important part of editing—making the content match the promise of the book and its emotional payoff—is all but forgotten to endlessly argue about comma placement and word choice with the author.

Timothy Dexter was born in Massachusetts in 1747. A real-life Ron Swanson, he became an uneducated farm laborer at the age of eight. At sixteen he became a leather worker. After the Revolutionary War, he invested every penny to his name to buy "worthless" Continental currency, which he promptly sold to the U.S. government for over ten times what he had paid. He used the profits to launch a shipping export business that was tremendously successful. Many lords and business moguls mocked him and tried to steer his business awry, but he always outwitted them. At the age of 50, to establish his immortality, he self-published his memoir, *A Pickle for the Knowing Ones or Plain Truth in a Homespun Dress,* wherein he eccentrically complained about the church, businessmen, politicians, and his wife. The book contained no punctuation and seemingly random capitalization. The book has sold hundreds of thousands of copies.

Based on his experiences, Dexter had a general distrust for educated people. With his substantial wealth, he began referring to himself as a lord and felt like he was just as significant as the literary heavyweights of his day. He was a talented salesman and the first edition was tremendously popular and sold through eight printings.

For the second edition, after numerous complaints about the lack of any punctuation, Dexter added an additional page containing thirteen lines of commas, question marks, periods, and exclamation points with instructions to the reader to "pepper and salt as you please." And, well, if Gertrude Stein and James Joyce can use experimental punctuation and have successful literary careers based on creating their own rules, why can't "Lord" Timothy Dexter? And indeed, his book remains in print nearly 220 years later—punctuation unchanged. Despite being barely functionally literate, Dexter's book sales were not hurt. His book had strong buzz and development. Readers bought it not because of the editing, but because of the emotional payoff.

Acquisitions

Ian Hamilton Finlay is the patron saint of difficult authors. He was a Scottish poet who came to prominence in 1958 when one of his plays was broadcast on BBC radio. In 1969, the rights to his successful book *The Dancers Inherit the Party* were picked up by Fulcrum Press, the premier small press of the era.

The book had already been published in two previous editions, so several new poems were added and the publisher marketed it as a first edition of a new title. It's easy to see why the publisher thought this decision was strategic and acceptable, Finlay did not agree and promptly wrote a letter to the Arts Council of Great Britain who had given a grant to his publisher. Finlay argued that public money shouldn't be used to "subsidize fraud." The Arts Council disagreed and told him to mind his own business.

Finlay next approached the Scottish Arts Council, who deferred to London's decision. Then Finlay wrote to the Association of Little Presses who correctly pointed out that Finlay was making more money *because it was* a first edition and, according to Finlay, told him not to "spoil a good racket." Eventually Finlay did convince the parliamentary ombudsman to investigate the British Museum and agree with him that the book could *not* be a first edition. Still, they refused to make a public statement, as did the National Library of Scotland.

The Scottish Arts Council tried to calm Finlay down by arranging a prominent exhibition of his work. Finlay failed to show up. When his readers and fellow poets pleaded with Finlay to give up this pointless fight against the country's most prominent indie press, who they all either worked with or aspired to be published under, he made a series of public statements that "Scottish poets...do not understand modern poetry at all."

To be fair, Fulcrum had plenty of warning about this kind of behavior from Finlay, who had a tendency to pick fights, such as his war not to pay property taxes by claiming that his garden was a secular religious institution. They should have communicated their plans and decisions with Finlay early on. Perhaps Finlay would have gotten on board with this marketing of his work to sell better if Fulcrum had involved him in these conversations or decisions. However, the relationship was unusual. Finlay was an agoraphobic and his publisher was an eminent psychiatrist, which I only bring up because the relationship between author and publisher can feel a bit like mental health counseling to begin with...even without the further stretch of this particularly strained dynamic.

Finally, Finlay convinced the Consumer Protection Department to take Fulcrum to trial. The court proceedings took two years and eventually ruled that the title was not a first edition and that the books should be withdrawn from circulation. The costs of the trial bankrupted Fulcrum in 1974, who were then forced to pulp all of their remaining books, including Finlay's. Finlay had won his lawsuit, but became the black sheep of Scottish poets, who he expected to revere him as a consumer champion.

Finlay's smirking face adorns the wall of our office as a cautionary reminder about the importance of how we represent our books, and of the reality that some authors are really quite ready to burn the whole thing down rather than face success. For many authors, publishing is more about their feelings than any logic or numbers or marketing or readership or even the mission of their book. Their dreams are rooted in a fantasy that never quite plays out the way that they expect. I can't even tell you how many authors have told me that they've prepared for what they'll say in imaginary interviews before they've written a single book or that holding onto a nonsensical title is more important to them than selling books.

We once had an author who sent a lawyer after us because she believed that a color illustration in her book looked too dark. Once the lawyer fully understood the dispute, he stopped engaging us, but the incident still proved to be a tremendous waste of everyone's time. We had another author who filed a complaint against us with the Better Business Bureau because he couldn't believe that his book had sold as few copies as we'd reported. You'll encounter many of your own difficult authors and the problems that I've had over the years will likely bear no resemblance to your own because each situation and interpersonal dynamic is different. Hold on to Finlay's story because it could have ended very differently. A positive author relationship is far more important than anything else about most books. No matter how famous the author, it's never worth it to be subjected to working with someone who will be obstructive, sabotage their own success, *and* leave you stressed out and questioning why you pursued this line of work in the first place.

Publish a Book Because It's Right for Your Press

We published a successful book about record collecting in 2015. The author frequently mentions in interviews how shocked he was that we offered him a contract based solely on a sample chapter rather than needing to read the whole book. The reason for this is that fundamentally the book was right for our press. We knew how to edit and market it. It did well in both record stores and bookstores. For the author's follow-up book, he pitched us a novel about a punk rock hitman. We explained that we don't have the skillset or reputation to publish fiction. He insisted that we read the whole thing and that we might like it. We might have—but ultimately what you publish is not solely an issue of taste. Taste isn't grounds for a book to sell. It's difficult for an author to understand that a publisher doesn't simply publish books that they like but rather ones that they know what to do with and that work within their list.

Know what *you're* looking for in an author. When Rupert Murdoch bought HarperCollins and began consolidating independents and creating the Literary Industrial Complex in 1989, he also skewed our perceptions of what sells and how many. Remember, you're a midlist publisher and you're throwing a party. Just like a party, if you only invite affluent, able-bodied white males, those will be the people who show up. And it's hard to make readers interested in more of the same old thing.

To attract the right talent, you have to clearly demonstrate to authors what you publish and act consistently. Bazillion Points has taken the model for golfing books (big trim, high price points, fancy production values, keepsake coffee table items) and ported those production values to heavy metal. Founder Ian Christe explained to me what he wants: "Authors with steamer trunks full of journals, photos, and lost wisdom offered us the chances to publish the definitive books on L.A. punk, Midwestern hardcore, New York hardcore, San Francisco thrash metal, Swedish death metal, Norwegian black metal, Seattle grunge, and so on. The decision then was whether the high cost of turning this into a book was worth pursuing, and in the end if it's something we want to read, the answer is yes. Otherwise, the form follows the function, but we try to make every book look exceptionally good."

Microcosm's own submission guidelines state "we double the industry standard in women authors…people of color are particularly encouraged to submit as is anyone whose experiences are not represented in the publishing world." I felt a little weird about this at first because it seemed tokenizing, like it was these signifying statuses we were seeking more than substance or ideas. But in our internal conversations, I came to believe that if we don't outwardly and intentionally project that we are explicitly seeking these perspectives, people will assume that we are upholding a microcosm of the sexism, racism, ableism, and classism that exists everywhere else in the world. In practice, our acquisitions process gives preference based on merit, substance, and following directions, but putting up these flags has increased the numbers of both women and people of color who submit. And the results have borne fruit.

Given the number of books published every day and the sales history of each, the likelihood of one of your books selling one million copies is only 0.07%. However, building a line and focusing on a niche will aid your efforts greatly. A focused, defined editorial vision and list allow targeted promotion and advertising your books together. If you make books about gambling, you could publish fiction and nonfiction. However, it will confuse readers if you suddenly add a book about the health benefits of smoking. Be clear and consistent. Repetition creates authority. If you are the company people think of when they want a Pilates book, authors will pitch those books to you. If you create murder mysteries set in 1800s Zimbabwe, you might feel a little confined but it will appeal to a certain type of reader. If you only publish BBQ cookbooks with beer pairings, that's how everyone will remember you and you'll have a clear specialty readership. Focus on your list's unified emotional payoff and benefits to the reader. List those front and center, always. Condense what is unique about each book into a five second pitch. Broadcast that language in bold type.

Put very clear submissions guidelines on your website and revise them based on feedback and results. My greatest piece of writing is our own submission policy and guidelines because I realized how much time I could save by revising them to do exactly what I wanted. If there is someone that you'd like to have as an author, don't be afraid to ask. If there are specific titles that you want written, you could propose them to specific authors. They may decline but oftentimes, even notable writers are happy to get involved in a passion project. But don't be fooled by big names. Contrary to belief, people with less experience tend to try harder or at least rely on their editor less. If you can afford to pay, even a little (see page 244), great. If you can't, be up front about this from the beginning.

You will still receive pitches that are outside of your niche. You'll receive far more submissions than you could possibly publish, even when you're just starting out. Compelling as they may be, if they are outside of your audience, ignore these pitches or refer them to appropriate publishers. Once you are five to ten years into the publishing, you may want to add imprints and expand your mission. But this is not to be taken lightly. You'll need to be just as committed to your main imprint as your new one and publish several books in each list per season.

There are so many authors and artists in the world with so much to express that you shouldn't ever take submissions that you don't like or contradict your mission. You'll also receive submissions outside your tastes. While your mission is a general guideline that drives your company's decisions, taste is a bit more ethereal and hard to pin down. Something can be perfect on paper but you might not like it. That's okay.

Some editors write personal rejection notes. Some send cold, professional rejections. It's kinder to scribble an encouraging and constructive line or two to personalize and energize your correspondence. I've begun to offer the option of submission feedback, and about a third of the authors request it. I don't send rejections unless the author requests feedback. This avoids hurting the person's feelings and prevents them from arguing defensively about why they should be published. Occasionally after being rejected and receiving feedback, an author will demand I put them in touch with an agent, but for the most part the system works well.

What Makes a Good Acquisition?

"I would like to say that you should only take a manuscript that you can sell so many copies of, but if you do that you aren't going to end up with the kind of publishing company that you would like. You also need titles that you can get passionate about and that you can get behind. You need an author who can be a real mouthpiece and promoter for the book as well," said Mark Suchomel. He has a point.

Ian Christe, publisher of Bazillion Points, explained what he is looking for in a submission: "Someone who is an absolute unassailable authority on a subject. Our AC/DC book is written by a member of the band during the period when they made their first five records. Our Nirvana book is written and photographed by Bruce Pavitt, who founded their label Sub Pop and is an integral part of their story. Our 750-page Norwegian black metal book was created by the guy who more or less started the movement. Writing a good book is a good start towards building a cult, anyway."

Build a relationship as you begin communications with an author. Relating to their life and experience will help them to see you as a person rather than an ATM machine with distribution. For some people, book publishing is an abstract academic argument about culture, and they want to argue about contracts all day long. These people exhaust me, so I avoid them. But maybe that's your motivation for becoming a publisher. The important thing is to work with people who have similar goals to your own and who you can communicate with easily.

The right acquisition is a book that you know how to talk about, how to package, and who you can sell it to, with an author who is motivated and cooperative. You want an author who is going to defer to your professional expertise and experience and who is not going to argue every point with you every step of the way. An author with a large platform is nice, but there's a reason that a popular author comes to a small press. Either it's because this particular book isn't as marketable as the rest of their catalog or because they insist on having ultimate control. If someone starts putting up red flags, consider walking away no matter how excited you are about the person or the project.

Joe Matthews told me that Independent Publishers Group received a submission from a small press for distribution that they were particularly excited about. It was a humor book by a former editor of *The Onion* about Trump before any competitive books had been published. Major account buyers look for any reason they can find not to purchase a book. IPG's special sales team gave the publisher the feedback that "We're afraid that buyers will open to page 42 [which featured the image of a penis] and decline your book for being objectionable." In traditional circumstances, a publisher is able to make that change. By the third meeting, the author revealed himself to be the actual publisher via a hybrid publishing program: a self-published author who hired service professionals. The author had the power and final say and was unwilling to make the requested change. IPG pitched the book to Hallmark, one of their largest specialty accounts, who rejected the book, specifically citing page 42. The rights to the book were later sold to Simon & Schuster for five figures. Rest assured that page 42 will be changed.

Perhaps, like Good Night's Adam Gamble, you intend to self-publish. Gamble has sold millions of books that he's written by being prolific but also by working with a professional staff that puts them through twice as much rigor. He explained, "I have always published first and foremost toward the question: would I happily buy this book? Do I want it? Then I look at known data such as the results of our previous publishing and of comp titles on NPD Decision Key or through anecdotal information. I've learned not to trust sales people in these matters, although I do listen to their feedback intensely and respect and appreciate it." You don't want to appear like a vanity outfit or even a hybrid publisher. You'll need to make sure that you aren't making emotional decisions and that your projects wouldn't even *look* like vanity work.

When you consider a book for publication, these are the criteria to think about most rigorously, whether it's your book or someone else's:

• How does this title fit your mission?

• Will this title consistently exceed minimum sales benchmarks over more than five years? (at least 1,000 copies in first year, halving for each consecutive year)

• How is this title notably different from existing work on the same shelf?

• Do we expect this title to turn a profit for the publisher?

• Is this work of particular merit? Why?

• Is there an identifiable and reachable audience of at least 5,000 people who will buy at least 3,000 books?

• Does this book challenge popular narratives about the subject?

• Will the author be cooperative and hardworking towards mutual goals?

• Have the competitive titles sold at least 3,000 copies in NPD Decision Key?

• Does the market allow U.S. based printing and production costs at competitive pricing to the comps?

• Does this book fit our core competencies? Does it fit on a shelf where we have existing recent work and are a known entity?

At no point are we looking for "good writing." Good writing doesn't tank or sabotage a project, but it only sells books in very particular genres, like literary fiction, where "pretentious" isn't a dirty word. Readers are almost always buying a book because of the emotional payoff and delivery promised by the cover and packaging. If good writing is a standard within that genre, readers will expect or even demand it. If it's not, you really want simple sentences that advance your narrative and its point and nothing more. Anything else runs the risk of alienating your base.

Even if you think you've acquired the perfect book, many things can go wrong. Once per year we will discover that we've signed a book where the author was very cooperative and seemed on the same page about the substance of the book until we are deep into the editorial process, and they reveal themselves to be unnecessarily meddling and self-sabotaging to their success. Sometimes we find out that the author has misrepresented their book, and changes the substance of the book after we acquired it. In years past, we made tremendous efforts to continue to work with these people but now we simply cancel the project. We are too busy, and there are nineteen other authors that year who are a joy to work with.

Sometimes the author is doing everything right but a major house releases a near-identical book with a much bigger budget nine months before we are ready or a book comes out and disrupts (or steals) our original research. We have to evaluate if it's still financially feasible to publish the book and what the consequences might look like. Are we involved organically enough in the community that the core audience will laugh at the imitator, or will the two books both halve their sales as a result? If so, is that still a sufficient quantity of sales to sustain our needs?

Again, a publisher's most important goal is to invest in books that readers want. Some publishers aren't great at making that determination, but planning and research helps you learn from prior mistakes, even if they weren't your own.

Once you've heard a pitch that you like, ask for a writing sample unless you are absolutely sure that the author can produce work to your standards or you are comfortable rewriting their work until it meets specification. Once you're at that point, complete a P&L. If the numbers are good, offer them a contract based on what you can afford. Once they sign the contract, begin the onboarding process and send them the author questionnaire.

Profit and Loss Statement (P&L)

While this might sound like a financial item, a profit and loss statement (P&L) is fundamentally an acquisitions issue. Creating a P&L for each book will ultimately tell you whether the title makes sense for you to publish. It's also the best way to determine how much you can afford to spend on each aspect of the project. To the right you'll see a copy of a spreadsheet that I created.[6] Thinking about each book in this manner will help you get your head around it.

The upper left hand corner begins with the title, author, and book's release season. Lines 7, 8, and 9 include retail prices for each format. If you aren't doing a certain format, don't include it. Lines 12-15 list the author's royalty by format as well as any advance payment that they receive. Traditionally this advance is your projected first two years of royalties paid in advance. For the sample book, you can see in G17 that anticipated royalties are $10,184. That is in no way guaranteed, and if you don't have the money to pay for an advance, many authors and agents understand.

---

6 Or get a copy here: Microcosm.pub/profitandloss

Line 16 is income from selling film or translation rights or foreign territory rights, but it's best not to plan for this in advance since even commitments can fall apart as the licensee changes their plans.

Beginning in column G, lines 6-8 predict what will likely be the sales in bookstores as well as returns and revenues. These numbers are based on your comparable titles and their selling habits. It's best to be conservative here so that your expectations are reasonable and you aren't shocked when you see your actual sales and returns.

Lines 10-12 predict similar sales in the direct market, which would include sales at your own events, via your own website, to non-trade stores that buy non-returnable, and books sold to the author. Again, these numbers should be conservative and based on figures in reality that you are seeing elsewhere.

Sample Profit and Loss Statement (P&L)

	A	B	C	D	E	F	G	H	I	J
2										
3	**TITLE**	**Cool Science Fiction**							**Developmental Costs**	
4	AUTHOR	Spacey			Units	Returns	Value		Editorial	$500
5	SEASON	F20		**Trade**					Copyediting	$100
6				Paperback	2000	400	$12,713		Proofreading	$100
7	Paperback	$16.95		Hard Cover	1500	300	$15,159		Indexing	$0
8	Hard Cover	$26.95		eBook	700	0%	$2,622		Photographs/Illustration	$100
9	eBook	$9.99		**Direct Market**					Permissions	$0
10				Paperback	1200	0%	$15,255.00		**Total Editorial**	**$800**
11	**Royalties**			Hard Cover	500	0%	$10,106.25		Typesetting	$50.00
12	Paperback	8%		eBook	340	0%	$3,397		Interior Design	$50
13	eBook	30%							Jacket/Cover	$500.00
14	Hard Cover	10%		**Total Sales**			$59,252		Type Output	$0
15	Advance	$0		Minus Returns			-$5,965		Advanced Readers	$0
16	Other Income			Minus Development			($10,055)		Database Service	$100
17	*8% Net Profit Royalty*			Minus Royalties			-$10,184			
18				**GROSS PROFIT**			**$33,049**		**Total Production**	**$700**
19									**Digital Conversion**	$100
20				Gross Profit			**52.17%**		Paperback PPB/Unit	$1.50
21				Bottom Line			51.89%		Hard Cover PPB/Unit	$2.15
22				Net Profit			0.28%		PPD Total	$7,855.00
23				Net Profit			$168.46		Freight	$600
24									**TOTAL COSTS**	**$10,055**
25				Gross Profit $			**$43,232.52**			
26				Gross Profit %			**72.96%**			
27				Bottom Line			51.89%			
28				Net Profit			21.07%			
29				Net Profit $			**$12,486.66**			
30										
31	*50% Actual Profit Roya*			**Minus Royalties**			**$6,243.30**			

Scooting over to column I, we're looking at the publisher's expenses for putting the book together from editorial to production to licensing to eBook conversion to paper, printing, and binding (PPB) costs. Fiddle with these numbers to see what you can afford for a project before committing with an author. You'll see as you plug in numbers that some factors are static. For example, you only have to pay to design a book once even as it continues to sell.

Next, back on column G and lines 14-18, we're looking at sales minus returns minus development costs minus author royalties. This will tell you what your gross profit is.

Next, we subtract operating costs ("the bottom line"), like rent, staff, telephones, envelopes, warehousing, etc. These should comprise every expense that you'll have to pay for even if you don't work on a book during a given month. At Microcosm, we've determined that this an average of 51.89% of our expenses. Subtracting your gross profit from your bottom line will tell you how much actual profit the publisher is earning from each book. In this example, it's less than $170. This example represents the most statistically likely outcome for a book like this. Publishing is about volume so to make up for these small margins, you can either produce many books (called a "paper mill" in the industry) or attempt to land a few heavy hitters every year.

Another vital purpose of the P&L is to evaluate a year or two later how well the book did against expectations. If a book does not sell as well as expected, it's important to figure out why. Was new competition added? Did interest in the subject fade away? Was it revealed that the author's cure for cancer was bogus? Was there a major developmental error in the cover/title/subtitle that confused readers about what the book offered or how it was unique? Answer these questions. If a book did better than expected, it's similarly important to figure out why and repeat this math with other titles.

If this math looks grim, consider that only 10% of books from major houses "earn out." Meaning that 90% of their books lose money and the remaining 10% pay for their losses. This is one reason that by being smaller, smarter, and more nimble, you can succeed. This is the reason that indies are gaining market share.

To demonstrate how these traditional contracts still benefit the author, I showed an alternate royalty model on G29 where the author takes 50% of the profit. But as you can see, comparing cell G31 to G17, 8% of the cover price ends up being *more* than 50% of gross profit in most cases until you really land a bestseller.

Due to Amazon's immense marketing budget and campaign to convince authors that publishers are greedy and obsolete, many authors don't understand why the traditional 6-8% paperback royalty is still much more in their favor than "70% royalties" from self-publishing on Kindle and CreateSpace, so I've made a chart for that too.

Expected Earnings by Publishing Type

Mode	Self-Publishing	Traditional
Likely Sales in Units	250	3,000
Likely Royalty	30-70%	5-8%
Likely Cover Price	$2.99-9.99	$14.95
Author Expenses	$1,500	$0
Likely Author Profit per book	-$1,275.75 — $248.25	$2,242.50 — $3,588
Likelihood of selling 100,000	0.07%	0.84%
Likelihood of selling one million	0.0035%	0.042%

Author Questionnaire

Once you're ready to sign an author, you'll want to prime them for what to expect next. An easy way to do this is through having them complete a questionnaire about themselves and their book. This is helpful for pushing the author to think about their book having an audience and what that entails. We use every answer to make their book successful, including developing the cover and metadata, marketing materials, writing and talking about the book, and spelling their name correctly on the cover. There's a sample version of the one that we use in the appendix (see page 401).

Pushing an author to think about and collect this data is not about saving the publisher the trouble. You will likely have to fact check much of this information and many things that the author considers notable will not be to the industry or the audience. But building this data is the beginning of cracking the author's vault of knowledge and making it work for their book's goals. You will likely need to ask probing follow-up questions, and eventually you'll take all of that information to build your metadata.

Metadata

Remember metadata? It's the data about your book's details that are broadcast to the universe. It's the excited blast that details your title, subtitle, series, and cover that clarifies any reason someone might want to buy your book (your marketing handles). There are the details that make a book successful and we cannot stress them frequently enough. As a result, the editor's priorities and time should be used like this:

1. 40 percent – Determining that an applicable niche exists (see page 250) and that your book can provide meaningfully unique benefits to readers.

2. 10 percent – Making sure that your book actually delivers on those promised benefits.

3. 50 percent – Clearly communicating those benefits in the title, subtitle, cover, data, and metadata.

If you did your title development correctly, your research should have steered you away from any parts of the shelf that are already too crowded or that have one celebrity author thoroughly dominating all sales. But even if you do your research, develop correctly, and the book is beautifully written and edited, you can still screw it all up with bad metadata!

Metadata directs the industry and, in turn, the reader. Book industry accounts review metadata on Edelweiss, a digital cataloging website for the publishing industry. When salespeople go out and meet with buyers, the process is accelerated. There are lots of books, and they are presorted by subject. The ones with the biggest marketing budgets get a few extra seconds. But if a book isn't correctly developed or is listed for the wrong shelf, the salesperson and buyer won't make time to let you know about the error—unless it's the only book being sold, they have large expectations of its sales potential, or you have a longstanding relationship with them.

This is where your comps—the books that a customer might buy instead of or in addition to your book—come into play. If you have access to NPD Decision Key software, look up what the comps are selling. Make sure that your comps are as successful as you suspect that they are. Many authors have argued that their book would be successful based on the success of another book, sending a link to a *New York Times* article about the book as "proof." When I look up this "well-received" book, I sometimes find that it hasn't even sold two hundred copies in NPD Decision Key! Sometimes so much effort is put into smoke and mirrors to create the illusion of success that publishers forget to actually make a book successful. Remember your research hack for a successful book: find Amazon subjects where the top four titles are in the top 100,000 and the category is not controlled by a single expert or celebrity.

By looking at the metadata, you can see what is working for your comps. What keywords are readers searching for that direct them to that book? These words should appear in your title, subtitle, reading line, and jacket copy. The Book Industry Study Group (BISG) creates a list of approved shelving codes based on books currently being published and subjects no longer seeing new titles. Once enough titles exist, say, in "comics journalism," it will be a distinct category for new books. What BISAC shelving codes are your comps using, and where are stores actually shelving the book? Publishing industry software typically allows two to four shelving categories, and this information is propagated to a series of industry databases. Use them all!

The most telltale sign that a book is self-published or from a vanity press is that the back cover indicates a subject to shelve it in a place that simply doesn't exist in the bookstore[7]. Similarly, I've had to explain to many authors that while their idea is unique, clever, and important, we can't package it the way that they want to because "essays / general" or "world history" or "memoir" just aren't magnet

---

7 Review a current list of all BISAC shelving codes here: http://bisg.org/page/bisacedition

destinations in any store. They are huge dumping grounds for books that don't fit on the shelves that readers frequent (or that, again, are dominated by a few celebrity authors).

Naturally, things can still go wrong. The worst horror stories feature the publisher making a series of intentional choices and inputting them correctly and Ingram or Baker & Taylor misinterpreting the data that arrives in their feed. Stores don't order a book about home repair if it's listed under "philosophy / hermeneutics." Though that might be an apt opinion about the book in question, no one is going to look for it there. This is why it's very important to routinely check your metadata on other databases. Amazon is another place where Microcosm's books have shown up as DVDs or under hilariously incorrect subjects. When Sarah Mirk's *Sex From Scratch: Making Your Own Relationship Rules* showed up on Amazon with the subject "religion / biblical meditations / Old Testament," I laughed out loud since the book is about rejecting religious dogma as the foundation of relationship choices.

Try to detach yourself from your personal relationship to the subject matter. Think about what you would be most excited about as a reader. Sometimes your metadata choices can become so robotic that the final product doesn't feel like a personal or creative work any longer. Review the cover and metadata with both industry professionals (ideally buyers) and people that read books like this for fun. You will likely be able to make simple fixes to avert huge mistakes. For instance, a beautiful, painterly book cover may not work on a title categorized as self-help / compulsive behavior / obsessive compulsive disorder (OCD).

Once you've done the homework of determining what the best keywords and shelving choices for your book are, visit two local bookstores that sell new books. See where books like yours are shelved in practice, and if you're the friendly type, talk to the staff people about why they they are shelved there. They will likely have hilarious personal anecdotes about what led to this decision-making, or in some cases, a political axe to grind about having to shelve Newt Gingrich's *Treason* in the first place. In any event, learning about how their decisions are made will better inform your choices.

Often making a few quick and easy changes will vastly improve your development before it's too late and you are hearing this same feedback from stores explaining why they think your book wasn't more successful.

Sometimes your vision for the book will come so naturally that the writing only takes a single draft and the development concept comes to you clearly and immediately. Even when this has happened to me, I am sometimes so excited that I still overlook important details—like making the title as readable as possible, omitting an unnecessary word in the subtitle, or neglecting to note the different meanings between "everyday" and "every day."

Sometimes you'll do everything "right" and the book still doesn't sell. While this can be disconcerting, investigate why this happened and learn from it. Similarly, sometimes you'll do everything "wrong" and the readers will find the book anyway and love it! Learn how to repeat this effectively.

Kinds of Editing

Based on your budget and the tone and feel of your company, you'll want to develop and hone an editorial style that's right for your list and your readers. As we touched upon in the job duties of the previous chapter, there are five types of editing: developmental, line editing, copy editing, proofing, and fact checking.

- **Developmental editing** focuses on the biggest picture and story, shaping the content cohesively. Ask why are we publishing this book? What benefits does it offer to the reader? How can the final product best accomplish this? What attributes are essential? Where does the narrative or arguments in the book fall apart? Is the tone and voice consistent throughout? What are its weaknesses, and how are they best minimized? What are the books strengths? How are they best highlighted? The developmental editor manages the relationship with the author and communicates desired changes, timelines, and expectations.

- **Line editing** evaluates style and begins looking at each sentence to see if it coherently explains what it needs and if it belongs at all. Does each word match its intent? Does it advance the narrative? Is it a random aside? Is it confusing? Does it fit the appropriate reading level? The line editor works through these issues so that you don't have to re-read paragraphs or find that information is repeated unnecessarily—or in the case of some "finished" books, that entire paragraphs repeat throughout the book.

- **Copyediting** checks consistency, grammar, spelling, word use, and that the publisher's style guide (see page 391) is followed.

A thorough copy editor may double check the work of the line editor, as well.

- **Proofreading** is reading the book very closely, line by line, to ensure that every comma is correctly placed, words are spelled correctly and not omitted, and that the correct dashes are used. They create and check the table of contents and double check footnotes' correct placement. Once proof corrections are made, a second proofreader will perform a "slug," checking to make sure that new errors were not introduced by those corrections. They may also be burdened with indexing the book.

- **Fact Checking** ensures the credibility of your book to its audience, that citations and facts are relevant, that text is not plagiarized, and that you are not opening yourself up to legal problems by publication. Sometimes this is a matter of calling up your sources, and sometimes it's a matter of scouring facts in source materials. Sometimes you'll need to hire a lawyer or other expert to review the manuscript.

Often an author will pitch a book as "edited and ready for print," but this is *never* true. The author may sincerely believe this, but you'll always want the book to go through all these steps, especially developmental editing. This is one reason that it can often be best to work with an author who hasn't written or finished a book yet in order to ensure that the final product is saleable and the author is invested in its success. If they haven't written the book yet, they won't fight you at every stage about every change because their emotional attachment isn't so developed. Their expectations will be different, and they'll understand the value of your skill and craft rather than perceiving it as meddling. Remember the story of my friend who was a volunteer editor without a high school education, knowing nothing about grammar or punctuation? Despite the prominent typo on the cover, the first book that he worked on sold because of its political mission and the idea that readers were supporting an underdog that needs your money. Publishers are often desperately afraid of a typo on the cover for fear that it will make them look like amateurs without credibility, but in reality it shows that you are passionately approaching your subject matter. Readers seek passion. Obviously, this isn't right for every book in every list at every house so pursue the style of editorial that is most appropriate for your press. If you aren't interested in doing this work yourself, you will have no trouble finding a competent editor. Ultimately, what's most important is choosing the correct kind of editorial style for your press.

Style Guide

A style guide explains to your authors and editors what basic formatting issues you use as a publisher. You'll want to be able to deliver a copy of your style guide to your author for them to process their manuscript through. There's a sample copy of Microcosm's style guide on page 391. Since a style guide cannot cover everything, you'll want to have a supplemental style guide for in-house use, such as *Chicago Manual of Style*, and a preferred dictionary for spelling and word use. This will prevent a proofreader from having to interrupt an executive and allow independent work with less chance that people will argue about it later.

Publication Schedule

Ian Christe feels out of sync with the industry norms. "We've sold a little over a quarter million books now, but I don't think we've ever engaged the sales cycle with full force. We simply don't have covers and galleys available six or nine months ahead of release dates. Oh how we've tried! I think our sales have been reliable, but I would love to make our sales and distribution partners happy with equally reliable advance information. Unfortunately, the way the schedules are now, we are often producing an entire book during the period when we are supposed to be sitting back and watching the preorders rise. Ultimately, we are confident the books will sell, and usually they do, but I'd like to relieve some of the stress on the buyers. Maybe next year!"

Once you have more than a few books, you're going to want to create a spreadsheet with all of these dates so you don't miss deadlines. This is because publicity, sales, and distribution are all matters of vital timing. Being ahead of schedule will give you freedom to publish one book sooner when another author is hopelessly missing deadlines. We tend to give the author a deadline a month before the actual deadline for this reason. Sometimes a sales opportunity will present itself if you have a book ready to go to print early.

Here's an idea of how a book moves from concept to execution:

1) Author proposes an idea or an acquisitions person solicits a project from an author. (3 years before pub date)

2) Marketing staff investigates size of market, existing competitive/comparable titles, sales history, NPD Decision Key figures, and various ways that development and packaging could be handled. Acquisitions staff then reviews the submission and approves it.

3) Contract is sent to author and terms of publishing terms are agreed upon and understood.

4) A publication date is scheduled approximately three years later and production dates are set. Marketing discusses the author intake form with the author for optimal success and how to think and write effectively toward that goal. Editorial discusses framing and outlining of the manuscript (MS) to specification on the agreed-upon timeline. It is very helpful for the author to complete this information before writing a book as it will help to think about the reader's experience and how to be distinct from similar books in print.

5) Editor works with author on the development process as they write the book, if appropriate. A due date is set for the updated MS in the production spreadsheet.

6) Staff compiles catalog data and production information to discuss with distributor's data submission team to determine outlets for the book and consider where it will be most successful, developing for those readers, in a last opportunity for editorial development. (fifteen months before publication date.)

7) Cover is designed, shared with the author and distributor, and approved by staff. (12+ months before publication date)

8) MS is completed and line edited by staff and necessary rewrites are requested from the author. If the author misses this deadline, delay the book till the next season unless you have a guaranteed and vital news tie-in. (11 months before pub date)

9) Quote is requested from the printer. Final retail price is determined.

10) Marketing submits distributor's announcement forms. (12 months before pub date)

11) Sell sheet and press release are built. (10 months before publication date)

12) Final text, line art, and photos (if any) are submitted to Designer. (11 months before pub date)

13) Edited text and formatted images are put into final typeset and design. (9 months before pub date)

14) Distributor lists book to trade and assembles preorders from all major book-trade accounts and size of print run is determined. (nine months before publication date.)

15) Uncorrected Advanced Readers Copies are assembled, printed, and mailed to all sales staff and national review outlets. (8 months before publication date, check exact date in Editorial Approval Sheet.)

16) A proof of typeset and designed book is sent to the author and editorial assistant in PDF format to identify and flag errors, proofread, and line edit (fix confusing elements). At this stage, edits should attempt to avoid matters of opinion or aesthetic disagreement and stick to denotative errors from the style guide. (8 months before pub date.)

17) One month later, staff and author feedback is due and edits are locked in. Proofreader begins to read for final typos. If the author so chooses, at this stage, they may express aesthetic concerns to their editor for consideration and potential for adaptation once all denotative edits have been locked in. (6 months before pub) Each proof reviewer indicates when they feel the manuscript is finished.

18) Book is sent to printer and book becomes available for preorder. (5 months before publication date ["pub"])

19) Printer sends proofs to editor who approves book for print. (4 months 3 weeks before pub)

20) Books ship to warehouse and author. Orders begin to be filled one month before publication so stores have time to receive and shelve them. (3 months before pub)

21) Quarterly sales reports are sent via email to author and royalties are paid every time publisher owes at least $100. (3 months after pub)

	Season	Title	Subtitle	Author	Contracted?	Contract signed?	Format	Pages	Trim size	U.S. Price	Canada price	Print/Case ISBN	Qty to print	Send to printer Date	Release/Publication carton Date	LoC CIP status	Print run due (author)	MS due (author)	Dev edits due	MS revision time before and after speak (author layout) due	Line edits due	MS revision time before and after copy edits due	All revisions or copy edits / Layout due	Front cover data finalized and image metadata pre-p due	Metadata/files uploaded and books due	Marketing conversion meetings	Ebooks	Ebooks publication
	Forthcoming																											
2	F18	*Unfuck Your Adulting*	Give Yourself Permission, Carry Your Own Baggage, Don't Be a Dick, Make Decisions, & Other Life Skills	Faith Harper, PhD	yes	x	PB	128	5x7"	$9.95	$14	978-1-…-6	88	6.9.18	10.17.18	rec'd	5,000	10/1/2…	8/1/201	8/1/203	9/1/201	9/1/201	10/1/…8	10/1/2…	8/1/201	8/1/203	9/1/201	6/1/201
3	F18	*Please Let Me Help*	Letters to the World's Most Wonderful Brands	Zack Stern walker	yes	x	PB	128	5x7"	$9.95	$14	978-1-…-6	88	6.9.18	11.13.18	rec'd	5,000	6/1/201	7/1/201	8/1/201	9/1/201	10/1/…8	10/1/…8	8/1/201	8/1/203	9/1/201	6/1/201
	In Print																											
4	W19	*This is Your Brain on Depression*		Faith Harper, PhD	yes	x	PB	128	5x7"	$8.99	$14	978-1-…-6	88	6.9.18	12.4.18	apply	3,000	11/1/201	12/1/201	1/1/2018	2/1/2018	3/1/201	1/1/201	3/1/20	1/1/201	2/1/201	7/1/201
5	W19	*A People's Guide to Publishing*	Build a Successful, Sustainable, Meaningful Book Business	Joe Biel	yes	x	PB	416	5x7"	$19.95	$27	978-1-…-6	44	8.9.18	12.4.18	rec'd	3,000	11/1/201	12/2/201	1/1/2018	2/1/2018	3/1/2019	3/1/20	10/1/201	10/1/2…	8/1/20	9/1/201
6	W19	*Space Race*	Book One of the Fifth Place Series	Set Sytes	yes	x	PB	150	5x8"	$11.95	$16	978-1-…-6	88	6.9.18	12.4.18	rec'd	3,000	11/1/201	12/2/201	1/1/2018	2/1/2018	3/1/201	1/1/201	3/1/20	1/1/201	2/1/201	7/1/201
7	W19	*Wulf*		Set Sytes	yes	x	PB	332	5x8"	$15.95	$22	978-1-…-6	32	6.9.18	11.10.18	rec'd	2,000	11/1/201	12/2/201	1/1/2018	2/1/2018	3/1/201	1/1/201	3/1/20	1/1/201	2/1/201	7/1/201
8	W19	*Faces in the Dark*	A Collection of Demented Fantasy & Horror	Set Sytes	yes	x	PB	140	5x8"	$12.95	$18	978-1-…-6	88	12.9.17	11.10.18	rec'd	2,000	11/1/201	12/2/201	1/1/2018	2/1/2018	3/1/201	1/1/201	3/1/20	1/1/201	2/1/201	7/1/201
9	W19	*Born to be Weird*	A Collection of Paranormal Horror	Set Sytes	yes	x	PB	150	5x8"	$12.95	$18	978-1-…-6	66	12.9.17	11.10.18	rec'd	2,000	11/1/201	12/2/201	1/1/2018	2/1/2018	3/1/201	1/1/201	3/1/20	1/1/201	2/1/201	7/1/201
	Out of Print																											
10	W19	*India, Bones & The Ship of the Dead*		Sytes	yes	x	PB	332	5x8"	$15.95	$22	978-1-…-6	66	12.9.17	11.10.18	rec'd	2,000	11/1/201	12/2/201	1/1/2018	2/1/2018	3/1/201	1/1/201	3/1/20	1/1/201	2/1/201	7/1/201
11	Not Active	*Flow Chronicles*		Urban Hermitt	yes		PB	200	5.5 x8.5	$10	$14	9781621062…	26	11.2.2														

22) After one year of sales, if there is more than two more years of inventory remaining in distributor warehouse, it is pulped or returned to publisher.

23) If, at any point, there is more than a ten-year supply of inventory on any title, the excess is donated to charities. If there is still excess, the remainder is given to customers who order using priority mail.

24) Book reprints once composite warehouse stock is reduced to one-month supply and sales remain steady.

25) New edition is considered if material becomes outdated or if sales begin to wane after a steady spike.

Homework

- Is highly refined editing a vital part of your publishing genre?
- How much time, money, and effort makes sense for you to put into editing?
- How will you acquire new books?
- What are the characteristics, network, and behaviors of your ideal author like?
- What are the characteristics and handles of your ideal book?
- How many books will you publish during your first year?
- What would it take for you to cancel an author's publication?
- Did you make a P&L statement for each one? (Please do)
- How do you need to prime your authors' expectations for publication?
- How will you handle propagating your metadata to the industry?
- What kind of style guide will you employ?

8

OWNERSHIP & RIGHTS

Legally Setting Yourself Up for Success

Rights sales help a book reach an audience that the publisher cannot reach on its own—whether that's producing a film, creating a television series, producing an audiobook, publishing the book in a foreign language or country, or being distributed to book clubs. Even if your book totally tanks and never makes money from being published and sold, sometimes you can still have a huge windfall success by selling publication rights.

This isn't outside the realm of possibility for a small press with a rights agency. For example, the book *Zero to Five: 70 Essential Parenting Tips Based on Science* sold about 5,000 copies in its original, English language edition. That's not great but the publisher, Pear Press, also sold a Japanese edition and rights for 120,000 copies, which in turn sold rights in Korea and Taiwan. Pear has earned more money from rights income than book sales!

In a more extreme case, White Cloud Press's historical novel, *The Franciscan Conspiracy* came out in 2005 as the founder sold the press to a new publisher. The new publisher, this being his first title, hired a consultant to handle the book's launch. Unfortunately, the consultant only sold 200 copies. Fortunately, one person who did notice the book was Danny Baror of Baror International, who optioned the foreign subrights. Baror sold the book into seventeen countries, becoming an international bestseller and netting over $700,000 in foreign rights income.

In 1986, Doubleday, then the largest independent publisher in the U.S., published Winston Groom's fifth book. *Forrest Gump* was an absurdist tale of a savant character that interweaved fiction with history based on bedtime stories that Groom's father had told him as a child and characters based on his adult friends. The book depicts a kind savant, with a certain emotional intelligence, embroiling himself in all manner of important historical events. While the manuscript was still being developed, Warner Brothers purchased the film rights, retaining Groom to write the screenplay for $350,000 and a 3% share in the film.

Groom was convinced that this book was going to be an immediate bestseller, but the movie adaptation was delayed. While eating lunch one day in New York, Groom was accosted by a *New York Daily News* reporter who informed him for the first time that Warner had sold the movie rights to Paramount, who threw out Groom's version of the screenplay. It seemed unlikely that any film adaptation would happen. Despite being published by the largest publisher in the U.S., *Forrest Gump* only sold 30,000 copies, a commercial flop for a publisher of that size. That same year, Doubleday was sold to German global media giant, Bertelsmann, joining its ranks in the Literary Industrial Complex. Surprised and disappointed, Groom attempted to move on, changed publishers, and continued writing new books. Paramount eventually pulled the project out of retirement and hired Eric Roth to write a new script for *Forrest Gump*, who substantially changed the narrative and characters, removing Forrest's extensive sex life and storylines about wrestling, cannibalism, and NASA. Essentially, Paramount had bought Groom's worldview, characters, and concept. Eight years after publication of the book, the film rocked the box office, earning $330M dollars, winning six Oscars, and becoming the fourth largest grossing film ever at the time of release. Inspired by the characters in the book, Bubba Gump Shrimp Co. Restaurant & Market opened in 1996 and now has 39 locations worldwide. Not one for sour grapes, Groom earned his 3% and embraced the film's success even without it being artistically consistent with his book. Naturally, the book went on to sell millions of copies despite its slow initial release.

On the far other end of the spectrum, I've spent most of my career developing and packaging books in a way that no one else does. In many ways this has been a tremendous benefit to Microcosm. Being unique means that we have no competition, but it also makes it harder to sell our books into new bookstores because it can take time to understand our approach. Our uniqueness has made foreign rights sales, mass market sales, and mainstream channels especially difficult to access for some titles. Understanding this dynamic helps to make conscious choices. And like all things, there are tradeoffs either way.

Copyright

Many years ago I designed a t-shirt with the words "Put the Fun Between Your Legs" surrounding a picture of a bicycle. I used it in

Microcosm's advertising and printed the shirts in my basement. It was flattering when people started to bootleg the design until major corporations began to do so. Fed up, I filed a trademark in 2015, only to find out that a Mr. Nathan Gray had already registered my design as a trademark. I spent hours on the phone with the Trademark Office in Washington, DC. How could someone trademark something that is so clearly based on my work? Apparently he could by claiming to be unaware of my image, even though it had sold over 25,000 prints and reached all corners of the globe. With no irony, Nathan Gray informed me that he was raising money for at-risk youth and had no time or interest in talking to me. Fortunately, Mr. Gray had filed his application incorrectly, and it was rejected. I wrote him another letter about how I had grown up as an at-risk youth and would be the perfect recipient of his funds.

Some authors worry about major corporations stealing their work. Speaking purely along the lines of the law, these are not things to be concerned about. As soon as a work is published, it is protected. A copyright protects an original artistic or literary work—like your book. Any work created after January 1, 1978, is automatically protected from the moment of its publication and is ordinarily given a term enduring for the author's life plus an additional 70 years after the author's death. If you love paperwork or if your books are anthologies or contain combinations of multiple people's work, such as children's books with separate writers and illustrators dreamed up and interfaced by the publisher, you can complete Form SE at copyright.gov/forms/ or you can simply print a copyright symbol on anything you suspect would be stolen: "All contents Copyright © [year] by [your name]." You own your work either way but the difference is that if you register the copyright, you are entitled to easier and faster financial compensation if someone uses your work without permission. You are copywriting the final editing of your book as a literary or artistic work. Contributors to an anthology would continue to retain their copyright to their own work. If you really love federal agencies, send two copies of anything you publish to Register of Copyrights, Copyright Acquisitions Div., Library of Congress, Washington DC 20559- 6000, which creates a record in case someone steals your work or tries to dispute your ownership of it.

Approaching the same issue from the opposite perspective, if I were trying to decide whether or not I could print someone else's image in one of our books, I wouldn't worry about anything over twenty-five years old. This is where protections end for printed materials. The trick is to see if it has been re-published in that time period. HINT: When in doubt, alter the image. This may still be considered "derivative," but should cover you if you change it enough. Three notable changes is considered standard. For instance, many artists use photos from magazines as references for their illustrations, but in the interpretation of a photo to a drawing, you could put the drawing right next to the photo and see little resemblance. Some photos and illustrations are free to use because they have been registered as Creative Commons. Others merely require a one-time licensing fee without royalties for continued use. For example, when we were publishing *Everyday Cheesemaking*, it was much cheaper to pay $25 for an image of a cheese cave than to pay for a photographer to travel to take a photo. Sure, the same photo might appear in other books about cheese but that kind of credibility was not a concern since it is not an art or photo book.

A trademark is a phrase, symbol, or design which identifies and distinguishes a company in advertising. It's the recognizability of Nike's swoosh or the slogan on a ketchup bottle. A trademark must be used in advertising rather than only sold as a product. If "Put the Fun Between Your Legs" was only a t-shirt I sold, I could not have trademarked it. I had to also use it on my work to tell people what my values were. Unlike copyrights, companies are forced to protect their trademarks or lose the rights to them. Disney, eBay, and Starbucks are notably litigious. When it comes down to it, the corporation usually wins—through sheer volume of resources. Of course, it's okay to use an image that evokes the character you have in mind as long as the "average person" would not be likely to mistake your use as representing the actual brand or its trademarks. The axiom "it's only illegal if someone notices" may apply here.

We've been lucky enough to have a few designs in our catalog so popular that they get rampantly bootlegged, including our logo. When someone uses these images without our permission, they don't always realize that they're stealing. In reality, it's pretty much the same thing as if they came into our store and walked out with a bunch of books without paying. When they print our images on poorly made sweatshop t-shirts, it devalues our identity and our work. We spend a lot of time laying it out for folks, and so we were stoked to find Portland designer Erika Schnatz's infographics about the topic. She's created the clearest visual explanation we've ever seen of how you know what you can use and when, and how to register your own copyrights.

Erika kindly gave us permission to print her explanation of fair use (which answers the question: "Is it ok to use this thing I didn't design?") here. See it on the next page! You can also download an interactive pdf and see her other copyright flow charts as well as her diverse other design work (and hire her!) at her website.

To be clear, sometimes if writers or artists are publishing fan fiction or images based on your work, characters, or intellectual property, that can serve to promote and sell the original work. When producers began using beats that Jay-Z had recorded, instead of cracking down on them, he began selling samples that other artists could use legally. He turned an IP problem into a revenue stream. On the other hand, if bootleggers are merely selling an inferior quality version of your book, this is only hurting your sales.

Unless a book was written as a work for hire or the intellectual property rights were signed away, as many early Marvel Comics works were, the author owns the right to their work. And as I said, an author's work remains under copyright for life plus 70 years *unless* it has remained continuously in print and the royalties are paid to the author's estate. In this case, the publisher wouldn't maintain publishing rights until the work goes out of print or a legal determination finds an exception otherwise. If you want to publish a previously published book, you would first want to see if the rights have lapsed. Typically if they have, and there is any interest in the book, you'll know immediately because multiple editions from multiple publishers will be in print. If it's not in the public domain, the next step would be to contact the most recent publisher. If they own the rights, they would probably be happy to sell them to you. If they don't own the rights, they might be willing and able to direct

IS IT PUBLIC DOMAIN?

ERIKA SCHNATZ: ERIKASCHNATZ.COM

WANT TO USE SOMEONE ELSE'S ART IN YOUR ART? LET'S SEE IF IT'S LEGAL! *

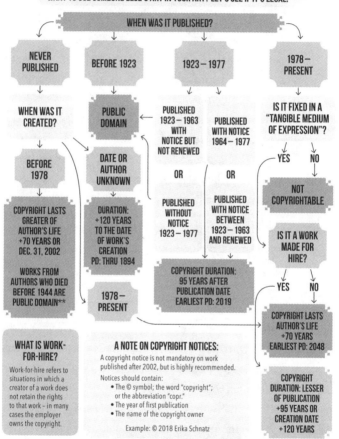

WHEN WAS IT PUBLISHED?

- **NEVER PUBLISHED**
- **BEFORE 1923**
- **1923 – 1977**
- **1978 – PRESENT**

NEVER PUBLISHED → WHEN WAS IT CREATED?

- **BEFORE 1978**
  - COPYRIGHT LASTS GREATER OF AUTHOR'S LIFE +70 YEARS OR DEC. 31, 2002
  - WORKS FROM AUTHORS WHO DIED BEFORE 1944 ARE PUBLIC DOMAIN**
- **1978 – PRESENT**

BEFORE 1923 → PUBLIC DOMAIN

DATE OR AUTHOR UNKNOWN
- DURATION: +120 YEARS TO THE DATE OF WORK'S CREATION PD: THRU 1894

1923 – 1977:
- PUBLISHED 1923 – 1963 WITH NOTICE BUT NOT RENEWED
- PUBLISHED WITH NOTICE 1964 – 1977

OR

- PUBLISHED WITHOUT NOTICE 1923 – 1977
- PUBLISHED WITH NOTICE BETWEEN 1923 – 1963 AND RENEWED

→ COPYRIGHT DURATION: 95 YEARS AFTER PUBLICATION DATE EARLIEST PD: 2019

1978 – PRESENT → IS IT FIXED IN A "TANGIBLE MEDIUM OF EXPRESSION"?

- **YES / NO**
  - NO → NOT COPYRIGHTABLE
  - YES → IS IT A WORK MADE FOR HIRE?
    - **YES / NO**
      - NO → COPYRIGHT LASTS AUTHOR'S LIFE +70 YEARS EARLIEST PD: 2048
      - YES → COPYRIGHT DURATION: LESSER OF PUBLICATION +95 YEARS OR CREATION DATE +120 YEARS

WHAT IS WORK-FOR-HIRE?

Work-for-hire refers to situations in which a creator of a work does not retain the rights to that work – in many cases the employer owns the copyright.

A NOTE ON COPYRIGHT NOTICES:

A copyright notice is not mandatory on work published after 2002, but is highly recommended.

Notices should contain:
- The © symbol; the word "copyright"; or the abbreviation "copr."
- The year of first publication
- The name of the copyright owner

Example: © 2018 Erika Schnatz

---

* This flowchart applies to works made in the United States. This visual is provided for informational purposes only. This flowchart does not constitute legal advice; proper advice from a legal professional should be sought when necessary.

** Public domain (sometimes abbreviated PD) dates are calculated from January 1, 2018.   © 2018 Erika Schnatz

Sources:
Peter B. Hirtle (2014) *Copyright Term and the Public Domain in the United States*
University of Montana (2014) *Public Domain and Creative Commons: A Guide*
US Copyright Office (2012) *How to Investigate the Copyright Status of a Work*

you to who does. If that fails, you can often find the author on their website or social media and contact them that way to inquire about publication. Most authors will just be happy to have their books back in print. If you are unsure about who owns a copyright or what a book's copyright status is, you can ask the Library of Congress to investigate for you or you can use a handy reference[8] that you can download from their website.

Perhaps the most common question we receive from authors is about quoting other people in their books. The particulars of how the law is applied are slightly complicated. If the quote is still protected under copyright, it is owned by the author and you would need their permission to include it in your book. The idea is that if you print a book of quotes from other people, the substance and value of the work is not your own work. People are essentially buying the creative work of other people.

There is one notable exception. You can use copyrighted work under the fair use clause, primarily for parody or criticism. This is how the *Onion* gets away with brutal satire of real people. Similarly, you'll notice many books will include a quote preceded and followed by the author's commentary about it. The legal interpretation of this use is that the value of the creative work is the author's commentary and the original quote is only included for clarity. A trademark works in a similar way but the owner has even tighter control over its use. If you're going to attempt parody or criticism of a trademark, do yourself a favor and hire a lawyer.

---

8 Copyright.gov/circs/circ22.pdf

Similarly, I published the book *Henry & Glenn Forever* in 2010, portraying parody personas of two living persons. The joke—which was vetted by innumerable lawyers—was that Danzig and Rollins' exaggerated public character personas were not as ridiculous as their real lives where all aspects of their public personalities were magnified even further. The joke resonated, the fans got it, and we sold over 150,000 copies of the books in the series.

Foreign Rights

The lowest hanging fruits of rights sales are foreign rights. This is where you sell the ability for a different publisher to print the book for sale in a different language or country. There are hundreds of thousands of publishers all over the globe looking for books that fit their catalog. Whereas many small presses outsource sales and distribution, buying publication rights is like outsourcing editorial. The publisher is trusting the licensee to do the diligence and turn a manuscript into content ready for publication. There are huge annual book festivals for selling foreign rights in Frankfurt and London. Publishers and their representative agencies will attend to meet with foreign publishers and discuss rights sales and showcase the same five-second pitches and sales handles that you would use at any other sales stage. Often, subrights agents will be present who speak the language of the acquiring publisher and understand what the right and wrong sales handles are.

The typical contract has the licensing publisher paying the licensee publisher 5-10% of revenues for hardcover rights sales and 5-7% for paperback rights. Unless the territory is very small or poor, there is normally an advance payment of a few thousand dollars. The rights sale typically has a period of two to three years before the rights revert. We've sold rights for a book to be published in Korea for a $500 advance. We've sold a book to be published in Japan for a $5,000 advance. Most are in the middle. We've sold rights for no advance and never been paid. Another time we received a check for $37 for Portuguese rights after the publisher had gone bankrupt. We recently sold non-exclusive French rights for 300 copies of a book to a micropublisher with the clause that we can still sell a proper French edition later. We've also sold rights several times where the licensor paid us but canceled publication of the book so we received the rights back and were able to sell them again to someone else.

This may sound like easy money, but a lot of work goes into it, and the money is normally split in half with the author, per the contract. I joke that the easiest way to close these deals is to answer the phone and check your email, but the joke is that it's true. Selling rights is about having the infrastructure in place to do so. Most of these deals come from foreign publishers coming across the marketing for a book that speaks to their list, not from aggressive solicitation.

There are many agencies with established relationships and networks that you can work with. The reason that rights agents are necessary is to get the best deal possible and understand the intricacies of the situation. They also employ subrights agents that speak the language and know the customs in foreign territories. This is work that it is often easier to outsource than to learn to perform effectively yourself if you have titles with foreign interest but don't have the contacts or relationships to make that happen on your own.

While the obvious French and Spanish editions come to publishers' minds for licensing, most graphic novels can sell Italian rights, where comics are respectable entertainment akin to Hollywood in the US. For many publishers, the easiest rights to sell are UK rights. While Microcosm remains a small press, we have received unsolicited interest for our books from Penguin UK, for example. While the language is the same, there are many reasons why a UK publisher would license a U.S. title:

- A UK publisher knows the British market better than you do.

- UK publishers have connections and relationships in their country that you don't.

- There are small language and cultural differences in the market that can be adjusted cheaply and easily. For example, bestselling author Karl Ove Knausgaard's books have not only different covers in England but titles and development so different that you would not realize they're the same books.

- UK publishers would purchase exclusive rights and better access and smoother turn times and material flow than importing. In short, if there's a significant market for a book, being able to control the means of production by printing and shipping in-country is almost always going to be smoother than importing, paying for freight, and hoping that the U.S. publisher has inventory.

- In most cases, a British publisher would buy the rights before publication and publish simultaneously to the U.S. edition so the two books are never competing.

- The cost to export to the UK can effectively double the list price of the book, making it prohibitive to purchase especially given the relative value of the pound at the moment. The Literary Industrial Complex is so big that the Big Five have years where they lose money solely because of fluctuations in international exchange rates.

- Often U.S. and UK publishers who are simpatico in their tastes and development can create a long term relationship to license each other's books.

Working effectively with a rights agency and developing your titles with translations, licenses, and foreign rights in mind can more than double your income in the span of a few years and will make the international growth of your list possible. In many cases selling foreign rights to one country will result in other countries in that region taking notice and licensing, as well.

Book Club Rights

Book clubs like Publisher's Clearinghouse sell a subscription service to consumers at deeply discounted rates. Book clubs once bought 10,000 copies for slightly more than the printing cost. Publishers printed them at the same time as the regular print run, saving money on the per-unit cost while landing a giant sale.

Unfortunately, Amazon has completely destroyed this market for most adult trade books, and book clubs have been cut to the bone. The remaining offerings are deeply mainstream because, similarly to how Target or WalMart think about book merchandising, it's simply too much work for the book club to worry about offending their customers with an off-beat book. The clubs do have secondary lists that you might be able to crack into, but the orders are small, 25-100 copies, and the discounts are substantial, 60-70%, so the effort and sale may not be worthwhile.

Asia Citro sold book club rights for five of The Innovation Press' children's titles to Scholastic. Scholastic controls literally a third of all children's book sales and much of that market dominance is through setting up book club event sales in schools. Citro did the research in advance, asking other publishers if this had negatively impacted their trade sales. It hadn't, and she's found that it's another way for parents to discover her books. It's a deep discount sale, meaning that her earnings per book isn't the same as if she had sold the same book to a bookstore, but the sales are non-returnable and, since they aren't poaching other aspects of her press, it makes good sense.

We've had more luck selling our books to subscription boxes where they are sold in thematic packs alongside other products that are not books. The sales aren't huge, but we can sell a few hundred copies to a bundle at 40-50% off. Similarly, thematic eBook digital bundles are a great outlet for bulk sales.

TV/Film Rights

Selling TV and film rights can ascend a successful book into a blockbuster. TV and film studios are looking for a certain type of writing, characters, and worlds that translates well to screen.

A book about wine and seafood pairing probably wouldn't be optioned or adapted. But a thriller novel with a unique world and memorable characters would be a strong contender. These deals can be incredibly lucrative not only in the profit from the selling the license but because they also all-but-guarantee a huge spike in book sales. That said, just because you've received an offer for TV or film for one of your books doesn't mean that it's from a major production company. The tastes and interests are also very fickle. A studio can be beating down your door for weeks and suddenly ghost you when you're trying to sign papers. Sometimes you'll be solicited for pay-to-play "deals" that promise to land you a major studio offer but really only list you in a database of available works. Sometimes you'll sell the rights to a small studio that will have a negligible impact on your bank account or book sales. Other times you'll sell to a company who merely wants to sit on the rights. They may want to wait for the right moment as the subject matter comes into fashion or to prevent their competitors from purchasing the rights. You should thoroughly research the company making the offer to ensure they are credible and could do justice to the work.

Many authors and publishers want to be brought on as consultants when studios or production companies buy the screen rights, but this is rarely considered. Production companies have specialists and experts in their craft and having additional story editors and consultants to run decisions through tends to muck up the works. Of course this can result in a production like HBO's *Dangerous Minds* where the author feels that the TV show bears little resemblance to the reality of her story or profession. This is because the studio is often more interested in buying the rights to your characters and world than they are in making something that is factually accurate or portrays the subject in the same manner as the book. So knowing all of this, make the choices that are right for you.

Audio/Other Rights Sales

The best titles for audio have very few images and occupy the key demographic for digital products: people who want to "read" while multitasking or driving, people who want to read the kind of books they'd be ashamed to be seen reading in public (romance, self-help, etc), and people that travel frequently and are too busy to read traditionally (business, self-improvement, personal finance, how to, etc). If you have books in these categories, it can still prove very difficult to produce, market, and distribute them yourself because it requires a whole separate set of relationships.

One busy weekend my business partner and I joined Laura Stanfill and one of her authors in her van down to Ashland, Oregon for a literary festival. Attending the same festival was the acquisitions agent for Blackstone Audio. We didn't meet him that day, but Laura put him in touch with me a few weeks later. He was interested in audio rights to seven of our titles in digital and physical formats and even pitched us his own book to publish. Similarly to Asia Citro's book club sale to Scholastic, working out the deal took hours of my time, but it was a substantial sale to a reputable company that won't eat away at our bottom line elsewhere. Blackstone is an industry juggernaut that is not affiliated with a Big Five house. While the Literary Industrial Complex tend to produce and manufacture their audiobooks in house, Blackstone is often outselling two out of five of them with audiobooks during any given year.

Similarly, we've had smaller licensing deals to excerpt a chapter of one of our books in a magazine or online. We recently received an offer to reprint an excerpt from *Bikenomics: How Bicycling Can Save The Economy* in an educational course text. They were only offering ten cents per copy but they produced 7,000 copies so again, the deal made sense because it would simultaneously promote the book without hurting us elsewhere. If you believe that a sale will hurt your bottom line, look at the costs and consequences. Will you earn 50 cents per book from the rights sale, but if you didn't sell the rights the customers would buy your book in paperback, netting a $2 profit? Sometimes you can ask the licensee to meet you in the middle. Other times you'll want to simply decline the license.

Selling All Rights

In 2011, Hugh Howey, author of *Wool* and the *Silo* science fiction series, followed in the tradition of authors like Amanda Hocking, who had been rejected countless times by publishers and earned $2.5M self-publishing on Amazon. But Howey changed the game, being wildly more successful than anyone before him with Amazon's publishing platform, selling millions of copies of his eBooks and documenting his progress. Howey was a beacon of hope to any author that had ever received a rejection letter that the whole system was bogus, obsolete, and sinking.

Within a year Howey began receiving licensing offers for movies. Even though he was published by the largest industry monopoly, he sold his print rights to The Literary Industrial Complex (Simon & Schuster, in this case) for six figures, finding "traditional publishing" to offer a better value and deal than Amazon. Then he built a house and sailing station in South Africa at age 40 and continued to collect his digital royalties.

The Howey Proverb convinces millions of self-published authors that they have a chance of retiring in luxury by self-publishing on Amazon and selling for six figures to the Literary Industrial Complex. But the reality is that Howey's imitators poisoned the market by flooding it with even more garbage than there was previously. The result has effectively reduced wages for authors across the industry. The Howey Proverb is a tired, though oft-repeated, one. The resulting crowded market reduced sales expectations for Amazon publishers from an average of 250 copies to below 100 copies sold in its lifetime and created odds for success so bad that, if the goal is to make money, authors are better off playing the lottery or looking for change on the sidewalk.

Amazon's PR team hoodwinking *New York Times* reporters into repeating false narratives about the state of the industry and the Howey Proverb are the reason that Amazon's marketing language is now cemented into the popular consciousness and the public has a general distrust for "obsolete, greedy publishers."

These methods are designed for authors that intend to flash bright and burn out hard. Still, it's virtually impossible to sell all rights for a title until it's already successful, at which point you have the choice to grow your press or sell your rights. Often, a midlist press cannot sustain a true bestseller (we'll revisit how to do this properly in Chapter 11). They either lack the financing to keep the book sufficiently in print and distributed or they overprint and suffer a crippling financial loss when the book stops selling. This is why, once a midlist publisher has a breakout hit, it is often easier for many presses to sell the rights to a bigger house.

So let's imagine that you want to sell all of your publishing rights to a major house and you've received an offer. How do you proceed? First you'll want to figure out the cost/benefit ratio. How much would you expect to earn if you kept the rights? Arguably, in many cases, The Literary Industrial Complex should be able to sell more copies of your book than you can and with greater efficiency. Why? They have much more infrastructure and the one kind of title that they do know how to manage effectively is a bestseller. Of course, they need a piece of the pie too but if this is your exit strategy, hold out for at least as much money as you would expect to earn on your own.

Homework

- Are you sure that you own copyrights to all aspects of your published work?

- Is there a publisher from another country who would be interested in your books at the right time?

- Do you have capacity to find and sell to them?

- What countries and languages are likely to be interested in your book?

- Is your book a good candidate for audio book?

- Is your book a strong contender to be optioned for TV or film?

- What are other likely areas for your rights sales?

- What would it take for you to sell all rights?

9

CONTRACTS

Outlining Your Agreements

The value of your publishing company is based on your contracts. While the point of publishing is to accumulate a collection of great information that stimulates the mind, the ability of your press to do this over a long period of time is secured by the quality of your contracts.

Like all good lessons, I learned this one the hard way. When I founded Microcosm, I stubbornly took my cues from Factory Records, the Manchester-based record label of Joy Division, Happy Mondays, and New Order. Formed in 1978 by Tony Wilson and Alan Erasmus, who infamously rejected contracts in favor of handshakes, the label claimed no publishing rights to recordings or albums. In 1980, "Love Will Tear Us Apart Again" by Joy Division broke the top 20 in the UK. Singer Ian Curtis committed suicide days before their first U.S. tour, propelling hundreds of thousands of album sales— that Factory Records had no way to secure the indefinite rights to. In 1992, when Happy Mondays spent £400,000 of Factory's money recording a disastrous album in Barbados, the label was propelled into bankruptcy. London Records was interested in purchasing Factory Records...until they discovered that the label did not own the valuable catalog of New Order, who could walk away with it at any time. The artists went on to sell over a million albums combined and, despite this, Factory no longer exists solely on the grounds that they rejected contracts.

Not one to be deterred, I adopted Factory's model of handshakes over contracts. To my credit, I didn't know the full story of how and why Factory Records ended until the *24 Hour Party People* documentary was released in 2002. Still, mine was entirely a pompous, emotional decision made as a pattern-thinking autistic teenager. I believed that by being fair and reasonable and focusing on the relationship with the author that all problems could be resolved and authors would *choose* to publish their books with Microcosm indefinitely. Microcosm's first ten books were verbally negotiated and agreed upon with the author. Sometimes we agreed to absurd things, like a book not having a cover or that a book could have multiple publishers or that the author could sell their books to the same accounts that we did, effectively competing with us. We let the authors design their own covers generally as most were artists, while we offered mostly financing, printing, and distribution. Later we began proofreading as well. Eventually authors would be so shocked by these policies that they would request a contract— or at least some scrawl on a napkin to outline what to expect for both of us from the interaction, and we began outlining terms and expectations casually. For our first ten years, this policy went remarkably well. Our books were developed so uniquely that not a single author left—because even if they had wanted to, there would be nowhere else to go with their book besides self-publishing, which was financially and technologically infeasible at the time.

By 2007, Microcosm had stumbled upon enough success that we began to have our authors poached. Newly infused with cash, a small press that had been founded by a friend was bought and gutted with old money in a strange attempt to turn the underground into the mainstream. For the first time, Microcosm had competition that was much more financially capable than we were. The other press began offering substantial advances to our bestselling authors, who we did not have under contract, luring them away one by one. At first this was scary and daunting, but also exciting—I expected that their new books, backed by marketing budgets dozens of times larger than ours, would propel our sales of their back catalog. This had worked for the independent record labels that had released early albums by Green Day or Nirvana after they sold millions of major label albums. Sadly, that never happened for Microcosm. This situation played out just before the giant stock market crash of 2007, effectively tanking sales of all of the poached books and saving us from their production costs! I was sad about the authors' decisions to leave, but I understood and went back to the drawing board of acquiring new first-time authors to publish new books with.

Slowly, I realized that every one of our bestsellers was by a first-time author who merely had a good concept and development. I realized that losing the authors wasn't a major blow as we had the tools to recreate similar successes indefinitely. We began implementing contracts for new authors that secured our rights as long as we upheld our end of the agreement. Later that year, *Make Your Place* was published and went on to become Microcosm's first book to sell over 100,000 copies. So we learned from experience and, fortunately, our story did not end like Factory Records' did. Ultimately it's better for you to learn these lessons from reading rather than from the experience of repeating the same mistakes yet again. If you ever have a book that sells over 25,000 copies, or want to sell your company on to its next proprietor, having good contracts will help your goals become a reality.

Creating and Negotiating the Contract

For most authors and publishers, thinking about themselves as any kind of business is terrifying. Still, when you're certain that you want to publish an author's manuscript, you'll want to create a publishing contract.

Even if you are the author and the publisher, you'll want to put yourself under contract. Absurd as this may sound, it's important. You may sell your company one day, effectively becoming an author at someone else's publishing company. Your press may take on a business partner or acquire financial backing or investment ownership. You may die unexpectedly and leave your intellectual property in an unsecured state, at risk of ending up in the hands of someone that you don't want it to go to. Putting the agreement between yourself and your press into writing is one way that the terms of the agreement are indisputable. I can tell you from experience that, decades down the road, nothing will happen the way you expect it to.

A contract is an agreement to license the author's intellectual property for certain uses. The contract outlines what happens in the future during best, worst, and most likely scenarios. It sets expectations and operates as your guide when the unexpected happens. Contracts work best when they establish necessary guidelines and expectations for a collaborative relationship. Most of your publishing sales will land squarely in the middle but you still need to prepare for all scenarios.

For most authors—as well as most publishers—an acceptable contract is the best one that is being offered. There's little reason for an author to hold out for a better contract unless there are reasons to believe that one exists. Publishing is saturated with supply: there are far more authors than publisher opportunities, so if you are making an offer that you believe is fair, it should be accepted. Of course, sometimes an author has no idea what a fair offer looks like. There are not many public resources or experts to refer to about contracts, so they will often inundate you with questions answered in the contract. Authors tend not to read their contracts and simply form their expectations and plans around what they have heard or experienced elsewhere. In this way, your reputation will serve you. As you publish more and more books, authors will expect that what you are offering is reasonable as other respectable names in your field have published with you. If an author is sending me demanding emails or transcribing their thought process to me in real time and I think it is unlikely that another publisher would make them an offer—or at least I wouldn't be upset if we lost a chance with the book—I wait a week to respond to their emails to let them process the decision on their own. This tends to de-escalate concerns or demands that they are making.

On the other hand, you want both the author and the publisher to understand the contract. Oddly, 90% of authors merely sign and return the contract faster than they could have read it. This creates problems when they begin asking questions a year or two later, and you discover that they don't understand how things have been working. My business partner likes it if an author asks a million questions because it means they are making an informed decision to work with us. I've found that the ideal author asks a few questions about the contract and requests a change or two, even if we cannot accommodate those requests. For example, if we think that publishing a certain book is a zero sum game financially, but we know that we can sell the Spanish language rights (see page 270), we aren't going to let the author keep those rights in the contract. I send them the contract with an email, encouraging them to ask me questions about anything unclear or concerning. If they sign and return immediately, I offer a brief synopsis of the terms and probable outcomes.

Recently we made an offer to a first-time prospective author who keeps an attorney on retainer. His lawyer requested five pages of new clauses—the revisions were longer than the original contract. None of the requests were unreasonable, but this was a red flag to me so I talked to the author on the phone and came to understand that his perspective wasn't to meddle or quibble, but that he had heard every negative experience imaginable and was trying to protect himself from them. I understood and respected him and his position, but ultimately you cannot legislate respect and trust into the author-publisher relationship. Trust must exist beneath the contract so that when something unexpected does inevitably happen, you know that you can work together in a way that is functional for all stakeholders.

The author-publisher relationship works best as a creative partnership, and contracts tend to be the least creative part of the process. In this case, I was comfortable to negotiate but the author decided to end negotiations and didn't seem hopeful that we would come to agreeable terms.

Often an author will ask for a new clause to be added during negotiation. If it doesn't cause any problems or works for you, it's in your best interest to comply. Making requested changes shows that you're a team player. And, to be honest, most clauses will never come into play but will build and embolden the mutual trust in the relationship. Remember that everything in a contract is negotiable (in theory). Wield that red pen responsibly and when there are disagreements, talk it over as a team, not as adversaries!

The basic components of a contract are:

- An outline of what the work is and what it will look like

- A plan and schedule to compensate the author

- A series of author obligations

- An outlining of territory that the contract pertains to (paper or digital, U.S. or world)

- A schedule for completing the work as well as various dates that the publisher is operating on

- Some expectations of what the publisher will produce (formats, if rights sales are lined up, etc.)

- How sales reporting will be done to the author

- An outlining of promotion, distribution, ownership (is the book a work-for-hire or does the author retain the work or is the work the composite of many people's contributions that creates an amalgamated new work?)

- What happens in various best and worst case outcome scenarios

In reality, every contract lays out "when you do this, these are the consequences." Some aspects benefit or protect the author. Other parts are obligations for each party. And other parts stipulate what happens if one party fails to do certain things or penalties for a lack of overall success, like having to pay back an advance or buy back unsold books before they are turned back into paper.

Even a solid contract does not prevent the chance of conflict or even going to court. A fundamental disagreement that has the ability to get this heated really comes down to who has greater resources, money, and stubbornness. The true goal of a contract is to create a mutually beneficial, long-lasting relationship in which both parties are happy. The nature of any dispute really comes down to expectations and personalities involved. You will probably be able to tell during contract negotiations if that's going to become an issue or not.

The Money

The most argued-about part of a contract is the advance: the amount of money paid for completion of the work in expectation of future success and royalties. Fortunately for your budget, advances have shrunk steadily over the last ten years. Only the major houses and fiscally independent mid-list publishers that operate on family money have enough cash flow to pay a substantial advance for a new book. As a result, even a relatively large indie will pay an advance to a first-time author of $0-$3,000. The advance is based on predicted sales for the first two years of the book, which is the lifetime of most books unless you've got an evergreen on your hands. These figures are based on conservative estimates from the P&L, generally 3,000 paperbacks or 1,000 hardcovers and 1,000 paperbacks. A more established author with a track record of similar work to point to will probably ask for an advance that predicts similar sales.

Some authors are represented by agents. Small presses often believe that if an author has an agent that they would require a large advance or that the agent wouldn't be willing to work with a small press. But that's simply not true. The agent's job is to place the book in the best (or only) house possible. If there are not competing offers from other publishers, the appropriately sized advance for anticipated sales will usually get you the contract. Even $500 is a good-sized advance for a book that an agent cannot sell elsewhere. We've signed books with large agencies for no advance because the author likes us. I'm proud to report that every time Microcosm has worked with an agent it has improved and smoothed over the acquisition process because they know what is expected, fair, and reasonable.

Of course that is not always the case. Noted ruthless agent Andrew Wylie supposedly said that "If my client's book earns out, I haven't done my job," meaning that he wants his author to earn more in advances than their books will earn in sales. Ultimately, you won't be and don't want to be working with agents like that. Asia Citro, who publishes books for children as The Innovation Press, has had a mixed experience working with agents. "I prefer unagented authors and illustrators because it's easier for me to get a feel for who they are as a person and whether or not they'll be a great fit for our company. I've had a few agents who were so aggressive that I moved on from their client simply because I didn't want to deal with that agent. Once we've signed someone with an agent, it can take weeks for them to review the contract when we've got a book we want to get to market quickly. I do have a handful of agents who are lovely to work with. They are honest, have reasonable expectations, and care about the project as a whole rather than looking out for just their client to the exception of everything and everyone else involved. They have a great feel for our company and our titles and are able to bring us clients who match our high standards and serious devotion to our young readers."

Even if you are not paying any advance at all, this choice does not communicate that you don't believe in the book. In most cases, it simply shows that you are bootstrapping and don't have money to fall back on in the event that the book does not recoup its costs. It's uncommon for the author to have to repay the advance if the book does not recoup, but your contract should specify if it needs to be repaid or, alternately, if they do not have to pay it back. If an author is demanding more money than your P&L deems possible, walk away.

Regardless of the advance, a much more important number is the royalty percentage. If the publisher will be producing the book in multiple formats, they should have a different royalty for each format. Hardcovers typically pay 8-12% of the cover price to the author. Paperbacks tend to pay 6-8% of the cover price. eBooks tend to pay at 15-30% of net profit. Translation rights can pay as much as

20-50% of the sale. Of course every contract is different and should improve with the author's track record.

Partially as a way of never losing money on a book that is selling well, Microcosm pays a royalty based on the net profit of each sale rather than a traditional royalty based on the cover price of the book. As the industry has continued to change dramatically over the past five years, publishers become responsible for more and more fees that used to be covered by vendors, such as freight costs to wholesalers and deeper discounts to Amazon. For example, if a publisher sells 1,000 books that retail for $20, the author's royalties would traditionally be 8% of cover, or $1,600. The publisher can run into trouble if it's only getting paid 30% of the cover price after a distributor's cut and Amazon's discount. You receive $6 per unit on your $20 book from Amazon. The author's royalty is $1.60 and printing costs $2 per book. Our staff, overhead, and bottom line cost 51.89% or $3.11. The remaining $2.40 wouldn't even cover that. We would be effectively losing $.71 on every book sold—let alone on the costs of unsold inventory. For this reason, many publishers are moving to a variable royalty model for Amazon sales, where the author is paid less on these sales. For example, if you paid the author 10% of net on this sale, you'd earn $6 - $3.11 bottom line - $2 printing - $.60 royalty = $.29 profit.

I have seen contracts where the author must pay a certain amount of money to be published or the publishers retain a certain amount of money for undefined expenses or undefined staff time. This kind of unaccountable cost for an author doesn't sit right with me. Typically "pay-to-play" contracts are scams that only benefit the "publisher." Don't include any clauses in your contract that you wouldn't be willing to sign as an author.

Obligations

Typically the contract will outline how much content (often expressed in a final word or illustration count) the author must provide and when it is due in various edited forms. It should also say if the author is responsible for indexing the book, as well as providing things like photography or art. Typically there is a deadline for a first draft, a follow-up deadline for developmental edits, a deadline for line-edit revisions, and a time for final proofing. If things like this are not stipulated in the contract, it's prudent to at least include them in email correspondence. If nothing else, make sure that you are on the same page.

Include clauses that establish that the work is original to the author. For example, they should promise to guarantee that nothing is plagiarized or used without permission. Some contracts stipulate that the author must secure permissions for content that they are including or that the publisher must secure permissions for content they want to include. It's probably a good idea to verify that the author did obtain said permissions—we've had authors lie to us about this in the distant past. Include language that certain standards of quality and consistency must be met in the final work so you can reject it if the quality is poor or doesn't match that of the sample or prior discussions.

It's standard to include an indemnity clause that releases the publisher from the legal consequences of the author's actions as well as the author from the legal consequences of the publisher's actions. Naturally, the law or a court may find differently and hold both parties liable, suggesting that the other party behaved irresponsibly to claim that the book cured cancer when it doesn't. When Tour de France bicycling champion Lance Armstrong admitted in 2013 to taking performance-enhancing steroids throughout his career, Armstrong and his publisher, Berkley, were hit with a class-action complaint. Former deputy chief of staff for Arnold Schwarzenegger asserted that *It's Not About the Bike*, a memoir detailing Armstrong's rise to success after beating cancer, was a fraud, violating consumer protection laws and exhibiting false advertising by claiming the stories told in the book were the cause of Armstrong's victory. Respectable presidential biographer Doris Kearns Goodwin allegedly plagiarized portions of *The Fitzgeralds and the Kennedys* and *No Ordinary Time* and confirmed in 2002 that she had paid a settlement to at least one author for doing so. James Frey went a step further, claiming that his fictional book *A Million Little Pieces* was actually his memoir. The mutual indemnity clause may not always protect you but still, it's important to include it as it will help more times than it won't. Also, do not do anything stupid and make sure to check easily verifiable details and claims in any book you publish.

Often the author will have obligations for how much they must promote the book, that they must take part in interviews that the publisher schedules, and even that public signing events or appearances at conferences or a book tour are required as part of the agreement. Some titles don't require this level of author support, but include language matching your needs about it in the contract.

Rights

You may ask for exclusive film/TV rights, eBook/digital rights, audio, hardcover, and paperback rights all over the world. This means that while the author owns the content of the book, only the publisher is allowed to sell it to other publishers in the above formats. Just because you received *some* publication rights doesn't mean that you own all rights to all formats. *Fiyah*, a "magazine of Black speculative fiction, made the mistake of issuing a collection reprinting writers' work from previous issues...without obtaining the authors' perrmission. They apologized to their fans and were largely forgiven, but it's an important lesson: get rights for formats that you intend to publish and secure new contracts if that changes. It's rude to take world rights in every language if a publisher isn't actually equipped with the resources to sell to the whole world. Some publishers will try to claim eBook and hardcover rights without plans of issuing those editions in order to prevent another publisher from publishing them. If you aren't represented by a rights agency and aren't actively pitching rights sales of the aforementioned formats and have no intention of issuing them yourself, it's difficult to make the argument that the author should sign them over to you. At the same time, even if you don't have these rights secured and you receive an offer for film or Italian rights, the author is usually inclined to add a contract addendum so that the license happens and everyone gets paid!

When is the publication date for each format? How will the book be distributed? How will you, as a publisher, do a better job of representing the book to market than the author could do on their own? Besides title development and market research, the reason that publishers exist is your relationships and resources that it wouldn't make sense for a single author to have. And even a brand new publisher has motivation and chutzpah and a valuable partnership to offer an author.

How does the contract end? Do the rights expire or renew in perpetuity? Does the author have the right to elect to renew or not with each printing, as is standard with graphic novels? Are there certain conditions that the author can terminate the contract under? Under what grounds can the rights be canceled or transferred to another publisher by the author or publisher?

After Publication

Plan for the worst-case scenario as well as the best-case scenario. The average book with publisher support sells only 2,000-3,000 copies in its lifetime. That means that plenty sell far fewer. A store can return books to the publisher for an entire year or longer after their order. Yes, you can prevent returnability, but you will also prevent stores from ordering in the process. Returns create a lot of unknowns about the success of the book during that first year.

How will sales be reported to the author? At what frequency? How much collaboration will the author have on marketing and publicity? Is there a way for the author to bring ideas and resources to the table other than promoting the book on their own platform?

Sometimes the most important parts of a contract are the parts that outline what happens if the book flops. Does the author have to pay back the advance? I've met too many authors whose book was deemed a failure by their publisher in the first year. Suddenly, they had to choose how many unsold copies to buy at 40% off because the rest would be pulped. Add a clause in your contract for how much the author buys dead stock for.

Books are highly emotional for their authors and often their behavior devolves quickly into illogical choices that aren't in their best interest (remember Ian Hamilton Finlay in the previous chapter?). For cases where you cannot functionally communicate directly with an author, you may want to include a forced arbitration agreement in your contract. Arbitration is legally binding mediation, but without a lawsuit or trial. Both sides state their case and grievances and the arbitrator creates a new contract to resolve the dispute with real consequences. Organizations like the American Arbitration Association[9] and local mediators can create binding solutions that are much cheaper and less stressful than a court trial.

Almost more Earth-shattering, what happens if the book is far more successful than anyone planned? Does the contract hold up? We once had an author request that he be paid in 20% of the books from each print run. That worked out great until we had sold over 40,000 copies and he needed to rent a storage unit for his 8,000 books. We renegotiated for an agreement that scaled better and worked for both of us. Often times, strangely, it's success that is most disruptive to a book. The strain of constant revisions, reprints, and financial management to make sure that everyone is getting what is owed to them is much harder on everyone involved but it's what we all dream of! So keep your agreements and financial records tidy!

---

9 https://www.adr.org/rules

Creating an Exit Plan

While 80% of "successful" self-publishing anecdotes aren't generating more than a month's income, there are plenty of authors who become proper publishers, realizing that publishing is more of a career than writing. Many of these proprietors find success beyond their wildest dreams...at which point the ad hoc publisher realizes that they don't actually enjoy the business end of publishing. Once they are a proven success, they may receive an offer either for their book or their whole press from a major house and leave the destiny of their work to the Literary Industrial Complex. In some cases, the publisher will sell the company to an outside investor who is not currently involved in publishing. If the entire press is sold, the proprietor usually stays as an employee of the company and makes flowery declarations to the press about how they can now just "focus on publishing great books."

If you have these pipe dreams, you'll need to include clauses in your contracts that they can be transferred to another party. Otherwise, the author can insist that they receive their rights back when you sell or dissolve your company. They aren't wrong, and this is one reason why planning ahead and thinking about contracts is vital. After 23 years, I have no intention of selling to an investor or vacating the company, but I know I won't be around forever, so I started to plan so Microcosm could continue even after I was gone.

When you sell your publishing house, even if you intend to stay as an employee, the cause for the sale is almost always a result of needing more financialization (see Chapter 11), either because of limits to growth or (much more often) general financial mismanagement. If the owner is selling the company for a reason beyond retirement, it often becomes quickly apparent that the problem wasn't having insufficient funds, but not knowing how to manage those funds into something greater than the sum of their parts. This is why you should start small with very small budgets to learn what you can accomplish from nothing. Because in 99% of cases, the owner sells the company and then it doesn't last a whole year under the new oversight and financial management. Ultimately, the same reasons that the company was sold are the reasons that former owner cannot work there any longer. Publishing is difficult and often the retiring founder had great creative ideas but ran the company into a financial black hole that it can't climb out of, driving a once-creative midlist publisher into the belly of the Literary Industrial Complex where its heart slowly withers.

In years of research, I found one glowing exception to this rule in Mitch Rogatz, founder and publisher of Triumph Books since 1989. Triumph publishes books about sports and trends. Before the World Series and Super Bowl each year, Triumph commissions books about both teams, arranges a printer that can turn around books in 24 hours, cancels the book for the losing team, and inundates the victorious market after game day. When fidget spinners hit the market, Triumph produced a book about them in weeks. They develop books for specialty mall stores like Claire's Boutique.

Mitch sold the company to Random House in 2006 to enjoy greater financing with himself remaining at the helm. In 2011, Random House decided to close Triumph and dismantle the brand. They gave Mitch a few months to find a buyer. IPG borrowed money and bought the company, allowing Mitch to continue his position as a very unique publisher. Joe Matthews, CEO of IPG, says he had weekly budget meetings in 2016 with Triumph and every week Triumph was wildly over budget. But the sales and revenue were worthwhile even though it makes planning difficult, and staff had to give up end-of-year bonuses as a result. Triumph remains IPG's most profitable department but in February 2018, IPG consolidated Triumph into Chicago Review Press and Mitch is no longer with the company. It was a rare and unique arrangement that lasted as long as it did because the publisher knew how to turn money into an investment.

Homework

- What is the most important thing that you are trying to accomplish with your contract?

- How will you communicate author understandings and expectations?

- What are the best and worst case scenarios that you can afford to give the author?

- What are you most afraid of going wrong in the author relationship that the contract can help with?

- What rights are a must-have?

- What rights can you part with?

10

PUBLICITY & LAUNCH

Growing Your Small World

T he most important part of publicity is building relationships. Your end goal isn't to land a certain review or event. It's to build a movement and connect with readers in a lasting way so that they are excited that your book exists and will spread the word about it. These fans will be your greatest advocates.

An interesting example of this is Robert Kiyosaki, the author of *Rich Dad, Poor Dad,* which was published in 1994. Kiyosaki explained that his publicity strategy for the book was to intentionally make divisive statements and create controversy around his work. He explains that you want 33% of people aware of your work to love it, 33% to hate it, and 33% to be indifferent. He insists that the strategy of making public statements to elicit reactions, creating controversy by sharing polarizing opinions, and being prepared for public media appearances will drive your work to the correct audiences. Through a partnership with Learning Annex, Kiyosaki landed on *Oprah* in 2000 and has sold over 32 million books to date. He went on to author eleven more books including *Why We Want You to Be Rich* with Donald Trump. Kiyosaki was a controversial figure with many critics poking holes in his claims and investment theories, but even when Learning Annex won a $24M settlement against Kiyosaki's shell corporation for unpaid royalties on its seminars, many fans continued to believe in Kiyosaki and his ideas.

Not every author has skin as thick as Kiyosaki's or wants to deal with the multitudes dissecting the validity of their arguments. But there's a kernel of truth to his ideas when you examine any successful author's launch plan.

The ideal outcome, of course, is to make everyone *else* talk about your book for you. I landed this feat with Tom Neely's *Henry & Glenn Forever,* depicting punkers Rollins and Danzig in a comic full of loving, romantic relationship moments and couples spats. The joke that these muscle bound, real-life cartoon characters who both exhibit larger than life public personas could be rewritten into slightly different personalities really resonated with the right audience. The idea was so odd and curious that fans of both real people felt the need to have an opinion about it—before they had even seen it. I was on a book tour when the copies came back from the printer. Before I could send a single promotional email or review copy, the book took off on its own. Someone talked about it on Twitter every day for nearly a year and it was picked up across the media, from *Rolling Stone* to MTV to NPR. In the first year we sold over 70,000 copies, most of them one at a time from our own website. Today we've sold around 150,000 copies of all the books in the series combined.

An even more successful example of this is the *Blair Witch Project,* which featured a trailer claiming to be made from "found footage" from three people who disappeared and were "presumed dead." The website featured fake police reports and news footage. Naturally, the public was confused if this was a true story or a fictional one built out of amateur shaky cam footage. The public imagination was captured and the results were stupendous. The film grossed $248 million at the box office. Of course when the studio tried to roll out a sequel, the film flopped. Hold onto that level of mystery, but don't pull the same stunt twice.

The *Guinness Book of Records* began in the 1950s as a marketing giveaway for Guinness Breweries. They sold 70,000 copies in the U.S. during the first year and the book now sells itself, even winning the world record for best-selling copyrighted book! Is it true? Maybe. It is it a scam? I dunno. Is it funny? Yes. And it stays relevant because it offers the chance for other people to get some press. If everyone's favorite subject is themselves, the *Guinness Book* appeals to the idea that you could appear in its pages. When I tweeted at them that I was sitting in front of the loudest snoring man on the bus, they sent me the actual world record. Brilliant social engagement.

Build Your Movement, then Your Catalog

For a book to succeed, you want to embed the author into the communities that would be interested in buying their book— or better yet, communities where you or the author are already invested and embedded. This projects the book's success beyond the initial launch and embeds it into the fabric of conversations in an organic community.

Think about where readers of your type of work socialize, network, and share information. Be active in those communities. Participate in your books' subject matter. If you're writing about bicycle advocacy, embed yourself in the social movement. If you're fighting against the over-prescription of antidepressants, rain leaflets down from the sky at psychiatrist conferences. If you're here to disrupt the science fiction world to become diverse, bring your posse to their conferences and social media groups. Be a contributing member of those groups. Let your fans know you and your work but **never, ever say "buy my book."** Make it implied. Participate just like every other active member of these groups. If you are insincere in your contributions, you won't succeed.

Don't just offer information; learn from other people. Talk about your theories and your qualifications, but focus on the community, not your ego. Keep links available to your website for people who want to investigate your credentials and publications, but forever think about what you would want as a participant in this community and social movement. Define the bounds of your subject matter. What won't you do? What will you embrace the most? A firm grasp of this is your best strength. Match every book to your mission.

Henry & Glenn Forever wouldn't have blown up out of nowhere if we did not have a giant mailing list, social media following, and appropriate infrastructure to manage the volume of hundreds of daily orders. By a stroke of timing and dumb luck, the book was not listed on Amazon so the only way to purchase it was on our own website. If we didn't have a secure shopping cart on our website, we wouldn't have received the orders. If we didn't have staff and procedures to fill them, it would have created massive problems. Perhaps more importantly, the book made sense to our audience and they were comfortable purchasing it directly on our website.

Make a Plan

Once you've got some books under contract—even before they are done being written—organize them into logical seasons together. It's much easier and more efficient to promote similar books at the same time. It's easier to sell books to an account when you have multiple books that the same account would buy. It's easier to promote your books thematically in your newsletter or solicit them to magazines. This is ultimately why most midlist publishers only publish one type of book that has one key audience. If you do, that's great. If you don't, do yourself the favor and group like books for publication during the same season. Think about all of this holistically and build a plan before you are neck deep in books.

Get your website online at least six months before your first book comes back from the printer. Why? Because that's how long it takes for it to rank on Google. In order to make a website, you'll need to know your mission and editorial focus and have some great language full of keywords that your fans will search. Just like your book's development, look at what words similar websites and blogs are using to target the same audience. Then you need to continue to add relevant blog posts and new book covers and other content at regular intervals so that your publishing website is obviously active and Google begins prioritizing you. Think of your website as your landing pad. Make sure that your website features, front and center, who you are and what you do with a descending hierarchy of information from there. As soon as you have a finished cover and product page for a new title, make sure there is a buy button on that page so that you can begin promoting the enthusiasm that you have for the book. Make supporting your books the easiest thing for your fans to do.

Getting all of this in order should help you to get your thinking in gear and hammer down some clear language and catch phrases. Revisit the first two chapters of this book, focusing on developing a niche and title development, to make sure that you are marketing yourself in the appropriate ways.

You're going to need to build and accumulate an email list any way that you can. An email list is the most efficient way to reach your most enthusiastic fans and build your sales funnel efficiently. Put out a sign up sheet at events. Solicit them on your website and on social media. Give the option to sign up when someone buys something. You're always wanting to connect with people that are interested in your work so make your newsletter itself interesting and only send genuine content and news. Encourage people to respond and engage meaningfully. Per Henningsgaard of Ooligan Press explains, "As a publisher you should have a lot of content and shouldn't be afraid to give it away for free in return for email addresses."

Most new publishers believe that they need to purchase advertisements at this stage to promote their company. Honestly, the science of advertising is shoddy at best. And you don't want to pay for advertising at all until you've got your plan and messaging dialed in.

Earned media is much more effective than paid ads. Make a list of organizations, magazines, websites, and outlets that would probably be happy to feature your book because it is relevant to their existing audience. Put them in sequence from largest to smallest. Create columns based on the various audiences that your book is relevant to. For example, our book *Feminist Weed Farmer* has five basic audiences: gardening, women, cannabis, feminist, and African American. These outlets would probably have some overlapping readership but not entirely so you would think of them as five different targets. Obviously, the book is of interest to people that are outside of these demographics too, but you still find and connect with those readers via these outlets because, for example, if you sent it to bow hunting magazines, they would think that you made a mistake.

Crowdfunding

Kickstarter and similar platforms are the superior versions of book launches, publicity campaigns, and buzz building. It's an engine to help you do what you already need to do. Yet, most publishers are somewhere between reluctant and terrified to use Kickstarter. I think their hesitation is because crowdfunding is not the kind of thing that you talk about at cocktail parties, and it does not fit well into the self-image of the Literary Industrial Complex. Wealthy people are not allowed to talk, think or be concerned about money. And to most people, Kickstarter is seen as a funding apparatus rather than a promotional or marketing tool.

To date, Kickstarter has funded over one hundred million dollars in publishing projects, but let's forget about the money for a minute. What Kickstarter helps you do best is build a campaign, spread the word, and create momentum.

Microcosm has run about 40 Kickstarter projects between our two divisions. It's these books that people come up to us at events and talk about. It's these books that the media contacts us about to feature in magazines and blogs. It's these books that are memorably burned into the minds of our fans.

Typically we aim to raise funds to cover our printing cost. While the average book costs us five figures to publish, we keep most campaigns around $5,000, mostly for the sake of our blood pressure. Granted, we also run several campaigns each year and we don't want to exhaust our supporters. Don't ask for too much money. Ask for what you need to close the gap of unreasonable risk. Use this as an opportunity to get feedback from your backers about your book. And don't send the book to print until the project is successful.

In return for readers' money and support, the primary rewards we offer are books. We typically offer the book at its list price (typically $10-15). It's a very bad idea to discount the book below cover price before it has been published because you are devaluing your own work and creating the expectation that people would not need to buy it at full price. While Costco, Amazon, and WalMart will happily battle to discount a new book into price oblivion, you are not operating on the same battlefield for future obsolescence.

From there, add additional tiers featuring the book plus logical add-ons. Brainstorm and arrange reward levels upwards from an eBook for $5-10, the book for $10-15, and upwards with staggered tiers at $25, $50, $75, $100, $250, and $500. Too much focus on rewards that aren't the book or are too expensive/time-consuming/complex to manufacture/ship/execute will quickly undermine your goals. So keep it simple. If you aren't an expert at making something already, don't include it as a reward. Otherwise you'll be over budget and behind schedule. Remember, your ultimate goal is to inspire your community to support this project a little bit at a time. Having too many reward tiers or making things too complicated will repel people. Most backers want to support your project because they support *you* or the author on a deep, emotional level. If someone wants something unique or special, create a custom reward or make special arrangements for them. Offer custom work done by the author for the highest tiers, even custom illustrations or a dinner or private Q&A with them. But mostly you want to create work that you can replicate and mail out easily, like books!

When we run a Kickstarter project, it takes over our office. It's like an Amish barn raising in that people who work in other departments chime in with ideas of where to promote it to. You start with hitting up reliable friends and then your mailing list and social networks. From there, the creative sky is the limit. The clock is ticking! And the enthusiasm is infectious. Here's a preview of the feelings, best practices, and work involved:

1. Joy. Receiving a steady stream of "You have a new backer" alert emails feels good. The idea that friends and strangers around the world believe in you, want you to succeed, and want to be part of the thing you're doing is pure magic. If you've ever needed a boost of confidence, a well-tuned crowdfunding project will do the trick. Enjoy this part! Say "thank you" a lot. And if there's a chance to get to know your backers by involving them in the project or rewards, even better.

2. *Range of emotions.* The thing that surprised me most about Kickstarter is how dang emotional it is to run a campaign. The above-mentioned endorphin highs are high... and then there are the days, hours, minutes that go by when nobody is backing your project. Projects usually start and finish strong, but there's an infamous slump in the middle when they're neither new nor about to expire. The self-doubt that results can be demotivating, but it's important to leverage it into new ideas and energy or you're toast—destined to be counted among the 60% of projects that don't succeed. Shorter projects are often better because they help maintain a sense of urgency and eliminate the dreaded middle slump—Kickstarter recommends 30 days or less.

3. *Hustle.* Running a Kickstarter is a publicity, marketing, and sales job. Some supporters find you organically, but you're going to have to reach outside your comfort zone and think outside the box every day of your campaign to put it in front of new audiences. You'll get comfortable fast with promoting your work, posting often on social media, and specifically asking people for help. You'll get turned down, you'll get ignored, and you'll also make awesome connections and build lasting relationships. There's also the constant scheming to come up with new ideas, new updates, new audiences, and new ways to reach them. Allocate at least a few hours each day to work on the project. You might get lucky and win big, but it's more likely that your luck will result directly from lots of hard work.

4. *Be organized.* Running a Kickstarter—and then coming out the other end of it solvent, on time, and without tearing out all your hair—is a logistical art form. The sooner and more thoroughly you plan, and the more diligent you are about maintaining your detailed spreadsheets, the better off you'll be at all stages. Plan for cost overruns, fees, late deliveries from suppliers, shipping logistics, and—most terrifying of all—the runaway success.

The Ground Game

Remember, the goal of all publicity is to make all potentially interested people aware of your publishing. You want your audience to be so invested in it that they spread the word about it. Born of my teenage years in punk rock music, I always focused most on what kind of experience I would appreciate participating in. As a result, I put together author package tours where we did comedy, zine making workshops, and martial arts incorporated into reading, and film screenings. On one tour we taught the audience to sing sea shanties so they could understand a book about commercial fishing. We had the chef prepare food for the audience to demonstrate cookbooks. We hosted screen printing demonstrations for a graphic novel about the printing process, bike repair classes for a book on the subject, and just about anything that I could think of and convince the authors to get in a van together and hit the road to promote. And of course I'd be joining them to sell books.

The reason that I chose these methods and stuck with them is because they work. They may not be traditional, but the proof is always in the pudding. Similarly, sometimes being the only vendor selling books at a conference or event gives you a tremendous leg up. Last Word Press, which operated a bookstore on 4th street in downtown Olympia, WA, would set up a book table in Red Square on the Evergreen State College campus. While their downtown bookstore would sell $400 on an average day, one table on campus would bring in $1,500. A bookstore can feel like an obligation, like a time-consuming venture to browse that you can put off and get around to when it's convenient. Bringing the books to readers in their present environment creates an immediacy. It's evident that a table of books in the middle of a piece of grass isn't going to be there forever. Similarly, if you're selling books at a conference or an event, readers feel the pressure, knowing that they cannot simply return later in the week to check our your wares.

Catalogs

Think of your website, first and foremost, as your best catalog with some additional content. Invoke the *Whole Earth Catalog* of the 1970s or the Loompanics catalog of the 1980s. Be conscious of your landing page and how it reads to someone who is completely unfamiliar with you and your work.

No matter what anyone tells you, you should make a paper catalog. There's a reason that direct mail has never died or disappeared: it works. Anyone with an office receives roughly 45 catalogs from one office supply company per month. The profit on the sales that result from those mailed catalogs are the reason another one will show up in your mailbox tomorrow. You would probably just make two trade catalogs per year: Spring and Fall/Winter. Apparently "summer" doesn't exist in publishing and books published in June/July/August are technically "Spring." Include a full page for each new title that season as well as a page for each subject of thematic backlist.

Make sure that both your paper catalog and your website are more than just a catalog. Tell your story. After years of gradually shifting towards a glossy trade catalog we started to also produce what we called a "consumer catalog," that resembled the kind of posters and catalogs our staff received from record labels that we liked when we were teenagers. One side of the poster shows all of our book covers arranged by subject with the size of the cover relative to how well the book had sold to date, including the title, price, ISBN, and a few words of description for each. The other side features a full-color comic drawn by Peter Glanting that tells both our story and that of the publishing industry as portrayed by dinosaurs. These were tremendously successful. We had dropped our print run of trade catalogs from 60,000 in 2007 to 2,500 in 2014. There was less and less interest in them and fewer copies were being distributed. Immediately after printing the consumer catalogs, the cause of our declining catalog distribution problem was apparent. We gave away the first 10,000 consumer catalogs in two months, couldn't keep up with the interest, and had given out 50,000 in the first year. That success let us know that we were back on the right track and the next year I collaborated with Trista Vercher to create a board game about personal growth where the players go on a book tour and learn about themselves. For this year, we are planning a new comic about the development of our value system.

Now that we are approaching 500 titles in print, we also make brochures breaking out a specific list like books that are of interest to record stores, comic stores, grocery stores, or bicycle shops. Our biggest growth in the past year is witchcraft stores, so we created a new campaign for them as well. And because we send out at least 25 packages to customers per day, we include any surplus brochures in there and produce postcards for new standout titles to promote through the mail as well.

Reviews

Reviews, once vital for a successful book launch, are a changing landscape. There are many more books competing for limited review space in fewer and fewer publications that are seeing fewer people reading those reviews. Still, reviewers put your books in front of people's eyeballs and into their consciousness, and the cost of printing and mailing a book or an advanced reader copy (ARC) is very cheap compared to many other kinds of publicity. Reviews are often an easy path towards the three-point saturation strategy of having your books seen at an event, in a magazine, and in a store by the same person.

There are effectively four kinds of reviewers:

- Trade reviewers: These are publications read by people who work in the book industry. Some trades include *Publisher's Weekly*, *Shelf Awareness*, *Kirkus Reviews*, *Rain Taxi*, *Library Journal*, *Foreword*, and *School Library Journal*. These publications alert key account buyers to the existence of your book and how it might fit into their part of the industry. Libraries especially are often required to reduce their liability by showing that they purchased a title because of an endorsement in one of these publications.

- General audience reviewers: The *New York Times, Time, Wall Street Journal,* or *Washington Post* are inundated with book submissions and represent the old guard of the gold standard of book publicity. They are read by the general, middle class, white public. Due to the volume of books being published today, these reviews do not have nearly the positive impact on book sales that they once did.

- Segmented reviewers: As much as they might learn something, not everyone reads *Ebony* or *Bust* or *New Noise* or *The Baffler*. Most national publications like these have a specialized audience and help you reach out to that segment of readers.

- Amateur reviewers: Many creative people build their brand by reviewing books on their personal blogs, YouTube, or on Amazon. Depending on your marketing and saturation strategy, this may be useful to you or not.

There are other ways to get coverage of your work that can be even more effective than reviews:

- Always write a post-it note telling a reviewer why your book interests their readers.

- Sometimes pitching profiles of the author or related subject matter is easier than a proper book review because there are many more parts of a publication where those articles can appear. An interview or article about the topic of their book with the author as an expert can be much easier for a reporter to find time for than a proper book review.

- Often even better, seek out media about the story of your press, its mission, and what makes it unique. This can be easier to pitch an article around than any one book and the results are often much more interesting to the reader.

While it's going to sound excessive, a good outreach goal is to try to submit to 300-500 reviewers per book. You won't land them all, but it's a good goal. Some reviewers won't see your book as relevant to their audience. Some will just be overwhelmed or too busy or uninterested. Sometimes your timing will be bad because they are committed to a theme issue or a current event in the news has usurped your moment in the sun.

Your best practice here is to invest in these writers by building strong, personal relations. This is not a one-sided affair. Begin by reading the publications that you want to be featured in and seeing how they approach coverage of books like yours. Maybe they prefer articles or interviews with authors or publishers over traditional reviews. Great! That's more ink for you. Understand the interests and tastes of each writer.

Presumably, since you're publishing in your field of interest, you are already familiar with some publications. So the next step is understanding how substantial the audience of each of these organs that feel so seemingly huge in your field actually are. How do you do this? You check how many followers they have on social media. You look at their engagement with their fans. Sometimes though, it's not always the size of the media outlet but rather how targeted it is. You wouldn't always want a publication targeting people who train psychologists to have millions of readers because there simply are not that many people in the field. It means that something is fishy. Often, you want a conference with hundreds of attendees over thousands to feature your author because they will have that much more meaningful contact and networking time to grow further publicity and marketing opportunities.

Once you have a good understanding for a publication and their interests, craft a pitch. You'll want a strong headline built from your five-second pitch that shows the editor or writer why your book connects with their readers. Make it clear and substantial. Journalists are inundated with pitches and emails so they tend to skim. As a result, make your press release very short and built up bullet points under your strong headline. You want to imply or state ways that the book has already been successful and has been accepted by others. Mention any awards or major sales or other publicity spots. Keep it simple. Tell them what they need to know and provide links to information and high resolution images of the book and the author. It's best not to include email attachments as it will clutter their inbox and annoy them. The best pitches tend to be two sentences with three bullets, if necessary, and one or two links so the reporter can investigate a bit more without having to respond to your email and ask for more information. I find it obnoxious when someone tells me what they want when it's rather obvious but reporters are often overworked and can benefit from a clear ask such as "I think this book would be great for a review in September."

The mother of all media for book coverage includes outlets like *Today, Good Morning America, The Daily Show, The View,* and *Weekend Edition* on National Public Radio. You may not land one of these programs, at least not right away, but you can likely land smaller variants of these programs like drive-time radio and local television or radio talk show spots.

Promoting Beyond Reviews

- A key reason for media and publicity is to mitigate returns by making your sales stick. Since book sales are returnable for up to a year and many distributors are lax and allow them for much longer, keeping the book in the media and talked about on social media is how you can drive your fans to stores.

- In some cases, the media spots can convince stores who have passed on the book in the first place to reconsider or to make a reorder.

- For most presses, the publisher's identity is irrelevant to the public, but you can effectively promote your company and its mission over any one title and subject and offer an easier handle for the reporter to find a news hook. I realized early on that getting publicity about Microcosm was the best way to promote the books because I could promote all of them at once. Figure out a consistent news hook that makes each book continuously topical every year as every relevant anniversary rolls around.

- We learned from the tech world that fans are particularly invested in a company whose narrative they are familiar with. Check out *How I Built This* podcast for unfamiliar stories of many familiar brands. Consider what's interesting or unique about your story. Consider what's interesting or unique about your press and its editorial focus.

- Is your author shy, uncooperative, or legitimately too busy to perform interviews to promote their book? That doesn't mean that you cannot leverage media. I once did a two-hour rush hour radio interview for all of Chicago's metro area about my relationship with the authors of *Dwelling Portably,* two offbeat individuals who live in rural Oregon on their income from mushroom foraging and who write a guide on how to recreate their lifestyle. Nine years later, I was asked to come back on the same station with Dawson Barrett, the author of *Teenage Rebels*, because the teenagers from the Parkland shooting were so heavily in the news. The host felt like it was relevant to include me to talk about my own teenage years and the press alongside the author.

Working with the Author

Many of our authors have no problem at all with promoting their work, and some have come to us with years of building up a successful body of work or a personal brand and are ready to grab a megaphone to tell the world about the book that they intend to write. Some write us every week asking what they can do to help their book succeed. Many others experience discomfort or even panic at the thought of standing up and talking to a room full of people about their book, using social media to broadcast sales pitches and positive reviews, or even telling friends and family that they wrote a book and that there's an opportunity to buy it.

Self-promotion anxiety is normal. That said, you and your author have gone through all this work to produce a book. The more comfortable you are with talking about it with friends and strangers alike, online or off, the more people who want or need to read it will be able to.

Here are some common concerns and what I've learned over the years, as a nervous author myself and working with many others, about how to tackle them:

Why do I have to tell people to buy my book?

- Explicitly telling people to buy your book is not in your best interest. Unless you've just delivered a speech to a full room who is clapping excitedly, you never want to say "buy my book." Instead, think about it this way: you just published a book about topics that you care deeply about. Other people who care deeply about the same things (or about you or your author) are going to be excited to find out about, buy, and read this book. Your promotional role is to find them and offer them the opportunity to do this as easily as possible.

- *Tip for authors:* Think about what makes this book exciting and interesting. Why did you write this book? When did the idea really come together? What have other people said that they like about the book? Write all of those things down and refer to them when you're trying to find something to say about the book other than "It exists! Buy it!"

What about people that don't want to read my book?

- We aren't concerned about them. You didn't create this book to please everyone in the entire world because no one would actually enjoy such a book. You published it for your readers. That's a very particular set of people and most of the job of promoting is finding them and talking to them (often about topics other than this book). Remember, you're part of a movement. Whatever this book is about—teaching in inner-city schools, making soap, cats, vegan cooking—it's now become a building block in that bigger movement, and you've become a leader of that piece of the movement (and maybe a much bigger piece than just the one covered by your book). So your job is less to find random people and tell them you have a book, and more to connect with your movement about your book and the ideas in and around it.

- *Tip for authors:* Starting a blog or forum where you write about many related topics (but keep a purchase link to your book in the sidebar) is one way to do this. Social media is another. For many authors it makes sense to bring readers into the conversation as much as possible. For others it works to share parts of their personal experience with the book. For yet others, the best strategy is to speak at conferences, write guest blog posts, and otherwise tap into existing platforms. Figure out what works best in your genre! Ask people who are already successful.

Won't people just discover and love my book because of its quality?

- If this were the case, all our jobs would be very different... as would the bestseller list. Hundreds of books are being published every hour, readers have more choices than they can even understand, and much as you have developed your book uniquely with its title, cover, marketing, and publicity plan, it is still necessary to go out there and tell the world why it's worth taking a look at.

- *Tip for authors:* Practice your five-second pitch. Find a friend, family member, or coworker who knows very little about your book and pitch to them. How do they respond? Adjust as necessary. Once you've mastered this, think about other things that people engaged by this will want to know. Prepare a 30-second speech with more details about the uniqueness of your book and, if relevant, how it fits into existing news stories and trends.

What if the critics don't like it?

- Yeah, reviews are scary. It's a mixed bag out there. Many famous and well-regarded authors have a policy of never reading reviews, and this is probably a good idea for your author, as this feedback can make them too emotionally reactive. The psychology of it is unfortunate—your ten good reviews might leave you cold, while the one lukewarm one could have you grinding your teeth for years. We keep track of reviews for all of our books so that we can tell the world about the good ones and issue corrections for the factually inaccurate ones. Reviews don't affect sales as much as everyone wants to believe (though bad reviews are better for sales than no reviews at all), so our advice is not to worry about them as much as possible. Easier said than done, we know!

- *Tip for authors:* When you're feeling down, Google authors that you think of as respectable and famous and read their terrible reviews. These moments are often revelatory.

What if I'm not really an expert or my book's not as good as we think it is? *(i.e. Imposter Syndrome)*

- A lot of people feel this way. Trust me, many accomplished people who seem utterly cool and collected on the outside are often a total mess internally when they're up on a stage, or doing an interview, or approached by a gregarious family friend at a party who wants to know all about their book. It takes courage for anyone to step up and promote their vision. You've already done a lot by writing a book about it—don't stop there!

- *Tips for authors:* Practice, practice, practice. It truly does get easier. It helps to have someone you can call on for supportive and encouraging words when you're experiencing self-doubt or stage fright. Also, figuring out exactly what you are promoting (It may help to think of it as not being *you* but rather your vision, your readers, and your movement) can help you take the stage as an expert in a way that feels supportive of your community of readers rather than uncomfortably self-aggrandizing.

Social Media

I gave a talk to Portland State University to about 50 students and prospective authors. When I told the story about how our bestselling author doesn't know how to use a computer and maintains no social media presence, I did not get the usual response of interest in her lifestyle. Instead, they were filled with hope at the idea that they would not need to cultivate tremendous social media fan bases as well as becoming the greatest writers that ever lived in order to get published. Social media doesn't sell books alone but it's part of a package for many authors that can create an effective marketing cocktail in addition to other efforts.

The best advice that I've ever received is *not* to sign up for and actively use every social media platform. Pick the ones that come naturally to you for daily, organic use without stress, panic, or anxiety. You want to incorporate social media about your books seamlessly without derailing the rest of your work or lifestyle. That said, if there's a social media where your audiences and fans are congregating already, it's worth your time and effort to understand it and make an appearance there every few days. On the other hand, if you're one of those people who loves exploring social media, then dive in head first. Otherwise, pick your battles wisely.

Consider who you're talking to

Your work is for people like you who presumably have similar interests and demographics. Where do they hang out? From there, branch out to other lateral communities that you can see an earnest interest in your work as well. When you are comfortable and confident talking about your work and topics that you care about, your communities will care and respond with enthusiasm.

Set your sights for where your readers already are

Where are your readers going to find out about and rabidly discuss your books? That's the place you need to be. To find out, choose one of your comps that came out in the last year or so and feverishly search every social media platform for the titles and authors.

Choose your social media platforms based on your readers rather than your subject matter. For instance, a vegan cookbook might well find its biggest audience on Pinterest where food photos reign supreme. But if their book's community is younger and hipper, use the newest social media that will be launched after this book is published. If you're trying to reach men, use Twitter or Tinder. One publicist posted her own novel to her personal Tinder profile and found that many men trying to impress her would purchase and read it.

The rule of thirds

According to Anna Bones, author of *The Culinary Cyclist*, when posting on social media in your professional capacity you want to follow these rough proportions:

1/3: Broadcasting: Promoting and linking to your own stuff.

1/3: Sharing: Posting links to other relevant news articles or ideas by other people, whether colleagues, fans, or experts that pertain to your subject matter or appeal to your audience.

1/3: Conversation: Engaging with your community about topics of mutual interest, including asking questions, or letting a bit more of your personal world come through.

Be image conscious

Include a link and an image with everything you post. Link to your website page for each book. Make it as easy as possible for fickle readers to order the book.

Even if a social media platform isn't entirely image-based, your posts will be seen by far more people if they center around an image or video with your commentary. Images can be literal, sarcastic, poetic, or ridiculous. We post photos of babies and cats on Facebook because it shows the results to the most viewers. Your photos don't have to be visual art—phone photos and screenshots are great.

Use videos

Aside from the rise of YouTube and Vimeo, digital video has emerged as a way to tell stories and get people excited about new things in a crowded media marketplace. Many authors are successful simply by talking about what they are passionate about, unscripted, into a web camera but I'd suggest to create a scripted and edited video that tells the story of your publishing in 60-90 seconds. You can take a look at four videos I made that people reference to me all the time at Microcosm.Pub/About.

Be prepared

Do you like social media a little too much? Don't want to spend your entire day clicking and scrolling? Just don't have time for this stuff? Once you've figured out where you want to be and have a basic understanding of how your chosen platforms work, then take a step back and do like the pros— make a schedule. For instance, maybe you've decided that three posts a day on Twitter at three different times is what's right for you. Draft out three ideas or topics per day for the next week. When you come across an article you want to share, see a review of your book go live, or finish a blog post, add it to your schedule instead of immediately logging in and getting caught in the vortex. Then at the appointed times, check your cheat sheet, log in and quickly post, respond to anyone who's engaging with you, and get out unscathed.

If you love planning ahead, then think about what you'll post leading up to your book publication date, your release party, or any relevant holidays.

Paying for social media advertising

In recent years Twitter, Instagram, and Facebook have all adjusted their metrics in such a way that virtually no promotional or commercial posts will be seen by even the majority of your followers unless you pay for them. Facebook is the best use of your money and you can focus intensively on any demographic from Danzig fans to people who play the clarinet to women over 80 in India. While you could write an entire book on the science of Facebook advertising, the cliff notes are that its a system that favors paid posts that are generating a lot of clicks and shows them "organically" (unpaid) to other users. For this reason, the cheapest way to advertise is to target the countries with the lowest cost per click. Once these users are seeing your post and clicking on it, it will be shown to the people who have elected to be in your network. Instagram uses a similar system but the users skew younger and have less disposable income which is why Facebook's audience is still king for advertisers.

Build it slow and steady

Be patient and consistent. Post every day. Try new things and keep doing them if they work. Engage with people as equals. Find people who do it really, really well and emulate them. Be yourself. Have fun.

Accept the limits

Social media is an odd beast. Even when you have thousands of interacting followers, it may not always translate to book sales. If they aren't buying, you need to engage those readers in additional ways, like placing coverage in magazines or blogs they read or stores they shop at. Perhaps you've not attracted followers that are interested in the right kinds of books or perhaps you've cultivated an environment that isn't about selling. So keep your subject matter and your books as your central focus. For this reason, it's important to reference your books and also request and accept feedback so that you can improve your approach.

Dealing with Negativity

During the course of promoting yourself, people are going to sometimes freely offer a knee jerk response that may be unflattering. Sometimes they are trying to help. Sometimes they are trying to hurt your feelings. It doesn't really make a difference either way, though it's probably a good idea to actively distance yourself from people that are actively trying to hurt you or who rub you the wrong way.

Sometimes though, negativity can be really helpful. It can help illuminate major deficits in your book cover or development. Once in the middle of a sales presentation that I was doing, a woman stood up and said "It's a terrible cover." As in those were the only words out of her mouth. I responded a bit defensively, trying to explain it to her as if that would help. She repeated herself. I merely said "thank you" and continued. Later, I internalized her feedback and thought about it. She was right. It wasn't the right cover for that book, and it wasn't visually gripping in thumbnail. It was high concept but a poor execution. I accepted it and made a note to update the cover when we reprinted. It helped our potential future sales as much as it hurt to hear it initially.

Reviews can be the same way. Sometimes a reviewer obviously hasn't read the book and written hurtful things because there's a certain jealousy or they are a frustrated creative person. In one case, we had a reviewer who relentlessly mantra'd "I could have written this book!" to no avail, because, well, he hadn't. But sometimes the reviewer's criticisms are spot on. One pointed out that one of our books lacked analysis in favor of exposition. I shook my fist at the page, then realized they were right and it was a poor choice. But truthfully, we hadn't thought about it at all. It was a strong lesson.

If you make a serious factual or attribution error this can be much more damaging than a poorly structured or executed book. *Fortunate Son: George W. Bush and the Making of an American President* alleged the story that G.W. Bush was arrested for cocaine possession in 1972, had a long history of bad decisions while drinking heavily, and had escaped consequences for his actions repeatedly throughout his life due to his family connections. Author J.H. Hatfield—whose previous books had been biographies of Patrick Stewart, Ewan McGregor, *Lost in Space,* and *The X-Files*—was hired to once again paste some standard news clippings together as a book but decided instead to take the jump from celebrity biographer to muckraking journalist. And he had promised big. But during the news cycle of the book's release, it came to light that Hatfield had been convicted for stealing money from his employer in 1992 and hiring an inept hitman to blow up his then-boss with a car bomb in 1988. Shortly before the book's release in 1999, its formerly independent publisher, St. Martin's Press, was sold to the Literary

Industrial Complex. St. Martin's immediately questioned Hatfield's credibility as a reporter and pulled publication to attempt to verify the book's many damning assertions. Hatfield claimed that three sources—including Karl Rove—had directed him to the cocaine story and a changed driver's license number as proof, asserting that GW's dad called in a favor to have a judge expunge the record for his son's arrest. Some news sources still claim that the cocaine bust is true, but it's very hard to prove. Hatfield pointed out St. Martin's public statements prior to the controversy that the book had been "carefully fact-checked and scrutinized by lawyers." For what it's worth, it seemed that Hatfield had turned over a new leaf, but St. Martin's got cold feet as the Bush machine brought a battery of lawyers to the fight.

The book was already on the *New York Times* bestseller list when St. Martin's decided to recall 70,000 books and leave 20,000 more in storage. Free from his contract, Hatfield was approached by fledgling publisher Sander Hicks of Soft Skull Press, who agreed to republish the book. Hatfield wrote a new introduction acknowledging his criminal past and PGW covered the cost of printing in anticipation of book sales. The book's future had seemingly been restored through the powers of independent publishing. And then the unthinkable happened again: Hatfield claimed that his boss' boss was actually the one who had requested that he hire the hitman to kill his boss and that he never intended for the bomb to succeed. Whether this is true or not, the attorney of his former boss' boss rightfully prosecuted Hatfield for libel since these were unproven, damaging claims about a living person. Another entire printing of the book had to be removed from circulation and destroyed. Within another year Hatfield was found dead in a hotel room from an apparent suicide. Publisher Sander Hicks took a leave of absence to mourn the death of his friend and the board of directors promptly pushed him out of the company he had founded. George W. Bush was somehow re-elected.

This is a story where everything that could go wrong, did. Granted, it was a difficult battle against a powerful foe. But many mistakes were also made. If you are ever in the position of publishing damning assertions about a powerful public figure, make sure they are reviewed by a lawyer. It might cost you an arm and a leg, but it will protect you from so much liability later. If you make a mistake, admit it, apologize, and move on. If you associate yourself with someone that you find is not the person that they presented themself as, it's better to sever those ties than to suffer the continued reputation of that relationship. These choices linger around you and the amalgamate aspects of the press will affect how people perceive it even in ways that don't feel fair to you.

I used to believe that all of our books were great and that everyone would realize that with time. But the truth is we have a logical growth and progression. We are gradually refining our skillsets, getting better and better at publishing. Part of that is realizing your mistakes in the past and learning from them, rather than insisting that everyone else is wrong.

Sometimes this information doesn't reveal itself to you immediately, and you need to seek it out to understand why a title isn't working. Sometimes asking your fans and the people that are most invested is the way to obtain this feedback and sometimes it's a matter of asking a professional or a reviewer or an editor. They probably all have strong opinions and when you ask explicitly, they will likely be happy to share. Own the parts that you feel are true and reject what you feel like is their own self expression and feelings. You'll be a better publisher for it.

Events

Every author with an ego dreams of doing a big release event in a bookstore. There are great reasons for this aside from the emotional and experiential ones. A successful reading event in a bookstore will create long-term loyalty between the store and the book and the store and the press. The store will make a substantial order, and publishers will often use the tactic of organizing numerous events at stores to show a large number of preorders for a new title. The store's staff will be familiar with the book and recommend it to customers. I have avoided this tactic myself as these sales are returnable, but there is wisdom to this method if you have an evergreen title that could benefit from bookstore-clerk familiarity. Larger indie bookstores are now charging "co-op fees" to cover their costs for event staffing and advertising fees. Honestly, there is no way that the math can work out favorably for a publisher paying co-op for an event. So you can approach this issue either as paying a healthy donation to your local bookstore for the good that they do in the world or by haggling with them about doing favors in other ways. To help explain this aspect of publishing, I've brought in book wizard and publisher Laura Stanfill to help explain the fine art of bookstore events to you:

Organizing a Bookstore Release Event

Independent bookstore events rally readers around a new title, boosting cash register sales and social media buzz while giving local newspapers a timely hook for coverage.

It's crucial to pitch events in places where you can earn a strong turnout. Bookstore staff will announce the event in newsletters and through store signage, but ultimately authors and publishers are expected to fill chairs.

Here are some tips about approaching your local indie for a reading:

Get to know your local booksellers. Stopping by with an event request works best if you are already known as a customer and as a supporter of other authors. Ask for staffers' names, and remember them or write them down, so you can greet them with a genuine hello next time. Note which booksellers are writing shelf talkers—the handwritten endorsements for books on bookstore shelves—for titles like yours, and then offer those staffers ARCs or galleys they might enjoy.

Be respectful. If you feel more comfortable with an in-person ask, stop by and ask if the events coordinator happens to be available; if not, ask where to address an email pitch. Remember, booksellers don't work for you. They aren't obligated to stock your book, take time away from other customers to listen to your pitch, or offer you a spot on the store calendar.

Be prepared to answer distribution questions. Is your book available for a standard discount? Can it be ordered through a distributor, print on demand, and/or wholesalers such as Ingram or Bookazine? Books need to be returnable; if the store brings in thirty copies of your title for an event, and three people show up, the staffers don't want to be stuck with the merchandise. If you get a distribution-related no, don't take it personally, and instead see if there's a way you can meet the store's preferred terms by taking the risk yourself.

Attend other publishers' events. What formats work well? How long do the authors read versus talking off-the-cuff, thanking people, and taking questions? Watch for signs of inattention in the audience, and try to diagnose why it occurs—and how you and your authors can avoid that kind of lag. Who gets good turnout? How does an author graciously handle a smaller-than-expected crowd? Communicate what you learn with your authors to prepare them to deliver a powerful presentation.

Avoid scheduling back-to-back events at your local bookstores. Portland, Oregon—my press's home base—has lots of indie bookstores, but a local author who speaks at three in a row will significantly damage the chance of a decent crowd. We tend to spread our readings out over the course of a few months, and usually pair an author with others for the later events. For visiting authors, we pick one bookstore to host and then tack on additional opportunities, perhaps a college visit, a library, a book club, or a radio interview. In some cities, and with authors with gigantic fan bases, closely-clustered events can build momentum. Knowing your community, your author's reach, and the book's audience will help you make the best decisions.

Out-of-town events can be tricky, because often the booksellers receiving your queries have no connection to your press or your author. Here are some thoughts on how to ask professionally:

Use a standard, business-related email address. Many bookstore event coordinators don't respond to queries they're not interested in. Writing from an email address that is clearly from a publisher (rather than random character strings or a Gmail address) helps avoid the hassle of wondering whether you've been rejected, forgotten, or filtered into a spam folder.

Only pitch bookstores in places where you have a strong potential audience, and articulate that information without exaggerating. If you or the author have a handful of friends in a certain city, that's not enough people to fill chairs. If those supporters are bringing their book clubs, inviting their students, or offering major community outreach to build buzz locally, then mention that. My author Ellen Urbani, author of *Landfall*, excelled at mobilizing former classmates, friends, sorority sisters, Peace Corps members, writers, and friends of friends to support her national book tour in 2015. Long before the tour began, Ellen detailed her potential audience in each place, and I used that information to successfully book her events in twenty cities, most of them at independent bookstores. Even better, the projected audiences actually showed up and bought copies of her debut novel.

Remember to include pertinent information in your query. Distribution, endorsements, an author bio that speaks to the person's knowledge of subject matter and/or public speaking ability can help your proposal stand out.

It's essential to follow up. Booksellers are busy; if you haven't received a response, reach out and nudge after a week or two, preferably with an exciting new piece of information about the book. I tend to pitch one store at a time, then follow up, then move on to the next if I still don't hear back, but that can take a while, so plan ahead. Four months is generally a good bet, but it's best to check with the store—or a publisher friend who has successfully held an event there.

Invite people personally—and with plenty of advance notice. Social media outreach can help spread the word about events, but reaching out directly to potential audience members can be even more effective, whether that's through email, a quick reminder phone call or text, or sending postcards in the mail. Labels or stickers can help customize one book postcard to promote multiple events. Postcards or bookmarks can be pinned on coffee shop bulletin boards or dropped off in small stacks at arts centers or libraries—by you, your author, or someone who lives in that city. If you have a newsletter, make sure you promote your events in a way that urges your core supporters to spread the word instead of just marking it on their own calendars.

As far as the events themselves, not all readings are created equal. Some authors are ebulliently articulate performers; others are shy, or even alarmed by the idea of using a microphone. Whatever the situation, build the event around the author's comfort level. A quiet author may prefer to appear in conversation with a more experienced one who can guide the conversation. Group readings and panels often draw a bigger audience; especially for out-of-town events, consider partnering with a local press to increase your reach.

Keep the reading short. Most bookstore events are an hour long, and the author should spend a good chunk of that time talking—whether to the audience, another author in conversation, or about the topic of the book or the details of its creation. Long, straight-up readings can exhaust people, and if the author mumbles, you can lose book sales instead of earning them. If your event ends at the 45-minute mark, with everyone feeling exhilarated and inspired, it's way better than running all the way to the end of the hour with fidgeting, uncomfortable guests trying to hide their yawns.

Add a dash of magic. This is the author's time to shine. If you make a habit of encouraging your authors to do something unexpected or special, word will get around that you create can't-miss events. Serving outside food and drinks can be an issue; many bookstores have strict rules, so be sure to ask if you hope to serve food. My authors and I have offered trivia questions with prizes, ticketed raffles, themed cupcakes, small giveaways on every seat (such as origami cranes or octopus tentacles), book cover posters, and pre-packaged baked goods. Author Stevan Allred hired a silver-painted street performer—who inspired one of the characters in his debut short story collection, *A Simplified Map of the Real World*—to entertain the crowds before his launch at Powell's Books.

Have someone take photos and/or video clips. Getting quality images of an event can maximize its range and impact. People who missed it will enjoy seeing the photos, and those who weren't initially interested may attend the next event or buy the book. If you don't have a decent camera or smartphone, ask around, and see if a friend will volunteer.

Sometimes things go wrong. We can't control all the logistics. The sound system might get wiggy. Unexpected construction could make the venue much less accessible than usual. Sometimes you'll be hit with extreme weather conditions. Bookstores estimate event orders, and sometimes end up with too many copies—or too few. Whatever the issue, congratulate yourself for creating an experience for your readers and try to stay present in the moment. At an indie bookstore event, you can see the relationship between author and reader develop, right there in front of your eyes, and it can be absolutely electric.

Laura Stanfill is the publisher of Forest Avenue Press, and the founder of the Main Street Writers Movement.

Organizing a Book Tour

Many authors get stars in their eyes at the thought of a book tour and have a very hard time understanding the scale of such an undertaking. They expect that a book tour will sell thousands of copies and that audiences are just starved for entertainment and content but the opposite is true. Audiences are overwhelmed with content and entertainment options. You must create that immediacy and desire to become a part of your movement.

Since Microcosm began as a record label, it came naturally to me from the beginning to run our book tours more like music tours. At first we asked for a suggested donation of $3-5 from each person who attended the event. Later we started charging outright at the door, sometimes on a sliding scale in the $5-12 dollar range. Yet later, we asked our cookbook author and traveling vegan chef Joshua

Ploeg to join our touring team. Including a seven-course meal from Joshua in the price of admission not only kept the audience happy and focused at the event, it made it reasonable to charge as much as $25 for tickets—and that's not including the books, t-shirts, stickers, and DVDs people often chose to purchase during or after the events.

Katey Schultz wrote about her book tour on the money blog, *The Billfold*[10] outlining her costs and rewards. Reading the article I paused and then was alarmed. Schultz's book of short stories *Flashes of War* was published by a small university press. Schultz's basic costs were:

+ $5,000 on a publicist
+ $2,000 on a tour manager
+ $5,000 for airfare, luggage fees, cab fare, meals, gifts for hosts, gas, car rentals, entry fees, shipping fees, etc.
=========
$12,000

Schultz doesn't seem particularly disappointed with the costs or the results of the tour but it is clear that her resulting book sales have failed to meet expectations. Let's compare Katey's tour with the Dinner & Bikes tour where Microcosm authors traveled with a chef who cooked dinner, charged admission for events, and sold books from our entire catalog. Here's a look at our tour expenses for a month on the road:

$2,340.38	Rental Car
$1,656.85	Groceries
$100.00	Posters
$661.15	Gas

10 https://www.thebillfold.com/2014/06/what-it-costs-to-diy-a-first-book-tour/

$57.11	Hotel
$11.58	Cable Adapters
$12.00	Parking
$87.12	Speakers

For a total of $4,926.19.

So, just like Katey Schultz, we spent $5,000 on incidentals (though we each paid for our own non-event meals out of pocket). We've been more frugal in the past and toured with four people in a subcompact car for around $700 but we've found that a minivan is more suited for the amount of merchandise that we sell on one tour and gives us a little more room to breathe.

One of us does the booking for the tour, in exchange for a 10% cut of revenues. We write a standard press release and provide promotional language and high-resolution photos, and then either we or our promoters can customize this for local media in every stop on the tour. We generally ask the promoter to find us a place to stay, normally in someone's house, as part of putting on the event. We've almost never had a problem with this, and it allows us to focus on the other point of a book tour: meeting incredible people doing neat things in faraway places that inspire us at home.

On this particular tour, we sold $6,661 worth of books and were paid $11,655 from ticket sales. We conducted a raffle each night where we sold tickets for $2 and raffled off books from every authors on the tour and overstock titles. About half of the money from book sales goes to paying for printing, author royalties, staff time, shipping everything to the tour, and the various reprints that are necessary afterwards. We split a 25% sales commission for doing the work of selling, and the remaining $1,555 is kept by Microcosm to make more new books. We deduct the tour costs from the ticket sales and then divide what's left evenly between the four people on the tour, including our roadie who does the loading, driving, and selling of raffle tickets. The raffle ticket money is divided between the books we are raffling so the result is similar to selling them.

In the end, we are each paid for a month of work just like any other month. For most of us, it's higher than what we earn in a month at home, but it's also quite a bit more work. With this model, we now find that the audiences get a little bigger and we sell more books each year. And the best part of all is that, with a credit card and some free time, our touring style is exportable to other authors doing book tours!

It's brave of Katey Schultz to tell the story of her own tour and how it paled in comparison with her expectations. She reveals that in her first year, her book sales hovered around 1,500 copies. Her investment of $12,000, which was only one small part of her marketing plan, helped to sell only 1,500 copies during that entire year, probably profiting her under $3,000 in hard cover royalties...or losing over $9,000. Worse, I suspect that Schultz's math is probably par for the course. Our industry could use a lot more frank talk about finances, as most authors and many publishers find the business side of things to be completely incomprehensible and often are left to make decisions based on guesswork. Our method of touring absolutely isn't for everyone (and we often find it exhausting, ourselves), but we do want authors to know that they have many options for successfully promoting their work and themselves without going into debt.

The book tour as envisioned by the book industry is based on an outdated model. The idea is that the author works for free, someone pays to fly them all over to events with unpredictable attendance, and the publisher hopes that the tour publicity makes enough of a splash to justify the whole matter.

This seems to be based on an implicit class-based romanticization of the Literary Industrial Complex. An author writes a literary work in a certain nostalgic style that is approved by certain establishments. Then they make the rounds signing said piece of literature in book stores for adoring fans. It's an attractive fantasy, but these days it's fiscally out of reach for all but the most mainstream of authors.

We've likely all heard of or attended book tour events where the author shows up, chairs are arranged, and they wait out the evening while no one shows up to hear them, or worse yet, only family and friends do. They are patted on the back, told that this is all part of climbing the ladder and cutting their teeth, and the whole thing is somehow talked about as if it's not a waste of time and money.

The positive aspect of this kind of book tour is, as I mentioned earlier, the fact that book stores tend to order 25+ copies per event. This can create the impression of a very successful month for the book. Unfortunately, the way the industry works is that bookstores are encouraged to order more copies than they can sell, and then allowed to return the unsold books, resulting in return processing fees from the distributor—so the illusion of an event's success is often fleeting. Signed copies of a book can be returned but "personalized" copies are not supposed to be. Meaning that if you write a message longer than just your name in each book, the store will display the books prominently instead of shipping back the overstock.

Simply to break even on the expenses of a traditional book tour, based on the average author's royalty of around $1/book, the tour would actually need to sell over 12,000 books, or around an average of 400 per event. That is also still assuming that the author is working for free.

Rather than continuing to try to work within this model, clearly authors and publishers need to build viable alternatives. In the original author tours that Microcosm organized, we sold our own titles and also diversified the zines and books that we had for sale at our events. This did take attention away from the title(s) featured on the tour, but it also meant that we maximized sales in others ways, which is more important to us.

We did some events at bookstores, but this proved difficult as traditional book tours are also unsustainable for bookstores, whose only way to pay for staff time, rent, and inventory is to sell books. Given that hoped-for sales at an indie book event hover around ten books, bookstores are also left in the lurch too. The stores needed to take 40% of our merch sales to make it maybe work out for them— and then it didn't work for us. Similarly, for a musician or label touring with a new album, this arrangement with retailers would not be acceptable. But that's partially because even musicians have better pay scales than authors, and music venues earn money from alcohol sales and by charging admission. But it is assumed that most author events are free to attend and that if an audience member has an enjoyable time, they can purchase a copy of the book. For more established authors, the bookstore will simply roll the cost of the book into the ticket admission cost. If the book is $27.95 the ticket will be $25 and includes a copy of the book, the author's speaking and reading performance, and a chance to meet them and get the book signed.

Over the years, we did events in rad DIY venues, historic punk clubs, people's houses, and infoshops. We quickly gave up on doing straight-up readings and signings—we found those undynamic, and it turns out that our audiences were also more excited about multimedia presentations on topics that related to our books. But it felt like a looping vacuum. We were reaching the same people in the same city each time we visited and while the quality of our performance and books improved every year, it couldn't grow our audiences in venues like these. So my business partner Elly Blue pioneered a new innovation for our tour in 2010: we could work with nonprofits and advocacy organizations, however small, to bring our tour to their cities. The organizations benefit by demonstrating their message and mission to their members and residents. Often, the organization can also use the event as a benefit for themselves once our fees are covered. And unlike booking at colleges, the people who attend are intimately engaged in the subject matter and buying the books as a result.

We benefit because they have a mailing list to promote the event to and working with them adds legitimacy to our tour even if someone hasn't heard of us, Microcosm, or our tour. It's truly a win-win-win for us, the organization, and the audience.

Another difference—the traditional author tour involves flying between a few major cities. While we occasionally do a big city event, we've found that piling into a van and driving between small towns and cities, avoiding the well-worn paths and the busy, hectic schedules of urbanites, yields better events, more excited audience members, better attendance and book sales, and lasting friendships with people whom we meet along the way.

Other Events

Often new publishers feel like they will make major headway by spending thousands of dollars on a booth at the American Library Association conference or BookExpo America. Success at these events is built on repetition and relationships. If you're attending for the first time, you may end up with some positive outcome, but it likely won't offset the cost of participating. There are regional trade show events as well for announcing new titles, having meetings, and writing orders. These events work similarly but the stakes are much lower. Still, the book trade is a crowded market and fiercely competitive against the Literary Industrial Complex who is much better funded than you are. For that reason, it's often better to set your sights elsewhere.

This past year we sold books at RollerCon in Las Vegas, the Oregon Law and Mental Health Conference, the National Bicycle Summit, Denver Independent Comics and Art Expo, Pride festivals, VegFest, BikeCraft, tech conferences, Deluxe Winter Market in Oklahoma City, the Bay Area Book Festival, our local neighborhood street festivals, Crafty Wonderland, the Why Not? Minot punk music festival, and many more. In most cases, we are the only vendor at the event selling books. And sales are good. We only do an event again if we earned at least $600 from the previous one and we can gross $4,000 in a weekend. When you are starting out, you may want to choose a lower metric. There are years where we've done over 100 events. There are also years where we've tried a lot of new events and many of them have not penciled out. Sometimes you'll lose money on an event but feel like you have strategically promoted yourself by passing out catalogs and collecting members for your email list. That may be true, but ultimately you shouldn't plan to do this. You can strategically promote your press while putting money in the bank. Losing money on conventions and having a stressful, slow weekend more than a few times will burn you out fast. So talk to other people that you trust about events you are considering before getting in the van.

Homework:

- Will you adapt a controversial media strategy or a friendly one? How will you cultivate it?

- What unique publicity ideas will you use to launch your book?

- Where do your readers socialize?

- What social media should you be using?

- What key terms and phrases belong front and center on your website?

- What is your launch plan?

- Who are our various audience segments?

- What is the ideal sequence of publicity coverage for your book?

- Which of your books strengthen each other's publicity by being published during the same season?

- Would crowdfunding make sense for your book?

- What are some likely publications or blogs to review your book?

- What unique ideas do you have for your catalogs?

- How will you work with your author to organize interviews and coverage?

- What are some great event ideas for your launch?

- Does an author tour make sense for your book? Who could you partner with?

- Where will you launch your Ground Game from?

- What non-trade events would love your books?

11

MONEY

Understanding & Planning Your Press' Future

P er Henningsgaard of Ooligan Press explained it best, "Publishers think of themselves as words people, not numbers people." Money is terrifying for many publishers, but you need to get comfortable with the numbers if you're going to succeed.

The hardest lesson to learn in publishing is that you can almost always do more with less money. Adam Gamble of Good Night Books wistfully appreciates this struggle: "Not having capital was a great gift in retrospect." Similarly, I financed Microcosm's launch by tucking away $100 from each paycheck at my restaurant job. Believe it or not, this was more than sufficient to fund a gradual launch of everything we needed to get going. Today, most of my deep work is digging into our inventory numbers, sales figures, returns, revenues, and historical monthly incomes to find patterns, changes, and emergent trends. My staff jokes that I have plans A-Z ready to implement in every scenario as the previous ideas prove untenable. I believe this is my primary job skill: to think through possible outcomes, hedge my bets, and plan for the best and worst case scenarios.

First, you need a clear plan for how to efficiently achieve your goals. Building your press from nothing forces you to get your house in order before injecting it with finance. Publishers constantly complain about needing more money and being under-financialized, but almost always the biggest problem is that they aren't properly spending and budgeting the money that they do have. If they had more money, they would expend it in the same manner. Having too much money causes you to spend too much, which causes more failure, which distracts from the priorities of publishing.

Even if you don't understand the intricacies of your daily finances, a publisher needs to understand what they are doing that is working and why, so that it can be endlessly replicated. Eventually you'll want a good accountant to do your taxes and maybe even an accountant to handle your bills, payroll, loans, and cash flow, and keep everything up to date. But especially when you're outsourcing this stuff, it's even more important to understand your bottom line and why it's working for you or not. Often the results are surprising and it's a collection of small titles that quietly and consistently turn over a little more every month.

Structuring Your Finances, Finding Income Streams

Haymarket Books has been a 501(c)3 nonprofit since day one in 2001. Co-founder Julie Fain explains, "We always knew we wanted to accept individual donations and foundation grants, we had a clear mission of social justice publishing, and we were willing to accept the tradeoffs in limiting the political work we could do in terms of supporting legislation and candidates. So it made a ton of sense to us. It's meant that we can sometimes acquire a book for political or mission-driven reasons, even if we know we'll subsidize its publication. It also means there are discounts on stuff we use, like our email service or event ticketing. There are reporting requirements that can be a pain, and we have to have an annual audit. And our finances are public information. It's not for everyone, for sure, as it can be expensive to apply and many people don't pay a ton in taxes anyway."

Haymarket employs a financial and publishing strategy unlike any other small independent publisher that I've interviewed or examined. They publish about 50 titles per year, with most selling between 2,000 and 5,000 copies. They sold over 240,000 books in 2016, with roughly 48% of those being titles from the current season, and have only a single title that has sold over 100,000 copies in its lifetime. So while each book earns a very small profit, they have built a backlist of 318 trade titles and 211 academic titles relatively quickly. Producing and distributing this kind of volume relies upon having a competent and sizeable staff and a good partner distributor to handle the sales, warehousing, and fulfillment of the books. In many ways, it would be much more difficult for them to handle this on their own, as they would need an astronomically large and efficient warehouse. They are doing a great job of implementing the variable cost benefits of being distributed by Consortium.

C. Spike Trotman, publisher of Iron Circus Comics has a diametrically different financial strategy that might feel closer to reach. She believes in the "1,000 fans theory." She told *Black Girl Nerds*, "all you need to take care of yourself as an artist is to have

1,000 fans willing to spend $100 on you a year to live comfortably. I have friends who get to do what they love, and they have 10,000 followers on Twitter, and that's all they need." Iron Circus is now distributed by Consortium as well but Trotman employs this strategy very differently than Haymarket, with distribution as the icing on the cake rather than the primary sales channel. She presells most of her new work on Kickstarter and is very popular at comics conventions and tech conferences.

Even closer within reach than establishing 1,000 fans or 10,000 Twitter followers, Kickstarter lets you test interest in a new title, especially if that title is outside of your reputation, audience, and comfort zone. You can show a potential new title to your fans and appropriate parts of the general public and see if it's something that they will buy or are responsive to. The profit margins are so small in publishing and investments are so large that market testing is vital. Microcosm does this by publishing a low-stakes version of a title, typically a zine, where we invest about $100 and see what the reaction is like. Sales are not always great, but that isn't the point. We are testing because we don't know and cannot afford to risk the $10,000-20,000 cost of publishing a paperback or hardcover edition. And often, if we have a huge zine breakout hit we receive vital feedback on how to develop the paperback!

Financially Microcosm is organized similarly to Haymarket, without being a legal 501(c)3. Becoming a 501(c)3 seemed to be costly without offering tangible benefits that we need and requires outside management who are not employees. In the vast majority of cases that I've seen, outside management eventually results in a board that is not intimately familiar with what the organization fundamentally does, resulting in confused management and internal conflict. So we picked a halfway point. We are managed by staff and just like a nonprofit, we publish our finances publicly each year on our blog and adhere to a mission statement. The transparency is appreciated by fans and onlookers and we have nothing to hide. Maximum transparency and public scrutiny may not be right for your press. You may have personal assets or financial partners that you may need to protect by incorporating your business. This subject is too complicated to fully unpack here. If you have reasons to be seriously concerned about this, hire a lawyer to set up your corporate structure. If you intend to remain a small hobby press and have no assets to protect from legal or financial liability, you can simply file a few documents with your local municipality or do nothing at all.

Know Your Numbers

There are many mathematical formulas that the pros use to make sure that their numbers are moving in the right direction. And now that you're fast-becoming a pro, you'd better get used to making sure your foundation is secure.

First, calculate your **bottom line**. This is what you'd be responsible to pay if you published nothing next month. It includes things like your office rent, phone lines, storage/warehouse space, employee salaries, and anything you pay for monthly whether you use it or not, like software subscriptions, equipment losing value, or licenses. You would not include contractors that aren't on retainer. This figure is calculated as a percentage of your average month's sales. So add up all of these monthly expenses. Then add up your annual sales and divide by twelve. Then divide the first number by the second number to find your bottom line. So, for example, let's say that your press earned $100,000 in income last year, you paid yourself a $40,000 salary, paid $1,000 for Internet and phone service, $5,000 for office and storage rent, and $600 for your Adobe Suite. Your total expenses would be $46,600. Monthly average income would be $8,333.33 and your average monthly expenses would be $3,833.33 so 46.6% would be your bottom line (3,833.33/8333.33 = .466). At Microcosm this number is 51.89%.

Your bottom line is important because your minimum gross profit on every book needs to be more than that or it doesn't make sense to publish the title. Remember your P&L? (see page 244) A fundamental part of publishing is that since the profit margin is so small, you have to make sure that you are actually making more money after income, bottom line, returns, and expense from each title.

This is why your gross profit on each book should be 50-65%, or at least greater than your bottom line. Gross profit is calculated as sales minus returns, printing, royalty payments, and development expenses for that title like design, editorial, research, etc. You can find the calculated number in cell G20 on the sample P&L. If you add up all of your printing costs, royalties, and development expenses for a successful title and divide by your sales revenue, you should come close to 58%. If you can produce these numbers consistently,

Balance Sheet	Value 2016	Adj Value	Value 2017	Adj Value	Value 2018	Adj Value
Current Inventory	$274,112.50	$274,112.50	$349,379.66	$75,267.16	$529,379.66	$180,000.00
Assets	$12,500.00	$12,500.00	$39,919.67	$27,419.67	$48,184.27	$8,264.60
Accounts Rec'able	$438,670.02	$438,670.02	$486,214.02	$47,544.00	$606,214.02	$120,000.00
Accounts Payable	-$420,963.93	-$420,963.93	-$416,596.97	$4,366.96	-$212,242.27	$204,354.70
Total Value	$304,318.59		$458,916.38		$971,535.68	

your titles are earning revenue for you and you'll simply need enough of them to be financially successful.

You'll also want to create a **balance sheet**. It might take a while to gather and count up all of your numbers but understanding a balance sheet is easy. There are essentially four parts: your **inventory** (the replacement value of your books), your **assets** (computers, equipment, real estate, etc), **accounts receivable** (money owed to the press), and **accounts payable** (money that you owe to others). These values are added up to demonstrate how stable the company is.

Plan to Grow Your Back Catalog

New publishers misunderstand the slow staccato rhythm of how money moves in publishing, so they spend relatively freely in their first year, trying to see what works. According to Joe Matthews of Independent Publishers Group, publishers really need a five-year business plan with adequate funding so that they can ensure that the economics will pencil out, and they won't run out of money prematurely. While it's tempting, don't publish more books until you've hit every audience and channel for what you have in print. This assures that you're being thorough and not getting in over your head too fast, publishing for the sake of publishing. Joe Matthews suggests, "Run the numbers, get an accounting system."

Most publishers finance new title development from their backlist: sustained sales from books published prior to the current season. While publishers like Triumph can exist on 90% frontlist sales, this is only because they are being financed by IPG instead of by their backlist catalog. This means that Triumph books do not continue to sell after the season they are released. For a small press, attempting to do this would be a dicey and unsustainable proposition because your first major mistake would bankrupt you. Instead, you want to create a steady cushion of bestselling backlist to pay for your fixed monthly expenses and the costs of reprints and new publishing. Matthews suggests that 65% of a publisher's revenue should be from backlist. This is an excellent goal.

Understanding what makes a good backlist title is vital. *Eight Steps to a Pain-Free Back* is a great example of a very strong backlist title. It's an evergreen title that will never lose relevance or go out of date, as long as people have bodies. Adam Gamble of Good Night Books points out that developing a solid backlist title is not solely a product of logic and mathematics. "The buck ultimately stops with my gut, and that of our publisher. If it wasn't that way, then CPAs would all be successful book publishers." After a year, you need to shift from following your gut to letting the data evaluate your gut health. And then use the data to deliver future decisions in addition to your tastes. Per Henningsgaard explains, "you need to be able to understand what it is about each book that appeals to readers and not in a patronizing way."

Julie Fain believes the secret sauce to making backlist stick is that "our books have ideas that may be timely, but also stand the test of time." Other publishers side more with Gamble's view. Adam Parfrey, late publisher of Feral House explained to me that he solely followed his gut and did "no market research at all," as long as he remains "personally interested in every book and its subject matter." Naturally, Feral House publishes books that no other publisher would consider which makes market research less necessary. Similarly, Ian Christe, publisher of Bazillion Points, believes: "Emotional distance is way overrated! Such a large part of the reward for writing books is glory, it's good to be emotionally invested."

Still, the changing nature of the industry leaves many gambles to have really unknown consequences so test the waters and tread carefully. Fain of Haymarket explains, "We still struggle with knowing in advance which of our books will break out, and we have found ourselves sometimes going back for second printings immediately after launch—up to three or four times in the first year. We also have books that have only ever sold 500 copies. Determining a book's print run is an elusive mix of art and science, but it's a process that indie publishers have an edge in. We're a lot closer to our audience because we get to know them in various ways—we meet them in person at events, we follow them on social media, we see their reviews on Goodreads, we know when they assign one of our books in their classes, we see what they buy in our online store, and so on." Longtime distribution president Mark Suchomel joked in our 2018 interview that so much of a publisher's money is tied up in inventory that you should determine a book's print run by asking the author what it should be and then cutting that figure by 2/3. Jokes aside, it's best to be conservative. Mark Suchomel explains "The biggest mistake that I see publishers make, over and over, is printing *way too many*. Be very cautious. Let the market tell you what you need to know instead of making assumptions. Judge the saleability of a new book by listening to the sales reps, the buyers, or the consumers. Price it to the market, not to the package. Build a book for the consumer, not for the author, the account, or for your ego. Successful titles are put in cautiously and built up from there."

Microcosm recently shifted gears around this issue. We used to optimistically print a three-year supply of each new title, since all of our books are designed not to be time-sensitive, but evergreens. But sometimes even a "sure" book would not land correctly and we'd end up giving away thousands of overprinted copies to our fans. So we now print 3,000 of almost every new title unless we are seeing very generous interest and advance ordering. Sometimes this means that after all costs we know that we will lose money on the first printing. But even in these cases, it's better to make this decision consciously, knowing that if the book sells, we can recover the costs on subsequent printings. And if it doesn't sell through, we've

Sample Frontlist vs. Backlist Sales Projections

	Sales Type	JAN	FEB	MAR	APR	MAY	JUN	JUL	AUG	SEPT	OCT	NOV	DEC	TOTAL
1						Key	Spring	Fall	Winter	Analysis				
2	Frontlist Sales minus Returns/Units	466	292	308	362	1141	840	411	462	308	471	816	216	6093
3	Percentage	42.60%	51.14%	31.62%	33.49%	64.03%	46.26%	33.63%	33.45%	23.57%	34.58%	32.71%	18.20%	37.11%
4	Frontlist Sales minus Returns/Dollars	$3,500	$2,700	$3,000	$3,500	$10,000	$8,000	$4,000	$3,500	$3,000	$4,500	$8,000	$2,500	$56,200
5	Percentage	46.67%	51.92%	33.33%	33.33%	62.50%	47.06%	33.33%	28.00%	25.00%	31.03%	34.78%	21.74%	37.39%
6	Backlist Sales minus Returns/Units	628	279	666	719	641	976	811	919	999	891	1679	971	10179
7	Percentage	57.40%	48.86%	68.38%	66.51%	35.97%	53.74%	66.37%	66.55%	76.43%	65.42%	67.29%	81.80%	62.89%
8	Backlist Sales minus Returns/Dollars	$4,000	$2,500	$6,000	$7,000	$6,000	$9,000	$8,000	$9,000	$9,000	$10,000	$15,000	$9,000	$94,500.00
9	Percentage	53.33%	48.08%	66.67%	66.67%	37.50%	52.94%	66.67%	72.00%	75.00%	68.97%	65.22%	78.26%	62.61%
10	Total Units	1094	571	974	1081	1782	1816	1222	1381	1307	1362	2495	1187	16272
11	Total Dollars	$7,500	$5,200	$9,000	$10,500	$16,000	$17,000	$12,000	$12,500	$12,000	$14,500	$23,000	$11,500	$150,700
12														

reduced our losses by thousands of dollars. It allows us to make changes between printings, correct errors, and add new review blurbs. Presently we have a book that we've been reprinting 10,000 of each month.

No matter the method or madness that is right for you, let's take a look at your data. At your current rate of sale, how long will it take to build up your publishing program where 65% of your income comes from backlist? I made you a spreadsheet to calculate this.[11] Input sales minus returns from the current season as frontlist and sales minus returns for all other titles under backlist. The sheet will add up the totals. I've color coded months by season and so when the color shifts, those titles are now backlist.

Now make a similar chart with all of your titles listed individually on it. How many copies of each title do you reliably sell year over year? What factors can you point to that make a book stick for you as backlist? Are you increasing backlist sales with time or are newer titles not sticking? If your new titles aren't sticking like your old titles did, Joe Matthews believes he might know why. "Good books stick as backlist. Typically, underperforming publishers aren't creating frontlist that is as good as their backlist. The publisher may have lost the passion. Budgets have likely been reduced. Good books matter. Jaded publishers don't make good books. When less money is invested in book development and marketing, books don't sell as well."

---

11 http://microcosm.pub/backlistsales

Build for Long Term Financial Health

The fear of creating and sticking to a budget has been the death of more great publishers than I can count. The behavior of avoiding information in a manner that is actively harmful to you is so common that psychology has a term for it: **Active Information Avoidance**. Just like running out of gas only because you didn't bother to check the fuel, ignorance does not change your reality or shield you from its consequences. For this reason, I've created a budget spreadsheet[12] that you can download, make a copy of, and populate with your own estimated numbers. This will help you to understand the impacts of your publishing and spending decisions.

The figures on the sample budget represent a healthy company about five years in business that publishes about fifteen titles per year with three employees. Your mileage may vary. Ideally, your direct sales would outpace your distributor's, but that strategy is up to what works best for you. Depending on your list, your actual development or printing costs may be much higher. Perhaps you sell subrights or film rights monthly and that comprises the bulk of your income. Whether your numbers are much bigger or much smaller, this is a starting place to begin to understand these numbers.

While I'm going to let most of these terms be self-defining, you may need to hire a tax accountant or a lawyer to review your general contracts rather than a specific book. I called those "professional services." When you pay a percentage to a sales person for soliciting and closing a sale, those are "commissions." When you purchase a booth at BookExpo or the mental health conference or the local

---

12 http://microcosm.pub/budget

Sample Monthly Budget Projection

	Projected Monthly Total	Actual Monthly Total	Projected $ vs. Actual $	December	November	October	September	August	July	June	May	April	March	Feb	Jan
INCOME															
Frontlist Direct / Dollars Sold	$3,500.00	$3,958.33	-$458.33	$3,500.00	$10,000.00	$8,000.00	$4,000.00	$3,500.00	$3,000.00	$2,500.00	$2,000.00	$4,000.00	$3,500.00	$1,500.00	$7,000.00
Backlist Direct / Dollars Sold	$9,000.00	$10,000.00	$8.33	$7,000.00	$21,000.00	$15,000.00	$15,000.00	$9,000.00	$9,000.00	$8,000.00	$7,000.00	$12,000.00	$10,000.00	$8,000.00	$7,000.00
Subrights Sales	$2,000.00	$2,041.67	-$41.67	$2,000.00	$3,000.00		$1,500.00	$1,500.00					$300.00		
Distributor Direct / Dollars	$15,000.00	$13,166.67	$1,833.33	$12,000.00	$11,000.00	$10,000.00	$13,000.00	$12,000.00	$10,000.00	$10,000.00	$15,000.00	$21,000.00	$18,000.00	$15,000.00	$15,000.00
Distributor Payment/Dollars (Distributor Pay Schedule~120 day delay)				Avg Sales	July Sales	June Sales	May Sales	Apr Sales	March Sales	Feb Sales	Jan Sales	Dec Sales	Nov Sales	Oct Sales	Sep Sales
Total Income	$29,500.00	$29,166.67	$350,000.00	$24,500.00	$45,000.00	$33,000.00	$27,000.00	$26,000.00	$23,000.00	$20,500.00	$26,500.00	$47,000.00	$29,000.00	$23,500.00	$23,500.00
EXPENSES															
Book Printing	$9,000.00	$9,083.33	-$83.33	$7,500.00	$17,000.00	$14,000.00	$13,000.00	$7,500.00	$9,000.00	$8,000.00	$6,500.00	$8,500.00	$7,000.00	$6,000.00	$5,000.00
Book Development	$1,000.00	$991.67	$8.33	$1,500.00	$2,000.00	$1,400.00	$1,200.00	$750.00	$750.00	$600.00	$550.00	$700.00	$900.00	$800.00	$700.00
Shipping	$1,900.00	$1,891.67	$8.33	$2,500.00	$4,000.00	$3,000.00	$1,800.00	$1,600.00	$1,500.00	$1,200.00	$1,100.00	$1,500.00	$1,200.00	$1,800.00	$1,500.00
Royalties	$2,500.00	$2,500.00	$0.00			$9,000.00		$8,000.00				$7,000.00		$6,000.00	
Supplies	$200.00	$214.58	-$14.58	$200.00	$400.00	$300.00	$300.00	$200.00	$175.00	$150.00	$200.00	$200.00	$100.00	$150.00	$100.00
Professional Services	$100.00	$100.00	$0.00	$100.00	$100.00	$100.00	$100.00	$100.00	$100.00	$100.00	$100.00	$100.00	$100.00	$100.00	$100.00
Editorial Salaries	$3,000.00	$2,833.33	$166.67	$1,500.00	$4,000.00	$4,000.00	$4,000.00	$3,000.00	$3,000.00	$3,000.00	$3,000.00	$3,000.00	$2,000.00	$2,000.00	$1,500.00
Marketing Salaries	$2,500.00	$2,383.33	$116.67	$2,500.00	$4,000.00	$3,500.00	$3,000.00	$3,000.00	$2,500.00	$2,500.00	$2,500.00	$3,000.00	$1,000.00	$300.00	$300.00
Production Salaries	$1,000.00	$1,025.00	-$25.00	$1,000.00	$1,400.00	$1,300.00	$1,200.00	$1,000.00	$800.00	$1,000.00	$1,000.00	$1,000.00	$1,000.00	$1,000.00	$1,000.00
Sales Salaries/Commissions	$3,000.00	$3,041.67	-$41.67	$1,000.00	$7,000.00	$6,000.00	$5,000.00	$4,000.00	$3,000.00	$2,500.00	$2,000.00	$2,000.00	$2,000.00	$1,000.00	$2,000.00
Building/Rent/Storage	$900.00	$900.00	$0.00	$900.00	$900.00	$900.00	$900.00	$900.00	$900.00	$900.00	$900.00	$900.00	$900.00	$900.00	$900.00
Events	$300.00	$275.00	$25.00	$100.00	$600.00	$500.00	$400.00	$300.00	$200.00	$200.00	$200.00	$300.00	$400.00	$400.00	$0.00
Travel	$250.00	$225.00	$25.00	$200.00	$500.00	$400.00	$300.00	$300.00	$200.00	$200.00	$0.00	$300.00	$100.00	$100.00	$100.00
Phone/Internet	$100.00	$100.00	$0.00	$100.00	$100.00	$100.00	$100.00	$100.00	$100.00	$100.00	$100.00	$100.00	$100.00	$100.00	$100.00
Advertising	$500.00	$508.33	-$8.33	$300.00	$1,000.00	$800.00	$600.00	$400.00	$500.00	$500.00	$600.00	$500.00	$300.00	$300.00	$300.00
Taxes															$1,416.96
Organizational Memberships	$250.00	$118.08	$131.92	$25.00			$50.00							$50.00	$300.00
Meetings	$100.00	$104.17	-$4.17	$50.00	$300.00	$200.00	$50.00	$100.00	$100.00	$100.00	$100.00	$50.00	$50.00	$50.00	$0.00
Insurance	$115.00	$114.49	$0.51	$100.00							$100.00			$1,284.00	$89.85
Website	$250.00	$241.67	$0.51	$100.00	$200.00	$300.00	$300.00	$400.00	$300.00	$200.00	$100.00	$100.00		$600.00	$600.00
Total Expenses	$27,015.00	$26,676.32	$338.68	$19,450.00	$43,500.00	$45,800.00	$32,400.00	$23,550.00	$31,350.00	$19,825.00	$19,200.00	$28,900.00	$17,050.00	$15,384.00	$22,106.81
Need Daily Revenue	$885.74	$874.63	$20,115.81	$627.42	$1,450.00	$1,477.42	$1,080.00	$739.68	$1,011.29	$694.17	$659.35	$963.33	$570.86	$713.12	
Avg Daily Revenue	$967.21	$956.28	$350,000.00	$790.32	$1,500.00	$1,064.52	$900.00	$866.67	$766.67	$683.33	$806.45	$883.33	$1,035.71	$783.33	
Returns	-$1,500.00	-$1,395.83	$350,000.00	$400.00	$600.00	$800.00	$1,000.00	$900.00	$800.00	$750.00	$1,000.00	$1,500.00	$2,000.00	$3,000.00	$4,000.00
Bad Debt	-$100.00	-$93.75	-$6.25	$0.00	$25.00	$50.00	$25.00	$75.00	$0.00	$0.00	$0.00	$100.00	$150.00	$300.00	$400.00
Dead Inventory	-$600.00	-$591.67	-$8.33	$200.00	$400.00	$400.00	$300.00	$400.00	$300.00	$400.00	$300.00	$300.00	$600.00	$1,000.00	$2,500.00
Excessive Author Advances	-$200.00	-$196.83	-$4.17	$300.00	$1,500.00	$100.00	$50.00	$0.00	$300.00	$100.00	$0.00	$50.00	$50.00	$600.00	$50.00
Profit	$85.00	$213.27	$2,559.19	$4,150.00	-$1,025.00	-$14,150.00	-$6,955.00	$1,941.67	-$8,883.33	-$1,585.83	$4,500.00	$4,430.00	$28,766.67	$10,060.57	-$4,723.48

farmer's market, those costs file under "events." When you pay fees for professional associations like Pubwest or Independent Book Publishers Association (IBPA), those are "organizational memberships."

At the end of each month, fill in your actual income and expense figures and at the end of each year, spend some time with your staff explaining what happened, what went well, and what should be avoided in the future, along with why.

After each title has been in print for a year, open up your P&L again and replace your estimated projections with the actual sales data and the current projected trajectory. As Per suggests, this is a great time to transition from your gut to what the data is telling you. This is also a good time to establish some realistic goals—for that backlist title and for your overall publishing program. What is your ideal annual sales volume in dollars and books? Figure out how much income you need from the press. Then figure out your bottom line costs. Calculate what each book costs you in production expenses. Then figure out how many books you'll need in print in order to pay for those things based on the sales data that you have. What do you need more of? What do you need less of? Where were your flops? What channels are your books selling best in? What channels are there room for growth in? What can you learn from evaluating this data? Here's another handy chart to estimate your sales by channel[13]. When failure occurs, take copious notes about how it happened to prevent it from repeating.

From there you can figure out what your ideal frontlist volume looks like. In 2012, Microcosm published 42 books. This proved too

13 Microcosm.pub/salesbychannel

many for us. We could not keep up with distributing and promoting each of them as much as they deserved. We cut down to only fifteen titles in 2013. That felt like too few so we published 20-27 each year from 2014 to 2017. But looking at the numbers, it became clear that we had the greatest financial stability doing eighteen strong titles each year. This allowed our development and marketing staff to make each book as awesome as it could be, avoid sloppy mistakes, and to focus on each book's individual success. Some publishers find that they make more money simply by publishing more books. Others balk at the expense of frontlist and cut it back or eliminate it completely. But this is foolish if your numbers don't support it. Cutting your publishing will cut your future income. So determine your correct volume of frontlist that will create the greatest return on investment. Play around by reducing your budgets and projected income. What amount of reduced expenses will substantiate the lost income? Is this temporary while you rebuild cash flow or are you finding that your press is insolvent? What change in strategy

Sample Sales By Channel

Channel	Units Sold	Units Returned	Net Sales Units	% in Net Sales	Dollars Sold	Dollars Returned	Net Sales/Dollars	Net % in Dollars	Dollars per Unit
Direct Sales	500	0	500	6.89%	$7,500.00	$0.00	$7,500.00	13.69%	$15.00
Wholesalers	1000	400	600	8.27%	$5,000.00	$2,000.00	$3,300.00	6.02%	$5.50
Barnes & Noble	600	300	300	4.14%	$3,000.00	$1,500.00	$1,500.00	2.74%	$5.00
Books-A-Million	300	150	150	2.07%	$1,500.00	$750.00	$750.00	1.37%	$5.00
Libraries	800	0	800	11.03%	$9,600.00	$0.00	$9,600.00	17.52%	$12.00
Indie Bookstores	600	120	480	6.62%	$5,400.00	$1,000.00	$4,400.00	8.03%	$9.17
Amazon	2000	300	1700	23.43%	$10,000.00	$1,500.00	$8,500.00	15.51%	$5.00
Canada	300	75	225	3.10%	$1,800.00	$450.00	$1,350.00	2.46%	$6.00
UK	300	50	250	3.45%	$1,800.00	$300.00	$1,500.00	2.74%	$6.00
Australia	100	25	75	1.03%	$750.00	$150.00	$600.00	1.09%	$8.00
Other World	100	25	75	1.03%	$750.00	$150.00	$600.00	1.09%	$8.00
Special Sales	1000	0	1000	13.78%	$7,000.00	$0.00	$7,000.00	12.77%	$7.00
Gift Sales	1000	0	1000	13.78%	$7,000.00	$0.00	$7,000.00	12.77%	$7.00
Institutional Sales	100	0	100	1.38%	$1,500.00	$0.00	$1,200.00	2.19%	$12.00
Total	8700	1445	7255	100.00%	$62,600.00	$7,800.00	$54,800.00	100.00%	$7.90

will help? Do your readers respond better to a few meticulously developed books or producing an enormous volume of new titles?

Do you have a new book that is selling consistently well and could benefit from a new edition every few years to show that it's updated and current? If so, raise the price 10% each time. These books are your bread and butter and can be used to pay for developing new titles. If a book is successful, it means that the audience is receptive to it and increasing the price by a dollar or two each edition will demonstrate that value to your audience.

Make a Budget

As Mark Suchomel pointed out, the worst mistake you can make is grossly overprinting. You can also grossly overspend on other aspects of publication, like design, advances, or publicity. So create a budget and always work within it. Perhaps you'll have to delay publication of some titles until you have the cash flow on hand, but often this is best. Publishing is a slow, long game. If you are in a hurry, you're in the wrong industry.

To get a better understanding of this, project some numbers on the predictive cash flow chart[14] and get a better understanding of your future. This helps you know what you should be paid when and to look at your whole year and how much money you should have when the dust settles.

Stores typically pay for books after 30 days. In the publishing industry, many stores pay late, often as much as 30 days or more, and they can return books for up to a year. This means that the cost

14 http://microcosm.pub/accounting

of returns is deducted immediately, while you don't get paid for that original sale for months. Sometimes a store pays for new books by returning old books. Barnes & Noble was notorious for doing this, returning books off the shelves to manage their cash flow. This makes your finances hard to predict since you are shouldering their risk. You can refuse to accept returns, but in an industry where other publishers are accepting them freely, that means many bookstore accounts will refuse to order from you.

If you work with a distributor, the wait to get paid is even longer. Your distributor pays you about 100 days after the end of the month where the sale occurred, so it can reasonably take 130 days to get paid for a sale.

This creates a lot of predictive math on your part. While your distributor is robust enough to get paid and is required to pay you even if they do not get paid, they tend to accept returns even after a year has passed to maintain relationships. Over the past 20 years, many distributors have grown financially insolvent and gone through bankruptcy, taking down many great publishers with them, relying solely on their monthly check. As Ian of Bazillion Points pointed out, the sole benefit of leaving PGW was receiving daily checks from vendors instead of a single monthly check. That made them quite a bit more stable and simplified their cash flow management. The chance that your distributor may go bankrupt is another good reason to always keep some of your own inventory where you can physically touch it.

And indeed, your inventory is probably your second greatest asset behind your contracts. Popular wisdom is that the total value of your inventory should be 12% of your sales. So if you are selling $100,000 per year, the cost to reprint your entire inventory should be $12,000. These numbers are very thin, hard to manage, and assume frequent reprintings. While you'll be sitting on a lot of money, it can be sometimes easier to be closer to 25% if only not to have to be constantly reprinting something or another.

Your **receivables**, the money owed to you at any given time, should be 18% of your total sales. Since you are financing the sale of your books—paying for all costs even while they are inventory in someone else's stores—to every one of your retailers and wholesalers, this ensures that you aren't in over your head. If you give a little incentive, such as free shipping or a larger discount, you can often get your stores to pay in advance. Granted, being owed no more than 18% of your sales is a goal and not always possible, particularly during the busiest time of year, but it'll give you a sense of your overall financial health.

Nowadays, even with remarkably different frontlist every year, our sales remain remarkably consistent. If you're publishing a lot of seasonal books for holidays, you'll see trends and strong months around those dates. To make better use of this predictive data, I begin each year by duplicating last year's balance sheet. I replace every outlier with a realistic estimate. For example, if we had a one-time rights sale, I don't include it when projecting income for the following year. Being overly optimistic will not do anything but disappoint you. Being conservative will delight you as you grow a bit each year. Last year's numbers are very useful for understanding this year.

Sample Daily Balance Sheet

check #	description	reference/invoice #	date	debit	deposit	cashed?	balance after	Total
			$45,382.61	$688,978.93	$734,361.54	12/31/	$49,977.53 total year	$688,978.93
	Deposit		12/8/2017		$13,254.14	X	$54,902.00	$19,584.00
7092	Editor	paycheck	12/1/2017	$728.00		X	$54,174.00	$15,568.00
	Deposit		12/11/2017		$2,000.00	X	$56,174.00	$19,847.23
	Book Printing	Book Printing	12/10/2017	$1,700.00		X	$54,474.00	$45,382.61
	Publisher	paycheck	12/10/2017	$1,300.00		X	$53,174.00	$688,978.93
	Deposit		12/12/2017		$2,458.34	X	$55,632.34	
	Deposit		12/13/2017	$10,000.00		X	$45,632.34	
	Deposit		12/13/2017		$5,765.04	X	$51,397.38	
	Deposit		12/14/2017		$6,000.00	X	$57,397.38	$2,011.95
	Book Printing	Book Printing	12/13/2017	$17,000.00		X	$40,397.38	-$3,759.26
7094	Sales Director	paycheck	12/15/2017	$698.31		X	$39,699.07	206.61%
	Deposit		12/18/2017		$3,191.77	X	$42,890.84	
	Deposit		12/19/2017		$8,000.00	X	$50,890.84	-100.00%
	Deposit		12/19/2017		$4,000.00	X	$54,890.84	$263.23
6803	Publicist	paycheck	12/16/2017	$1,160.00		X	$53,730.84	
	Deposit		12/20/2017		$2,825.77	X	$56,556.61	
	Book Printing	Book Printing	12/19/2017	$5,000.00		X	$51,556.61	
6806	Office Manager	paycheck	12/16/2017	$5,000.00		X	$46,556.61	
			12/16/2017	$1,140.00		X	$45,416.61	
6807	Marketing Director	paycheck	12/16/2017	$600.00		X	$44,816.61	
			12/21/2017	$2,328.63		X	$42,487.98	
6804	Sales Director	paycheck	12/16/2017		$2,992.80	X	$45,480.78	
	Deposit		12/22/2017		$1,182.18	X	$46,662.96	
	Deposit		12/16/2017	$812.00		X	$45,850.96	
6805	Editor	paycheck	12/16/2017	$198.00		X	$45,652.96	
7096	Author	royalties	12/26/2017		$1,732.10	X	$47,385.06	
	Deposit		12/24/2017	$1,300.00		X	$46,085.06	
	Deposit		12/24/2017	$1,564.00		X	$44,521.06	
6802	Rent	Building	12/27/2017	$200.00		X	$44,321.06	
	Publisher	paycheck	12/24/2017		$7,436.97	X	$51,758.03	
	Deposit		12/28/2017	$2,000.00		X	$49,758.03	
	Deposit		12/28/2017	$38.94		X	$49,719.09	
	Loan Pmt		12/28/2017		$570.79	X	$50,289.88	
	Internet	Phone	12/28/2017	$660.58		X	$49,629.30	
	Deposit		12/29/2017	$320.00		X	$49,309.30	
6808	Sales Director	paycheck	12/16/2017		$1,093.23	X	$50,402.53	
6902	Author	royalties	12/16/2017	$100.00		X	$50,302.53	
	Deposit		12/29/2017	$125.00		X	$50,177.53	
	Author	royalties	12/16/2017	$150.00		X	$50,027.53	$19,862.22
	Author	royalties	12/16/2017			X		$2,783.45
	Loan Pmt	royalties	12/29/2017	$50.00		X	$49,977.53	$2,121.37

Financing Your Growth

Self-financing means that you are gradually allowing your company to pay for itself rather than taking on an investment partner or taking out a loan. You don't necessarily need a lot of money to start, but it means you'll go slower. Eventually you'll need a staff, an office, and a proper bootstrapping plan, but for now we're just creating perspective.

When you put your money into a project, look at your return on investment. Let's say that you've sold some books and earned $2,000. You could spend that to print 1,000 more books that you could sell to earn $4,000 and then print 2,000 more books with that money, gradually building your way to having a substantial enough backlist. This is financing your own growth. This is how I grew Microcosm with $100/week from my job into $1M per year in sales 23 years later without ever having to take on capital investors or establishing loans.

But for some people this just won't do. If you need to grow faster, you'll need to borrow money and take on the corresponding risks. Let's evaluate how to determine that. Imagine that you didn't publish a single new book this year. How much profit would you have from your back catalog? Ceasing new publishing is generally a bad idea because your returns will gradually diminish and your back catalog will dry up as people forget about you. However, the revenue from your back catalog is money that you can use to fund new titles. How many new titles would this money pay for? Is that sufficient for your growth plans? If not, you'll need to slow down, re-evaluate, or borrow money.

Obviously the best loans come from people that appreciate what you are doing and won't charge you interest: friends, family, or fans. But if you don't have people like this available in your life, you'll need a more traditional route. Typically this is done by showing your plan to a bank with a request for how much money you'll need and the math to back it up. The risk is high, so to evaluate your success, especially before your model and methods are proven, you'll also need to add paying off that interest to your budget. If the numbers still work and you believe strongly enough in what you're doing financially, see if the bank agrees. The biggest trouble a publisher can get into is not planning expenses ahead, not being able to pay its bills as they come due, not having access to a line of credit, and having to charge everything to a credit card, which can eat several hundred dollars in fees each month out of your bottom line.

Before long, your publishing house will own many things, from cash to inventory to computers to real estate to equipment. These are your **assets**. The debts that you owe are your **liabilities**. If you divide your liabilities by your assets, this number is your **debt ratio**. If your total is larger than 50%, you are financing through debt. If it's less than 50%, you are financing through equity, value that you've created in the organization through prior successes. That means your company is now proven and older books are paying for newer books rather than borrowed money.

$$\frac{liabilities}{assets} = debt\ ratio$$

For example, let's say you have $2,000 in cash, own computers worth $4,000, furniture and shelving worth $1,000, and inventory worth $60,000. You currently owe your printer $5,000 and your bank $30,000. Your total assets are $67,000 and your total debts are $35,000. Your debt ratio is 52.2% so you are financing through debt. But once you pay the printer, your debt ratio will be 44.8% and you'll be financing through equity! Congrats!

Similarly, if you divide your net income by your assets, you will know the return on these assets (ROA). The higher the number, the better. So let's say your income is now $200,000 and you reprinted another bestseller so your assets are now $71,000. Your ROA is 2.82. This number shows how efficiently your assets are earning you more money. There isn't a "correct" number for ROA. The important thing here is that you want this number to improve every year. Otherwise it means you are becoming less efficient, typically meaning you are increasing dead inventory.

Exercises like this are helpful for understanding the health of your press and comparing to the same time last year. If you apply for a loan, a bank will review this kind of information so it's a good idea to have a firm understanding of how favorable your business is looking.

Remainders, Hurts, and the Pulpmill

In 1979, the U.S. Supreme Court ruled that Thor Power Tool Company could no longer undervalue its excess replacement parts. Taxes on inventory are based on replacement cost or market value, whichever is *lower*. So after 1979, in order to reduce inventory taxes, a company has to demonstrate that the market price was reduced or the goods are defective. Previously, management had taken a lot of liberties by reducing inventory value simply because something wasn't selling. The decision against Thor pushed publishers to take fewer risks and destroy excess inventory before the end of the financial year in order to write off the loss on taxes and not pay taxes on dead inventory. Previously, publishers would simply reduce the value of stock that they did not expect to sell but now they had to destroy it. This is why you will read stories of unsold books being destroyed in their first year.

Sometimes a book sells very well into its initial offering, but a year later you swear that more books have been returned than were even sold. Returns are a completely exhausting aspect of publishing and can destroy the best-laid plans. After a year, you may find that your distributor has more than a two-year supply of a book and is going to begin charging you for storage. Even if you handle your own warehousing, if a title has totally stopped selling, there are few reasons to store it for the rest of your life and leave your heirs to deal with it, other than not planning ahead.

There are many reasons to purge dead stock. There's no excuse to pay taxes on dead stock. It's taking up space that you presumably need for other stuff. If it's not selling, you definitely don't want to pay to store or move it.

To determine if you have excess stock, multiply the price by your inventory and find 5% of that number. Subtract that total from your sales in dollars over the previous year. The result is the value of excess inventory to get rid of.

For example, if you have 1,000 copies of a $10 book in your warehouse and you only sold $400 worth in net sales last year, it would look like this:

$$1{,}000 \times \$10 \times 5\% = \$500 > \$400$$

So you'd get rid of 200 copies (\$100 is 20% of \$500. 20% of 1,000 is 200 copies). That stock is dead and doing nothing is effectively costing you more than getting rid of it would.

So what do you do with it? Well, your distributor can probably pulp them—turn your books back into paper for new books—for free. But perhaps you are more optimistic about the value of the books. Is there a specialty customer that you could sell them to who wouldn't have seen the book before? If not, there are also numerous remainder dealers like Texas Bookmans (Half Price Books), Daedalus, and Symposium. Remainder dealers purchase large lots from publishers for anywhere between ten cents to three dollars per unit and have their own parallel distribution networks. You can be sure that if you remainder something the books will end up deeply discounted on Amazon and in Half Price Books stores, destabilizing a market for full-price copies. Typically your distributor will also force you to simultaneously put the book out of print.

Instead of pulping or remaindering, we give away excess stock with paid orders by simply including the additional book in the order for free. The customers are happy to get extra books, we promote the books, and we don't have to destroy anything we love.

Similarly, many returns will not arrive in resellable condition. Damaged returns are called "hurts" and the same remainder dealers will purchase these as well without them destabilizing your market. We deal with them by having a discount shelf in our bookstore and we sell random ten packs of hurt books on our website.

Your Successes Can Kill You

John Campbell is the publisher of *Sad Pictures for Children,* a comic about two characters working unfulfilling office jobs. In 2012 the book raised over $51,000 of an $8,000 Kickstarter goal. But two years later, all the orders for the books still hadn't been fulfilled. Campbell said that the IRS took $3,000-5,000 and he somehow spent another $30,000 printing 2,000 hardcover books. He also purchased dead wasps encased in plastic to insert into the inside back cover. He said he mailed over 750 books but about 150 were returned to him because the customers had moved in the two years since they had entered their addresses. Campbell received over 100 emails from unhappy backers who hadn't received their books. Even understanding that he was exasperated and fed up, Campbell's response to dealing with his tremendous success is still confusing. "After a decade of putting personal work on the Internet in public for free and realizing I didn't have what I felt that I needed, my online persona committed suicide," Campbell explained in an interview with DNAInfo. He claimed to have run out of money to mail the remaining books and finally set the rest on fire in an alley. He described burning the books as "like a weight lifted off of me."

Success had made Campbell miserable in perhaps the best argument against self-publishing that the world has ever heard. Not knowing how to source proper costs for printing books, not being efficient or organized, and suffering extreme mental duress as a result, Campbell's success could have killed him. In my alternate universe, Campbell hired a production manager to pay $2 to print each book and to oversee the scheduling and handling of shipping out books to customers while the artist stayed busy happily producing new work instead.

In a larger-scale example of the perils of success, All Romance eBooks, a publisher with over 5,000 erotic authors and $4.5M in income in 2012 went belly up without warning by the end of 2016. Not offering much in the way of explanation beyond the fact that customers cashed in more than twice as many gift certificates as they had the year before, the owner cited being unable to manage her overhead and claimed that she had only noticed her impending financial collapse six days before she abruptly shut down. She pleaded with her authors not to sue her lest they get paid even less of what's owed to them and tried to quietly disappear.

It's a confusing mystery to understand how a functional business could abruptly collapse after so many years but it's also an important lesson to keep your eye on your numbers and spreadsheets so you can see problems before they are upon you. Even a relatively experienced publisher like Soft Skull Press could have easily been put out of business by their debacle with J.H. Hatfield's *Fortunate Son*, despite the book selling hundreds of thousands of copies. Stay organized, plan ahead, predict the problems before they happen, do the math, and make sure that you can afford to succeed.

In a less dramatic scenario, my mentor had a runaway hit in 2001 when one of his authors made an incendiary remark on television and his book sales quadrupled. The publisher responded by choking the supply, only printing the number of backorders each month. This strategy made no sense to me. I asked why he didn't respond with tripling the print run, buying ads, and having the sales reps push the book. He explained that because the sales were all returnable it's easy to get caught up in a bestseller fervor and easily overprint and tie up all of your cash into inventory that is dead before you know it. He explained that by shorting supply, you force the wholesalers and chains to only ship books to the best accounts that are unlikely to return them later. While they might have lost out on potential sales from not overcommitting resources to this title, they continued to publish another day and had predictable cash flow across the next year. I fervently disagreed with him at the time but today, eighteen years of market changes later, I think this is the correct strategy. Dip your baby toe in first and proceed with caution until your sales are sticking.

IPG uses a similar strategy with their Trafalgar Square Publishing program, wherein they import books from British offices of the Big Five publishers. They create a catalog, solicit orders, and bring over a shipping container at a time. By the time the inventory arrives, the books are sold and more orders are solicited. There is no inventory to store and while they may be risking potential sales, this just-in-time inventory model seriously mitigates risk.

Similarly, when not managed properly, a single bestseller can kill your whole company. A bestseller creates all sorts of problems like underprinting, chains and wholesalers over-ordering and then doing massive returns after interest fades, financing huge print runs, the book being unavailable while demand is at peak, and overprinting after the book ceases to sell. Sometimes you won't have the ability to borrow enough money to cover your print runs or find that you now have an unrealistically demanding author. For these reasons, a bestseller is sometimes best handled by selling the rights to a bigger house.

Evaluating Your Own Success

While there are many forms that can help you determine your business' value, ultimately if that's what gets you into publishing, you're going to be disappointed; the profit margins are slim and the work is difficult. If you're into metrics, here's one basic balance sheet to get you started on thinking this way.[15] But don't hold yourself only to financial goals. Keeping your head above water can be hard enough.

Before you need guidance, develop a mentorship relationship with a publisher who is more experienced and knowledgeable than you are. Don't bother them frequently, but develop specific questions about where you're getting lost or stuck. Once you have enough information to know your blind spots and what you are ignorant about, you can make efficient use of everyone's time and develop a mutually fulfilling relationship. If you want consulting time don't just ask them to go to tea unless you are already friends and very clear about your intentions. If you want an hour of a professional's time, offer to pay for it. They may decline your money but you will maintain your relationship. And they can be the most helpful in evaluating and recognizing your own success.

Adam Gamble explains that he evaluates success in these terms: "If I'm proud of it and it loses money, it's a failure. If I'm not proud of it and it makes money, it's a failure. From there, the degree of

---

15 http://microcosm.pub/balancesheet

success is a function of those two factors." Essentially Gamble has to be proud of the book *and* it has to make money. You may not be so hard on yourself but it may motivate you to do great work.

Ian Christe thinks of success a bit differently: "I want to see our books visibly in retail stores, referenced on social media, and of course selling lots of copies. For each author, I've seen different dreams kind of come true, whether it's bringing back together a defunct band they were in, giving them a status to immigrate to a different country, putting them in touch with their heroes. Each book is wildly different in terms of what gift it has given the author."

Perhaps you will watch your goals and plans change over time as the industry continues to evolve. The number one question that I am asked about Microcosm is if someone else could create a similar organization today. I'm not sure if I could. We had established an e-commerce site and built an audience at a time when Amazon didn't control even 10% of book sales. We had tremendous consistency and financialization which allowed us to build infrastructure, like training long-term staff, owning a warehouse, and building our own software and databasing to manage all of our own operations. The climate is different today.

In our interview, Joe Matthews contemplated how hard it would be to create a company like Microcosm today. "Microcosm organically evolved into a publisher in a grassroots manner with a slow build-up at an interesting time." That's a polite way of saying that even with the same skills, I'd be hard pressed to sell three million small-trim paperbacks if I started today. The market has changed. This doesn't mean that you won't succeed or shouldn't try. It means that your story will be different, as will the things that do and don't work for you.

Perhaps your goals are more modest or more ambitious than the publishers profiled here. That's fine. Don't judge yourself based on their accomplishments. You know what's right for you and I wish you luck on your own terms.

Homework:

Starting out

- Who would be a good mentor for your press?
- Where will your seed money come from?
- What legal structure will your company use?
- How will you manage initial print runs?
- What is your plan for building stable backlist?
- What is your strategy for managing excess inventory?
- What kind of accounting system will you use?
- How frequently will you run and review your numbers?

Long term planning

- How does the next 90 days look for your cash flow?
- What books do you need more of? What books do you need less of? Where were your flops?
- How does the next year's cash flow look?
- What is your ideal number of frontlist titles?
- What factors can you point to that make a book stick for you as backlist?

- Do you have books that are ideal for new editions every few years?
- Are you increasing backlist sales with time or are newer titles not sticking?
- What sales channels are your books selling best in?
- What channels are there room for growth in?
- Can you afford to finance your own growth or will you need a loan?
- How can you hold onto your passion every day as a publisher?

Playing with your numbers

- What is your ideal annual sales volume in dollars and books?
- How much does your bottom line cost?
- How many copies of each title do you reliably sell year over year?
- At your current rate of sale, how long will it take to build up your publishing program where 65% of your income comes from backlist?
- What is your asset/liabilities debt ratio?
- What is your return on your assets?
- What percentage of your sales is the value of your inventory?
- What is the ratio of your receivables to your total sales?
- What is your average gross profit on each book?
- What consistent patterns are you seeing in your historical sales data?
- What emergent patterns do you foresee to become consistent in your future sales data?

CONCLUSION

The Future of Publishing

Publishing has more new competing products introduced every year than any other industry in the world. The volumes of new work being published increase rapidly every day even while sales are flat. Each breakout successful book is harder to achieve than the last. Many categories are well past saturated, and it can feel harder every day to sell books. Your solution is simply to avoid crowded categories and not aim for bestsellers.

There are plenty of other things that you can do to improve your own odds of success:

- Follow your passions.

- Focus first on your core audiences and your author's network and platform.

- Focus on audiences that will enthusiastically spread the word about your books.

- Keep your investments small and grow gradually.

- Forever be creative and thoughtful, thinking outside of the box and ahead of your competition.

- Aim for special sales markets as they are growing, easier to break into, and much more consistent than other channels.

- Represent an area of diversity that is lacking in publishing and in which you feel authoritative.

The industry is changing. If publishing is consistent about anything, it is the fact that it's becoming more diverse. The overwhelming evidence of the lack of representation in publishing, both in terms of authors and staff, have changed the conversation. The Literary Industrial Complex is even taking notice as they realize that, for example, the Black interest titles that they used to think of as niche titles are now clearly mainstream.

The public's relationship to African American authors has evolved tremendously over the past 100 years. When Black olympic athlete Major Taylor self-published *The Fastest Bicycle Rider in the World* in 1928, he employed the same hand-selling methods that Timothy Dexter used for *A Pickle for the Knowing Ones or Plain Truth in a Homespun Dress* in 1797...which bear remarkable resemblance to the methods that still work well today. Both authors relied upon their reputations, grit, prior accomplishments, and skill at selling. But despite being a world champion, Major Taylor fell into severe financial hardship upon returning to the U.S. and self-publishing his book, dying four years later from heart disease. Unlike the white Dexter, Taylor's book remains out of print today. Despite setting numerous world records, his story is largely forgotten and the U.S. sports franchises and the Literary Industrial Complex rejected him.

Still, African American publishing had thrived since the 1960s, existing as an intellectual microcosm of the industry. By 1992, publishing's interest and relationship with the politics of race was changing.

Annie Elizabeth Delany and her sister Sarah Louise Delany, the Black daughters of a slave, published their memoirs, *Having Our Say*, as they were both nearing 100 years old. They weren't celebrities and their lives hadn't been particularly eventful, say, compared to Major Taylor's, but they sold over a million copies of their book and the world revelled in their compelling storytelling.

Fast forward 25 years and Nigerian author Chimamanda Ngozi Adichie has sold millions of copies of her books. Adichie is published by Anchor Books, whose mission is to "make inexpensive editions of modern classics widely available to college students and the adult public." Anchor is an imprint of Knopf Doubleday, which is now part of the $9B/year Penguin Random House juggernaut. Naturally, the widespread acceptance and commercial success of authors like Adichie turned a lot of heads and caused even the Literary Industrial Complex to look for talent in authors outside of well-monied, white gentlemen in Manhattan.

Today, the people most likely to purchase and read books are young, educated Black women[16]. And while the industry's acceptance of this revelation has been slow and awkward, the gears of change have gradually begun grinding to understand how to cater to it. And with change comes pushback. "I love when people talk about [diversity] inclusion as pandering because the same people who say that are the ones who've been pandered to for years," C. Spike Trotman told *Black Girl Nerds*. Per Henningsgaard agreed that publishing is going to continue to shift away from the industry staff being 82% white and embrace the many audiences that it has historically ignored and been closed off from. He was also quick

16   TheAtlantic.com/entertainment/archive/2014/01/most-likely-person-read-book-college-educated-black-woman/357091/

to point out how myopic publishing is in the U.S., "Literature and publishing aren't seen as part of the arts in the United States in the same way that people look at theater, museums, or the opera. The U.S. is one of the few countries with a lack of government subsidy for publishing and the Big Five have such a giant presence in the U.S. that Americans rarely think of small publishers. When Australians think of publishing, they think of small presses."

Find an audience that has been historically ignored, in the way that the majority of Microcosm's customers are low-income, queer women of color with little conventional education. Find an audience that makes you feel grateful about your work every day.

You don't need to react the same way to anything as the rest of the industry does. You get to write your own story with all aspects of how you run your press. In 2007, HarperCollins, very proudly and very late to the game, introduced their first retail website to compete with Amazon. Barnes & Noble tried to introduce the Nook e-reader to the marketplace in 2009 and reinvent themselves as a "technology company." These efforts were too little, too late, trying merely to offer the same services that had been available for years elsewhere with superior quality.

The rise of digital printing alongside Amazon's market dominance of around 35% of book sales has led to a major disruption in the business. Still, the Literary Industrial Complex is not going out of business. While the Big Five don't have the stranglehold on the industry that they once did, they still are better financialized with more long term contracts for the most successful backlist in the industry than any independent press. These backlist titles create so much financial stability that these houses can afford advances for guaranteed bestsellers by people like presidents and celebrities...or to buy the rights for the next *50 Shades of Grey* from a small press. Ian Christe mused to me, "I don't understand big money advances for books that will clearly never sell nearly enough to break even. But that's such a different realm than what we deal with. It's just that we compete with actual sales with those books, why don't the big publishers take a smaller risk and pay more royalties like we do? I guess that's a mystery about the book industry." The short answer is because they develop every single book to become a bestseller and they have the finances to make this happen. At the same time, Christe is right and many of these books are increasingly unsustainable.

And that's where you come in.

There is so much room for new voices and talent in publishing with little barrier to entry. While eBooks failed to catch on in the way that the industry expected and/or feared, and earning a living from self-publishing an eBook is now less likely than winning the lottery, there is still infinite room for introducing new midlist publishers to the market and physical books are not disappearing or even slowing.

If you can figure out how to sustain your expenses while selling 3,000-5,000 copies of each book, you can seize a piece of this dream. If you find a vacant niche, follow your passions, understand who your audience is and how to respectfully communicate with them, and publish great work consistently, you'll have a bright future. And you get to touch people's lives and have the best job. That's the biggest victory of them all.

do it
5% BETTER
every year

APPENDIX

List of Full Service Trade Distributors

Baker and Taylor Publisher Services (previously Bookmasters)
Offers the greatest access to the library market.
501 S. Gladiolus St.
Momence, IL 60954
Phone: 800-775-2300
BTpubServices.com

Cardinal Publishers Group
A smaller distributor than most, Cardinal is focused on indies interested in carving out their own niche and their lead titles are focused around health, fitness, diet, travel, writing, and sports.
2402 N. Shadeland Ave., Suite A
Indianapolis, IN 46219
(317) 352-8200
Cardinalpub.com

Consortium Books Sales
Now owned by Ingram, Consortium has wonderful leadership and remains a strong choice for small presses with several new titles per season and a consistent backlist.
34 Thirteenth Ave NE, Suite 101
Minneapolis, MN 55413
(612) 746-2600
Cbsd.com

Diamond Book Distributors
Specializing in graphic novels as a spinoff of Diamond Comics, has the market monopoly on non-returnable sales to comic book stores (referred to confusingly as "The Direct Market").
10150 York Rd Suite 300
Hunt Valley, MD 21030
Diamondbookdistributors.com

Ingram Publisher Services (IPS)
Largest supplier of books to bookstores, retailers, schools, etc. IPS wants publishers selling six figures annually.
One Ingram Blvd.
La Vergne, TN 37086
Phone: (855) 867-1920
Ingramcontent.com/publishers/publisher-services

Independent Publishers Group (IPG)
Oldest independent book distributor in the U.S. featuring a wide variety of publishers in many categories.
814 N. Franklin Street
Chicago, IL, 60610
(312) 337-0747
ipgbook.com

Midpoint
With a primary focus on the East Coast, they are a starter distributor for new publishers.
27 West 20th Street, Suite 1102
New York, NY 10011
(212) 727-0190
midpointtrade.com

National Book Network
Best suited for publishers with a very mainstream list and self-explanatory titles.
4501 Forbes Blvd.
Lanham, MD, 20706
(301) 459-3366
nbnbooks.com

Penguin Random House Publisher Services
The largest distributor with the most infrastructure for independent publishers that is also the most choosy.
1745 Broadway
New York, NY 10019
Fax (212) 782-9622
distribution@penguinrandomhouse.com
Penguinrandomhouse.biz/publisherservices/

Publishers Group West
Now owned by Ingram, PGW is familiar and comfortable handling quirkier and edgier titles for publishers doing six figures annually.
1700 Fourth Street
Berkeley, CA 94710
(510) 809-3700
PGW.com

SCB Distributors
Located on the west coast and focusing just on a few dozen small publishers with four or more books per year.
15608 S. New Century Drive
Gardena, CA 90248
(310) 532-9400

scbdistributors.com

List of Book Wholesalers

American West Books, Inc.
Sells books to mass market accounts like Costco.
1254 Commerce Way
Sanger, CA 93657
(800) 497-4909
AmericanWestBooks.com

Baker & Taylor
Public and school libraries.
1120 Route 22 East
Bridgewater, NJ 08807
800-775-1500
www.btol.com

Bookazine
75 Hook Rd,
Bayonne, NJ 07002
(800) 221-8112
Bookazine.com

DeVorss & Company
Metaphysical, spiritual, and self-help.
P.O. Box 1389
Camarillo, CA 93011
(310) 822-8940
Devorss.com

Gem Guides Book Co.
As in books about rocks; also history and regional interest.
1275 W. 9th Street
Upland, CA 91786
(626) 855-1611
GemGuidesbooks.com

Ingram Content Services
With warehouses in Pennsylvania, Oregon, and Tennessee, Ingram is the
largest passive supplier of books to bookstores in the U.S.
One Ingram Blvd.
La Vergne, TN 37086
Phone: (855) 867-1920
IngramContent.com

New Leaf Distributing Co.
Specializes in books about Spirituality, Metaphysics and New Age. Also carries
self-help, gardening/herbs, and conspiracy titles.
401 Thorton Road
Lithia Springs, GA 30122
(770) 948-7845
Newleaf-dist.com

Sample Screening Interview Questions for Intern or Employee

• **What obstacles did you overcome to arrive at where you are now in life**?: (I
added this question at the suggestion of Mark S. Luckie, the first Black employee
of Twitter. It helps to fundamentally understand someone's privilege and how
much hardship they've had to endure towards their goals.)

• **Can you talk about your dream job**?

• **Why do you want to work in publishing**?

*(impose reality of publishing—8,000 new books published every day, 90% of work
is administrative and involves more than just "good books," especially researching
a niche, P&Ls, etc)*

• **How familiar are you with [your press]**?

• **What is most important to you, your values**?

• **What are you looking for in an internship**?

We divide internships as 25% publicity / sales / marketing / editorial, or 20%
Adobe Indesign if there is interest and experience. You would work on real
manuscripts so it's important to preserve the author's voice and help them to
sound more like themselves and express their narrative and viewpoints in the
most coherent manner rather than overwrite their voice with your own. This

can be difficult around issues of creative work for some people. **Would this be a problem?**

• **Do you have experience taking instructions, following directions, working independently and to spec**?: (we receive many intern applicants who have not had previous employment or who haven't previously had to work on projects that would be used in the world. We now stress that *successful publishing employee requires Common Sense / problem-solving / figuring out shortest path to goals & Hard Work, as well as learning new things and practicing those skills. There is no busy work because we are too busy. We often teach and test attention to detail by having interns count T-shirt colors, styles, and sizes. It's the publishing version of Daniel painting the fence or Luke training with Yoda on Dagobah.*)

(at this point I insert a pop quiz where I show covers of a dozen different books and ask the interviewee to identify what benefit each one offers and who the audience is. This determines if they understand title development fundamentally.)

• **What were your favorite/least favorite projects that you've worked on and why**?

• **Do you have experience speaking up when you have concerns**?: (this question is important for understanding if someone will say something if they don't understand a task that you have explained to them and to emphasize that importance.)

• **What things do you excel at**?

• **When do you have trouble**?

• **What motivates your best work**?

• **Do you have experience working with people with special needs**?: (we have several disabled employees and this is something else we want to prime new staff for as well as how to accommodate them.)

[and then as a transition I interject] *We try to have the most fun every day. You would be encouraged to participate and contribute in meetings.*

• **Do you prefer juggling many projects or managing a single project?**

• **Would you rather spend a few weeks with each dept or focus on the most pressing task each day?** (Emphasize minimum requirements, type of work environment, pay (if any), and opportunities.)

• *I think you'd be a good fit here. What kind of schedule would work for you?*

• **Do you have questions**?

Sample Style Guide

How to Write

1) Once you've laid out the bones, always be asking yourself how each sentence advances the narrative. If it doesn't, remove it, or add more to show how it's relevant. ("give or take")

2) Clarify sentences to be the simplest language possible and use active verbs (The person climbed the tree not The tree was climbed.).

3) Show why each new character is relevant. If you need to introduce an "expert," use the newspaper style of "Sam Adams, Mayor of Portland, said that he thinks fluoride is stupid."

4) We use William Zinsser as the general go-to when you have a writing or editing question. Either *On Writing Well* or *On Memoir*, as appropriate. Both are highly recommended books and excellently readable.

Formatting

Text should be single spaced with no blank lines between paragraphs. Format preferences the copy editor and designer should know about may be communicated separately in RED in ALL CAPS.

Block quotes: Quotes of one hundred words or more can be set off as a block quotation. These should have a single indent for the whole quote (highlighting the whole thing and hitting Tab once), not using tabs, spaces, or hard returns on each line.

Capitalization of titles: In general, all the major words are capitalized:

1. Capitalize the first and last words in titles and subtitles.

2. Lowercase the articles the, a, and an; and the conjunctions and, but, or, nor, and for.

3. Lowercase prepositions (except when used adverbially or adjectivally, such as up in Look Up, or on in The On Button).

4. Lowercase to and as.

Citations: A quick guide to Chicago-style references with examples is online at: ChicagoManualofStyle.org/tools_citationguide.html.

A few simple examples: We organize these as "references" in the back 10% of the book.

Citation:

Geoffrey C. Ward and Ken Burns, *The War: An Intimate History*, 1941–1945 (New York: Knopf, 2007), 52.

Abbreviated style for subsequent references:

Ward and Burns, War, 59–61.

Bibliography:

Ward, Geoffrey C., and Ken Burns. *The War: An Intimate History*, 1941–1945. New York: Knopf, 2007.

Dashes: The most common and versatile dash is the em dash, — (longer than the en dash, –). The Mac keyboard shortcut is Shift+Option+Hyphen. For the en dash, Option+Hyphen.

Both are formatted without spaces before or after—like so. The en dash (not a hyphen) is used for ranges of numbers such as pages and years (1968–2011). The double dash (--) is never used.

Diacritics, accents, and foreign words: These should generally be used when known to be part of a word or name. Foreign-language words used in books should include the correct diacritics/accents. Foreign-language words that are not proper names and that are likely unfamiliar to most readers should be in italics on first mention (a translation of the term into English may follow in parentheses and not in italics). Such terms used repeatedly should not be italicized each time once they've been introduced and the attentive reader will know what is meant. Latin phrases that are common in English do not need italics.

Ellipses: In general, use three points with spaces before and after each, like . . . this. When an ellipsis indicates an omission from a quoted passage, following a grammatical sentence, a period is used at the end of the sentence before the ellipsis, and the next sentence begins with a capital letter. For example: "This complete sentence

precedes an omission. . . . The quoted passage then resumes." To indicate hesitation and the like, no extra point is needed, even after a sentence. To prevent ellipses from breaking across two lines, it is best to use non-breaking spaces in Word (on a Mac, hold down Option when hitting the spacebar).

Endnotes and footnotes: For reference format, see Citations. We use Word's footnote/endnote system, with options set to default. It is preferable to place the note number after a sentence, not in the middle, except to avoid confusion as to what the note pertains to. Where multiple citations are needed for one sentence, combine these in a single note, separated with a semicolon. Discursive notes should be as concise as possible. To further save space, a reference can be abbreviated after the first citation (see Citations), except when there is no bibliography and the abbreviated note would be placed far from the original note. Ibid. (followed by page numbers, if different) can be used when the source is the same as the one preceding it. Avoid the term op cit. Cross references (for example: See also note XX.) can be useful to save space and avoid repeating lengthy material, but avoid cross references by repeating anything only one or two lines long, using the abbreviated citation style if appropriate. Numbers should be written as: XX.

Format: For nearly all manuscripts, the simplest format is best: a series of headings (see Headings) and indented paragraphs in the same font with uniform margins and tabs, no special characters, images, or text boxes (see Images). Section breaks where a special character should appear in the book can be indicated in the manuscript with three asterisks (***). Word has a Style feature (under format) for advanced formatting that can cause design complications, so please do not use Styles. See also Images and Spacing and indents.

Full capitals (a.k.a. "all caps") should be replaced with emphasis in italics: Full caps is only used to describe something written that way such as a sign or headline (for example: "A sign said, OPEN 24 HOURS.") and will later be converted to a font with small caps.

Headings: An author or editor can indicate desired levels of headings as follows:

Photo placement, designer notes, and sidelines should be indicated with red text in ALL CAPS on its own line. You can use [BEGIN SIDEBAR] and

[END SIDEBAR] and we should be all set.

Chapter Titles: FULL CAPS, BOLD

Level 1, headings: Bold, Headline-Style Caps

Level 2, subheadings: Bold, italics, sentence-style caps

Level 3, sub-subheadings: italics, sentence-style caps

Initials: A name with multiple initials has no spaces between them: C.L.R. James. A name that consists only of initials is set without spaces or periods (JFK), as are acronyms (NATO).

Interviews: An author's previously unpublished transcriptions of interviews may require a judgment call about how much to "clean up." While some transcripts must be an accurate record of what the speaker said, other (unpublished) transcripts can be edited for grammatical slips and elisions. More substantial changes may be explained in a note or preface. The book's author or editor may consult copy editors about what type of editing of this material is desirable, if any.

Books, periodicals, films, albums, plays, TV series, works of art, and longer musical works (e.g., ballets and operas) are italicized. Essays, short stories, chapters, songs, and poems are not italicized and placed in quotation marks.

Job titles, academic appointments, professional designations, etc.: These are generally lowercase: Smith is associate professor of history at UCLA. An exception is a named professorship (Edward Said was Parr Professor of English and Comparative Literature) or when it immediately precedes the name as a title (Professor Said).

Numbers: In nontechnical prose, zero through twenty are spelled out, as are round multiples of those numbers in hundreds, thousands, and hundreds of thousands (thirty-three thousand). Other numbers, such as 120 and 7,852, use numerals.

Possessive: For singular nouns, add apostrophe + s, including with ending in s (Williams's play).

Quotations: Comma and period go inside quotation mark.

Serial comma: we use serial commas, for example the final comma in "A, B, and C" (not A, B and C).

Spacing and indents: Manuscripts should be single-spaced. The first paragraph of a section is not indented, but subsequent paragraphs have an indent formed with a hard return (not a series of tabs or spaces) and a single tab. There should not be an extra line space between paragraphs.

A line space can be indicated with a bracketed note: [space]. Use a single space between sentences, not double. (See also Block quotes)

Spelling: Spell-checking manuscripts is a good idea, but consider Merriam-Webster's Collegiate Dictionary to be the final arbiter on spelling questions.

Words in all capitals: Use italics instead (for emphasis).

Underlining: Use italics instead.

U.S. and United States: U.S. (with periods) is generally preferred as an adjective, whereas United States is spelled out as a noun. However, U.S. can be used as a noun in looser, more informal styles of writing.

Sample Contract

Here's a sample publishing contract. You can download a copy from http://microcosm.pub/samplecontract

This agreement is made between Publisher and:

NAME (hereinafter called the "Author")

and

[YOUR PUBLISHING COMPANY'S NAME] (hereinafter called the "Publisher")

WHEREAS, the Author has created a non-fiction book tentatively called **Sample Book** (hereinafter called the "Project") consisting of text, lettering, and illustrations, and

WHEREAS the parties wish to respectively publish the project to exploit the rights granted in this Agreement and set forth in the terms below.

In consideration of the mutual promises and agreements of the parties hereto for the Project as hereinafter set forth, it is agreed as follows:

Printed copies: 1) Publisher, whose principal offices are located at [your address], will incur all expenses related to publishing and will plan each print run to satisfy at least two years of anticipated sales.

2) Publisher will provide the author(s), for free, with 5% of the physical copies of each printed edition, to be used as the author(s) sees fit, as long as the author(s) desires them. If the author has media relationships or knows blurbers, Publisher will produce review copies in advance for the author to promote the book six months before publication.

3) Author(s) may request copies against royalties or within royalties expected to be owed to them within one year.

4) Copies obtained from Publisher cannot be sold to stores or outlets that Publisher sells to directly (outside of author(s) events at said venues and book fairs, where both parties may be present). This is to protect the money invested, cost of review copies sent, and author(s)' royalties. **Author(s) Initials ___**

Profit and Accounting: 5) Publisher will provide the author(s) with a royalty of one of these options: **(check one)**

___ 15% of net profits (which are defined as revenue minus printing costs, eBook conversion costs, freelancer fees, freight costs, and invoiced promotional expenses, best choice for 95% of authors) -or-

___ 50% of actual profits (all sales minus all expenses including bottom line and staff salaries, best choice for our top 5% of bestselling authors whose book sales exceed 40,000 copies)

___ 8% of the cover price (best choice for authors who hate to check our math)

A one-time advance of $500 from expected royalties will be paid to the author, with half due upon signing of this agreement and half due upon approved submission of finished manuscript on schedule. Future royalties will not begin being paid to the Author until this amount has been recouped by Publisher. If the book never recoups the cost of the advance, the author does not have to repay it.

eBook royalties will be paid at 30% of net profit. In the event of additional printings that are not new editions, the author(s) will receive a 20% royalty on paperback net profits. (For transparency's sake, our operating costs for staff salaries, warehousing, and running an office are 51.89% of net sales. Our owners do not keep any profits. Any money left over after inventory and operating expenses is spent on new projects. We publicly publish our finances annually.) If Publisher can foresee a future expense on a book, the corresponding amount of author royalty may be withheld until after the payment has been made.

Due to book industry payment schedules, the average book sells enough to recoup its expenses and begin to pay a royalty after nine months. The author understands that some books recover expenses faster or slower and sadly it is possible that some books may never recover expenses. The average publisher-supported book sells only 3,000 copies in its lifetime and while 99% of Publisher's books exceed these sales, there are roughly 8,000 new books being published every day in the United States and thus there are no implicit sales guarantees.

6) Audiobook rights, foreign/translation or TV/movie rights, when sold, will pay author(s) a royalty of 50% of net receipts. Any additions, abridgments, subtractions, and artwork changes to these editions must be approved by the author with author's approval not unreasonably withheld.

7) Publisher will send the author(s), via email, an accurate statement (see Exhibit A) at least every six months with a record of sales in units and dollars. Every time at least $100 is owed, a royalty payment will be sent within 30 days.

1. Publisher will sell additional copies to the author(s) at "cost," determined by using this formula: (editorial cost + printing cost) / (size of print run - promotional copies) = author(s) unit cost, rounding up + shipping

8) Author(s) reserves the right to audit book sales history up to twice per year. In the event that Publisher fails at good faith efforts to pay royalties due to the author(s), Publisher will pay an additional 8% annual fee in interest.

Promotion and Distribution: 9) Publisher will distribute the work through whatever means are available; including but not limited to trade distribution, Turnaround UK, Baker & Taylor, Ingram, Barnes & Noble, Diamond Comics, New Leaf, Event Network, book stores, specialty retailers, gift shops, conferences/events, a printed catalog, and the Publisher website.

10) The author(s) will promote the work to the extent of their abilities—to colleagues, friends, professional contacts, and to build relationships with journalists and professionals writing about their subject matter and to complete any mutually agreed upon interviews that Publisher schedules. If the author cannot complete a sale themselves, the author agrees to direct their audience to purchase copies online from [your website URL] as it provides the best highest royalty for the author. **Author(s) Initials ___**

11) Publisher will make all efforts to promote the book to the best of its ability to all applicable audiences. Publisher will attempt to find the largest audience possible via marketing and publicity, given our resources.

12) The Publisher and any of its licensees or assigns shall have the right to use the Author's name, image, likeness, pseudonym if used, and biography in connection with the exercise of any such rights, and in advertising and publicity in connection therewith for the duration of the agreement. The Author shall provide at the Author's expense a reproducible photograph of the Author (accompanied by photographer credit) that the Publisher may use in connection in promoting the work.

Ownership and Rights: 13) Author(s) remains the copyright holder and owner of the contents and licenses Publisher worldwide exclusive rights to publish hardcover, paperback, TV/movie, audio, and eBook editions in the edited, finished form. Author(s) may choose to share their copyright under Creative Commons and retains subsidiary rights not mentioned in this contract. This contract may be transferred or assigned to another party at the Publisher's discretion based on their professional expertise and only for reasonable and customary rights sales, licensing, or contract transfers.

14) Author warrants that everything it gives Publisher to include in the Project is legally owned or licensed to Author. Author agrees to indemnify and hold Publisher harmless from any and all claims brought by any third-party relating to Author's Proprietary Material provided by Author to Publisher including any and all demands, liabilities, losses, reasonable associated costs and claims including reasonable attorney's fees arising out of injury caused by Author's Proprietary Material supplied by Author to Publisher, copyright infringement, and defective products sold as a result of Publisher's distribution of the Project. Publisher agrees to indemnify and hold Author harmless from any and all claims brought by any third-party relating to Publisher's negligent actions and all demands, liabilities, losses, reasonable associated costs and claims including reasonable attorney's fees arising out of injury caused by Publisher's negligent actions or copyright infringement.

15) Author(s) agree to submit a finished manuscript of approximately **40,000 words** each before November 1, 2021 for an expected publication date of January, 2023 or as soon as is practicable. **Author(s) Initials** ___

16) Unless these terms are breached by Publisher, the author(s) is contractually bound to continue to publish this work with Publisher, in whatever forms Publisher deems appropriate. In the event that Publisher fails to provide requested accounting details or required payments within 60 days after author(s) believe there is an error or funds owed, authors may give written notice to cancel the contract when the current printing is sold out or by buying it out within 60 days. Upon termination of this agreement, for any cause, all rights granted to Publisher shall revert to the author(s), subject to Publisher's continued participation in any licenses granted by Publisher.

1. Publisher has a duty to publish the work within the expected timeline stated in paragraph 15, given that the finished manuscript is delivered on time. If the manuscript is delivered late, Publisher can opt to reschedule for later publication. Publisher has a further duty to re-publish the book within six months of it going out of print (or one year in the case of a new edition) or in the event of a misprint which the author(s) has no fault in. If Publisher fails to publish the book within this period, the author(s) may cancel the agreement by giving written notice, at which time all rights for the book revert to the author(s).

2. Publisher can only decline to publish the work if the author is excessively uncooperative with editors, the finished work conflicts with its mission as a publisher, due to lateness of delivery, poor quality of finished work, final work not matching or representing the work agreed upon via correspondences, or because Publisher reasonably believes the work infringes upon the proprietary rights of someone else's work.

3. "Out of Print" shall be understood as "not available in physical copies through traditional channels in the U.S." When the number of in physical

copies falls below 100, Publisher will make good faith efforts to reprint as soon as possible or let the author(s) know if it does not plan to reprint the book, let it go out of print, and revert rights to the author(s).

4. Publisher has the right to final authority on the book's cover and Publisher will share drafts with the author(s) before the book goes to the printer.

5. Publisher has the right to final design and editorial changes to the book's content with the goal of making the work into the best book that it can be. Author(s) will be able to review and discuss final edits and cover design before the book is printed.

6. Author(s) states that they own the rights to use all content in the book or have requested and received specific permissions from the creator to use their work.

7. Author agrees to reserve all new content or changes to content for the new edition and will make any other paperback editions out of print through conventional book trade and retail channels nine months before publication.

8. Author can direct interested parties to wholesale large numbers of copies at volume discounts. For over 100 units, a 50% discount (before cost of freight) will be applied. For orders over 500 units, a 60% discount (before cost of freight) will be applied.

17) In the unfortunate incident that, after five years from the date of publication, the author is unhappy with the relationship, Publisher offers the author the opportunity to pay upfront for any remaining inventory + the cost of shipping. Publisher will not reprint more than two years of inventory, before a termination period. Publisher's license to publish the work would end, and all remaining copies and rights would be sent to the author. Termination can be given in writing at five years after publication.

18) This Agreement is governed by Oregon law. Any dispute arising out or in connection with this agreement including any question regarding its existence, validity or termination, shall be referred to and finally resolved by arbitration under the laws of Oregon. The place of arbitration shall be Portland, OR. In the event any party to this Agreement employs an attorney to enforce any of the terms of the Agreement, the prevailing party shall be entitled to recover its actual reasonable attorney's fees and reasonable associated costs, including expert witness fees.

19) Over and above the preceding agreement, the two parties agree to work together in the spirit of mutual respect and friendship, in mutual benefit, to quickly resolve any differences or concerns in good faith and assume that the other party has good intentions as we move positively forward. In the event

of a fundamental disagreement, arbitration will be brought in to resolve disagreements.

IN WITNESS WHEREOF, the parties hereto have executed and delivered this Agreement

_____   _____
("Author")   ("Publisher")

_____   _____
Date   Date

Sample of sales report:

The Book (Paper-over-board)

Your sales for this period were:

Month | Revenue | Sales in Units

• January: $16,397.75 (2694)

• February: $1,992.81 (331)

• March: $6,965.02 (1396)

Total Revenues: $25,355.58

Related Expenses:

• First Printing (Jan '17): $14,296.78

Total Expenses: $14,296.78

Statement Period Net Profits (Revenues minus Expenses): $11,058.80

You receive a 15% royalty so your royalties due are $1,658.82 (Revenues - Expenses * Royalty)

The previous total owed to you was: $433.13

So your current total owed is: $2,091.95

Sample Author Intake Form

Title: *Everyday Bicycling*

Subtitle: *How to Ride a Bike for Transportation (Whatever Your Lifestyle)*

Author Name (as it will appear on the book): Elly Blue

How do you pronounce your name?

Author's legal name (if different, for checks):

Pronouns:

Phone number:

Mailing address (let us know if you expect this to change in the next year):

Biography: Elly Blue is a writer and bicycle activist living in Portland, Oregon. Her work has appeared in the *Guardian, Grist, Bitch, BikePortland, Streetsblog,* and *Momentum*. She has appeared on Democracy Now!, in the Oregonian, on OPB, and in other media outlets. She blogs about bicycling and empowerment at takingthelane.com.

If any, list degrees, credentials, schools attended, cities resided in, and any other details that might help us publicize your book.

Do you know any friends who are reporters or have relationships or connections to people who work in the media? Please List:

What previous books have you written with ISBNs? How many copies has each sold?

Bikenomics, 978-1621060031, Microcosm Publishing, 2013, 12,000 copies

Everyday Bicycling, 978-1621067252, Microcosm Publishing, 2012, 17,000 copies

What makes this book special and different compared to similar books on similar subjects?

Set apart by its positive emphasis on the lifestyle and culture of bicycling, *Everyday Bicycling* shows that bicycle commuting can be something safe, convenient, and simple that you can structure your life around as a joyous, practical, and sane choice. Unlike other books about how to bike, this one assumes that the reader has transportation needs beyond commuting, like childcare responsibilities and household errands.

Three or four specific benefits to the reader of this book:

1.Practical instructions for learning to ride a bicycle, dress for bicycling in any weather, use safety gear, and carry cargo and children for daily transportation.

2.Encouragement for people new to bicycle transportation to incorporate riding into daily life and honest tips about choosing when and where to ride.

3. Entertainment is provided by personal anecdotes, stories of impressive feats performed by everyday people, and whimsical illustrations.

Any information pertaining to this title that will help it sell, such as statistics on trends, interesting factoids, trivia, etc.

In 2009, 1% of all U.S. trips were made by bicycle, an increase of 25% from 2001.

U.S. Department of Transportation and Federal Highway Administration, 2009

71% of Americans say they would like to bicycle more than they do now.

Royal, D., and D. Miller-Steiger, 2008

Book Description (100-200 words):

Everyday Bicycling is a guide to everything you need to know to get started riding a bicycle for transportation. Elly Blue introduces you to the basics, including street smarts, bike shopping, dressing professionally, carrying everything from groceries to furniture, and riding in all weather. With its positive, practical approach, this book is perfect for anyone who has ever dreamed of riding a bicycle for transportation.

Author tour? Dates and cities.

May: Seattle, Portland San Francisco, Los Angeles, San Diego, Dallas, Houston, Austin, Fort Worth, Oklahoma City, Tulsa, New Orleans, St Louis, Omaha, Lincoln, Kansas City, Chicago, New York,

Reviews of this book or similar work you've done, and/or three to five testimonial quotes about how great your book is from experts, peers, and contemporaries:

"One of the rare books that deserve to be called "perfect." I finished reading it and thought everyone, absolutely everyone, should read a copy. She concisely and humorously tells you everything you need to know about cycling safely and efficiently in traffic. Even controversial topics are treated evenhandedly and with a fact-based approach. Get copies to give to your family and friends."

—Jan Heine, Bicycling Quarterly

"Makes even this experienced cyclist feel as if I'm being let in on valuable secrets, yet in a comfortable, informal way." —Bicycle Times

"A succinct primer on the basics of cycling. Blue takes cycling and makes it digestible to cyclists and would-be's in a friendly, laid-back tone. Absent of any authoritarian voice, this is the book I wish I had years ago" —Urban Velo

"The tone is friendly and approachable, with the emphasis placed on the fact that commuting should be fun, easy, and not too expensive. Newcomers to the lifestyle will find this book a great tool for overcoming early barriers and initiating conversations about bicycling." —Momentum Magazine

"The relative virtues of messenger bags, backpacks, baskets, and panniers? Family bike logistics? How to avoid succumbing to road rage? What to wear in the rain? How to pick a seat that won't hurt your butt? It's all in here." —*The Atlantic Cities*

Who will be driven to buy this book? Describe the types of potential buyers, their levels of expertise, their typical job positions, conferences and shows they would attend, publications they would read, etc. Specific information on the size of the audience is also useful.

Buyers of this book will be adult men and women in the United States and Canada. The audience could be as large as the 70% of the adult population who say they would like to ride a bike more often. They are likely to live in cities or suburbs and be creative class professionals, civil servants, homemakers, and people who work from home. They likely read blogs and magazines about parenting, minimalism/simple living, urban homesteading, sustainable lifestyles, and environmentalism.

These readers are already concerned about societal ills such as pollution, public health and safety, social isolation, and climate change. They want to be more active and engaged in their personal lives, and if they have kids they want to set a good example for them. They may be disillusioned with measures like recycling and changing light bulbs. Riding a bicycle has occurred to them as a way to address all these issues, and they may already have begun riding occasionally.

Types of buyers:

- Someone (likely a man) who is already a regular bicyclist who purchase this book as a gift for a spouse or friend to encourage and help them to start riding. They would likely buy this book at a bookstore or a bike shop.

- Someone of either gender who is interested in bicycling and either hasn't yet started or has just begun and isn't sure what they're doing. This person is likely to buy the book at a bike shop, grocery store, a sustainable goods boutique, or online, or request it as a gift.

- Parents of young children who are exploring options for riding with their kids. They will likely find out about this book on a parenting blog and/or find it at the grocery store, at a specialty bike shop geared towards imported cargo bikes, or at a sustainability-oriented boutique.

- People who want to change their lifestyle for environmental reasons, to avoid stress, to simplify their lives, to work their way out of debt, or to be healthier.

Comparable/competitive titles. Please list three to five books that were published in the last three years that would be on the same shelves in the bookstore as you would expect to find your book and that would be of interest to the same readers. (Please steer clear of bestsellers or books from major publishing houses—we don't actually compete with them!)

- *On Bicycles: 50 Ways the New Bike Culture Can Change Your Life*, edited by Amy Walker. 978-1608680221 New World Library, 2011. $16.95.

- *How to Live Well Without Owning a Car* by Chris Balish. 978-1580087575 Ten Speed Press, 2006. $12.95.

- *Pedaling Revolution: How Cyclists Are Changing American Cities* by Jeff Mapes. 978-0870714191 Oregon State University Press. 2009. $19.95.

- *The Practical Cyclist: Bicycling for Real People* by Chip Haynes 978-0865716339 New Society Publishers 2009 $14.95.

- *Bike Snob: Systematically and Mercilessly Realigning the World of Cycling* by BikeSnobNYC. 978-0811869980 Chronicle Books 2010. $16.95.

- *The Art of Nonconformity: Set your own rules, live the life you want, and change the world* by Chris Guillebeau 978-0399536106 Perigee Books 2010 $14.95.

Please list as much of a finished table of contents as you have. (If you can, please include 1-3 sentences describing each chapter)

Introduction: Why we ride

Chapter 1: How to ride a bicycle

Chapter 2: Your life by bike: What to wear, where to go, and how to work it

Chapter 3: Bicycle care and feeding: Choosing and maintaining your steed

Chapter 4: Taking it with you: Carrying things large and small

Chapter 5: The family bike revolution

Chapter 6: Get organized! Finding fun, creating community, and bicycling toward a better world

Conclusion: Knowledge is power: Where to learn more

Glossary

Acquisition—a publisher acquiring rights and permissions to publish a new book.

Advance—Money paid to the author before any books have been sold. Some part of the advance is paid when the contract is signed, some when the book has been written, and the rest when it goes to print. This amount is deducted from future royalties.

ARCs (Advance Reader Copies or Advance Review Copies)—Unfinished versions of the book that are printed and mailed to solicit blurbs and reviews months before the book becomes available for sale.

American Booksellers Association (ABA)—Similar to a trade union, the ABA is a non-profit trade association to promote U.S. indie bookstores. Founded in 1900, ABA membership peaked in 1995 and once regulated the bookselling industry before monopolies began decimating the market share.

Author Services—"publishing" houses that charge fees to authors for tasks normally performed by a publisher, from editing to printing to marketing to listing the book on Amazon.

Authorpreneur—An indie or vanity author who pays for services that publishers usually pay for and oversee, such as editorial, marketing, distribution, and design.

Automation—Invented in the 1930s, a manufacturing process performed without human assistance. Normally the creator makes a prototype and oversees the process of engineering using various control systems. The creator then oversees creation while it is handled by a third party that specializes in this process. The major advantage of automation is efficiency because you are not learning a new trade but having the work handled by people who have equipment and experience.

Backlist (Back Catalog)—Books in print that were not published during the current season. These are usually among the most profitable for a publisher as expenses have already been paid for.

Bestseller—A subjective and meaningless term. Without a modifier that can be fact checked, such as "*New York Times*' bestseller" this term merely means that it has sold better than the rest of the catalog. Definitions vary so widely that it could mean anything from twenty to millions of copies.

Big Five—The five largest trade publishing houses; Simon & Schuster, Penguin Random House, Hachette Book Group, MacMillan, and HarperCollins.

BINC—The Book Industry Charitable Foundation is a safety net nonprofit that provides over $6 million to 7,300 families, supporting booksellers experiencing medical emergencies, severe hardship, or financial disaster from circumstances like lack of insurance.

BISAC—Book Industry Subject And Category codes that often appear on the upper-left corner of the back cover, and in your metadata. These are shelving codes that further clarify the subject and content of your book for account buyers. You must choose your BISACs from the BISG list found here: bisg.org/general/custom.asp?page=BISACSelection

BLAD (Book Layout And Design)—As opposed to an ARC, this is a small sample or excerpt of a to-be-released book with a cover proof (sometimes attached, sometimes not). BLADs are preferred for certain buyers, often in highly visual books like children's publishing.

Bleeds—Where images or text run fully to the edge of the page, done by printing a page that is larger than the final trim size and cut down to size.

Blurb—an endorsement for a book from a third party that adds both depth and praise for the work while clarifying what it is and what it isn't.

Book Industry Study Group (BISG)—A book trade association that offers standardization for best practices, as well as determining applicable shelving categories. BISG also analyzes industry data.

Book tour—A series of author events to create buzz, sales, and publicity for their book in a variety of cities.

Bowker—A private company that sells and distributes ISBNs to publishers.

Comps—Books similar (comparative or competitive) to the one you're looking to publish, used to guide decisions about placement, size and format.

Consolidated Conglomerates—Corporations that own controlling shares in and are made up of seemingly unrelated businesses, like General Electric owning publishing, television, and arms manufacturing companies.

Contract—An agreement outlining the terms, expectations, payments, territory, and rights between two parties.

Copyright—Legal protection of original artistic or literary work, specifically the editing of the finished work or image.

Development—The title, subtitle, tagline, and cover of your book that conveys the emotional payoff of your book to the reader and makes it appear comfortable and natural on the shelf next to the comps.

Digital Printer—Akin to a home laser printer with an attached bookbinder, this is a type of printing with a lower quality than offset and a higher per-unit cost. It is generally used for ARCs or books with very limited runs.

Distribution—The process of delivering your book to readers, most commonly via retailers.

Distributor—A company that specializes in distribution, generally working with multiple publishers and has a good working relationship with many accounts.

Distros—A slang term meaning a distributor that is not exclusive or full-service.

Division/Imprint—A subdivision of a publisher, generally specializing in different genres or subjects. An imprint or division utilizes most aspects of their parent publisher, such as as distribution and production.

Dumps—Cardboard stands to display your books.

Dust Jacket—A detached, folded paper cover to protect a clothbound book.

Economy of Scale—Reducing per unit costs by increasing quantities. E.g. Printing 2,000 for $1.50 each versus printing 5,000 books in order to pay $1.00 each.

Edelweiss—A private company that owns the premiere metadata feed and catalog for the book industry. All established publishers are expected to have their titles listed in Edelweiss, which is normally handled by their distributor.

Electronic Data Interchange (EDI)—Other than fax, this is the way that purchase order information is communicated in publishing. EDI eliminates the need for these orders to be manually input, introducing human errors, and automates them into warehouse software without the trouble of someone having to input them manually.

Evergreen—A book that sells consistently year-over-year because it remains timely and relevant to readers, not tied to current events.

Fair Use—Exemption in U.S. law that allows brief excerpts of copyrighted material to be quoted for purposes of criticism, reporting, teaching, and research, without the need for permission or payment to the owner.

Financialized—Access to capital in order to carry out intended plans through ability to borrow or having money.

Flagship Title—A publisher's bestselling book that becomes definitive of its brand, development, list, and the kind of pitches it receives. A flagship title will cement a publisher's credentials for sales and acquisitions in a genre.

Flood—Style of layout where the ink is reversed and most of the page is printed, meaning that everything but the image or text is black, and the image and text are the color of the paper. For an example, look at page three of this book.

Foreign Rights—An agreement to transfer the intellectual property rights to publish, export, and sell the book in other countries and languages.

French Flaps—A cover that extends past the trimline and is folded into the inside cover. French flaps add production value and are often printed to fold out and offer more information like maps, photos, or jacket copy.

Frontlist—Books published during the current season e.g. Spring or Fall.

Fulfillment Companies—Outsourced companies that perform storage, warehousing, and shipment duties for a publisher.

Fulfillment Strategy—Once the books have been sold to the customer, a plan for packaging and transporting them, along with the proper paperwork, to arrive in good condition.

Gift Sales—Books sold to retailers that specialize in impulse buys. These sales are generally non-returnable and are almost always displayed in a minimal selection with all books face-out.

Ground Game—Marketing books in real time, face-to-face, such as at seminars, conferences, speaking events, or music festivals. The ground game is a vital part of bringing your books to reach new readers to add them to your sales funnel.

Hurts—Books sold at a discount due to damage from shipping, manufacturing, or storage.

Hybrid Publishing—Combining the worst aspects of vanity and self-publishing, these downsized industry professionals are mildly selective about which authors' money they will take and create a professional book that is completely financed by the author. These books try to appear traditionally published but because the author has the final say and—even with the help of industry consultants—is too emotionally close to their own work to make decisions that would allow it to thrive on the shelf, these books often have fundamental development flaws, do not have proper distribution, and fail as a result.

Incidental Sales—These are passive book sales that are small in the grand scheme of things. In certain nonfiction and genre fiction, such as Romance, you will see larger sales from casual browsers that require no marketing or expense.

Indicia—Towards the front of the book, this page contains the copyright information as well as credits and rights holding information as well as vendor of record ordering data for industry professionals.

Indie Author—A term for authors published by independent presses that has been claimed confusingly by authors published by the non-indie industry monopolies such as Ingram/Lightning Source or Amazon.

Indie Publisher—Small publishing houses that are independent from the Big Five, often with a specific mission and list that drive acquisitions and sales. This term has also been confusingly cannibalized by non-indie self-publishers who use the corporate services of Ingram or Amazon.

Institutional Sales—Books sold to a government, corporation, or organization that will not be used for resale but will be re-distributed among constituents or employees. Sometimes they are printed with customization.

ISBN—An international standard book number; the universal unique identifier for each format and edition of a book. ISBNs are sold and distributed by Bowker.

ISSN—Magazines, journals, and periodicals use international standard serial numbers instead of ISBNs.

Just in Time Inventory—Instead of warehousing and managing months of inventory, to save on costs a wholesaler or retailer will plan their ordering to arrive restocks simultaneously as the sold product is shipped to the customer. Many third party Amazon suppliers sell books they don't have and then use Just in Time Inventory for fulfillment.

Kerning—The amount of horizontal space between characters on a line of text.

Leading—The amount of vertical space between lines of text.

Line screen—The number of literal lines per inch that determine the complexity of detail in a printed image.

List—A publisher's existing catalog, often used to explain the press's developmental strategy, sensibility, or tastes.

Literary Industrial Complex—The Big Five publishing houses and major corporate book monopolies as well as people who draw best practices and influence from them.

Market Share—A percentage of the total industry. For example, if one out of 1,000 books sold per month are yours, you control .1% of the market share.

Mass Market—Stores like Walmart, Target, Sam's Club, Costco, and airport stores. These stores price competitively against Amazon and have severe metrics required for a book to remain on their shelves.

Meet the Competition (MTC)—A result of the court cases involving the Robinson-Patman Act, in order for competition to be fair, publishers must offer the same terms to retailers of all sizes. Previously publishers had argued that it was cheaper and easier to deal with one buyer who orders for 600 stores than to service 600 stores individually and thus that they did not have to provide the same terms to all retailers. Now publishers request proof that a retailer or wholesaler is receiving equitable terms as what they are requesting from three or more similar publishers. This protects them legally and also allows the publisher not to offer discounts that are unreasonably deep.

Metadata—Data about the details of your books that is distributed to the industry so key account buyers can understand the price, trim size, page count, and emotional payoff of each book and make purchasing decisions. (similar to keywords or tags)

Midlist Publisher—A publisher with over $100,000 in annual revenue that is represented by a trade distributor with a defined and established reputation and niche. A midlist publisher would expect their books to sell 3,000-5,000 copies each. These publishers have begun to make a name for themselves in their chosen niche, generally have 3-10 employees and income up to a few million dollars a year.

Muse—Your comp title that you emotionally relate with and best serves as your guide for your own book's development.

Niche—A small, specialized subset of publishing. For example, while many publishers focus on the self-help genre, perhaps your niche is alcoholism treatment for the elderly.

Nonprofit—A legal definition for an organization that is tax exempt and reinvests all revenue surplus into the achieving the organization's mission instead of owner or shareholder profits. The understood vernacular is that a nonprofit performs work in the best interest of the public in the same way that the government would.

Non-Trade Publisher—Publishers creating books that aren't intended for a general audience, like textbooks or technical books for professionals in a specific field.

NPD Decision Key—A product developed by Nielsen, based on their popular Soundscan service, that records and reports book sales at register checkouts from reporting retailers. This is the reporting data used to appear in *New York Times* bestseller lists and is reviewed by industry staff to review a book or author's track record.

Offset Printing—The finest quality of printing that uses a relief process where oil and water repel each other to transfer images from metal plates onto paper. It is ideally suited for print runs of 2,000 or more. Offset also offers much greater printing options for maximum production value.

ONline Information eXchange (ONIX)—A computer transmission in XML language that communicates metadata about new frontlist titles or any changes to backlist titles. The information is communicated from one computer to another in order to prevent data entry errors as well as to distribute it to many vendors at once.

Out of Print—Not available through traditional commercial channels, such as Ingram or Baker & Taylor, due to lack of inventory because the publisher does not have plans to reprint or has lost the rights.

Pantone Matching System (PMS)—Similar to paint chips, PMS colors ensure that the color(s) printed in the book matches what you expect. The printer mixes inks based on PMS color so that the results are universally the same.

Paper Over Board—A hardcover book with a printed cover and no dust jacket.

Planogram—Used in chain and mass market stores—especially where books are mixed with other product types like plants or toys or china—these are models and diagrams for maximizing sales by arranging books with other merchandise and planning how much "white space" to maintain around them. Understanding a store's planogram will help a publisher to understand what books to pitch to them.

Print on Demand (POD)—A type of printer that prints books digitally one at a time. There is no set up or economy of scale with POD. It is equivalent to loading a file and hitting the print button.

Print run—The total quantity of a title that is printed at one time based on sales interest and to decrease per-unit cost.

Printer—The company that physically manufactures books for a publisher.

Profit and Loss (P&L)—A comprehensive analysis of expected sales based on comp titles as well as expenses that determine the feasibility of publishing a given title. P&Ls are typically done before making an offer or signing a contract. They show a publisher expected income and what they can afford to spend on a title.

Public Domain—After a copyright has expired, or if the copyright holder has given up the rights willingly, the creative work is owned by the public and anyone can publish it without needing permission.

Publisher—The company that handles buying the rights to a book, editing, layout, production, fulfillment, distribution, finances, and management.

Pulping—Turning unsold books back into paper in order not to be taxed on dead inventory.

Retailer—Online or brick stores that sell books to readers.

Returns—Unsold books shipped to retailers that are sent back to the publishing house or distributor.

Robinson-Patman Act—1936 U.S. law that protects small retailers from chain stores by forcing manufacturers to sell to all competitors at the same price and terms so some stores could not aggressively underprice their competitors. In 1988, a lawsuit was filed asserting that several publishers had offered price and promotional terms to chains not advertised or available to independent stores. The publishers argued that they were "meeting the competition" and claimed to have saved money by only meeting one buyer instead of hundreds. Essentially, their argument was "everyone else is doing it too." Consent decrees were signed and the industry created a formalized system of "meet the competition" requests. The American Booksellers Association, which had peaked at 7,000 independent bookstores in 1995, began to shrink rapidly as the Literary Industrial Complex seized control of the industry.

Royalties—The money owed to an author for book sales.

Sales Funnel—A business phrase for the process where customers become familiar with your books, develop an interest, consider a purchase, and eventually buy.

Shipped Books—Books that have moved from the publisher or distributor's warehouse but haven't been paid for and can still be returned without payment for a year or longer.

Showrooming—Customers seeing a book in a retail store and purchasing it elsewhere online.

Small Press—Books or publishers with a niche audience and lower sales expectations, often representing marginal subject matter, characters, perspectives, or narrow interests.

Special Sales—One aspect of selling books outside of bookstores by using books to communicate the mission of the business, which means there's strong thematic messaging in the book selection. This can be as diverse as "fishing," "history of music," "dogs of Oklahoma," "stories of The South," or even "coping with addiction." These books are always communicating their value, their audience, and what they have to offer them. These sales are often easier, more fun, and more lucrative than bookstore sales.

Spot Color—Areas of an additional pantone color, used to add production value and draw the eye to notice important design details.

Stock Transfer—Moving books from one warehouse to another without expectation of payment or invoice.

Stopgaps—A temporary solution to a one-time problem for obtaining materials in time to fulfill your usual methods. E.g. You are desperate for a reprint and your usual printer is delayed by three additional weeks or the Canadian post office is on strike and won't deliver your orders.

Style Guide—A publisher's guidelines for formatting punctuation, capitalization, abbreviations, spelling, and grammar rules.

Tagline—A single sentence that further clarifies the emotional payoff of a book.

Third Party Sourcing—Rather than purchasing through a Vendor of Record, a retailer intentionally buys through a different third party wholesaler. Normally this practice is done for the purpose of Just in Time Inventory or faster turnaround time.

Trade Distributor—A company to which publishers outsource sales, warehousing, metadata propagation, fulfillment, customer service, and debt collection. These companies use the combined catalogs from dozens of publishers to establish collective bargaining power.

Trade Publishers—Publishing houses that develop books for bookstores and the general public, such as novels. As opposed to technical or textbook publishing.

Trade Reviewers—Publications read by people who work in the book industry such as *Publisher's Weekly, Shelf Awareness, Kirkus Reviews, Rain Taxi, Library Journal, Foreword,* and *School Library Journal.* These publications alert key account buyers to the existence of your book and how it might fit into their part of the industry. Libraries especially are often required to reduce their purchasing liability by showing that they purchased a title because of an endorsement in one of these publications.

Turnaround Time—The time between when an order is placed and when it is received. Alternately, for a publisher, distributor, or wholesaler this term may be used as "turn time," meaning the average time frame it takes to sell a copy of a book. E.g. The turn rate is every 38.7 seconds.

Vanity Publishing—Going back to the beginning of private wealth, an "author" pays exorbitant fees for a "publishing" company to create a book-shaped object without the difficulties of writing something worth reading.

Vendor of Record—A clear listing of where a bookstore can order a copy of the book. This information is contained in Edelweiss and NPD Decision Key as well as on a letter distributed sent to trade accounts whenever it is changed.

Wholesalers—A company that fulfills existing demand for your books, rather than marketing or selling them actively. Some examples include Ingram, Baker & Taylor, Follett, New Leaf, Diamond Comics, Brodart, Bookazine, or Blackwell. They take a 50-60% cut of the cover price.

Zine—A cross between a book and a love letter about a subject of intense personal passion. Zines prioritize expression and building community over money. See my first book *Make A Zine: Start Your Own Underground Publishing Revolution.*

About The Author

As a publisher Joe Biel has sold millions of books over the course of his 24-year career. He is also an autistic writer, activist, filmmaker, teacher, founder of Microcosm Publishing, and co-founder of the Portland Zine Symposium. He has directed over 100 short films and four feature documentaries: *Aftermass: How Portland Became North America's Bicycling Capital* (2014), *If It Ain't Cheap, It Ain't Punk* (2010), *Of Dice & Men* (2006), and *$100 & A T-Shirt: A Documentary About Zines in Portland* (2004). He is the author of *Good Trouble: Building a Successful Life & Business with Autism* (2016), *Proud to be Retarded* (2018), *Your Neurodiverse Friend* (2018), *Manspressions: Decoding Men's Behavior* (2015), *Make a Zine!: Start Your Own Underground Publishing Revolution* (2017), *Perfect Mix Tape Segue, Bicycle Culture Rising, CIA Makes Science Fiction Unexciting: Dark Deeds & Derring Do* (2013), *Bamboozled: An Incarcerated Boxer Goes Undercover for John McCain's Boxing Bill* (2013), and *Beyond The Music: How Punks are Saving the World with DIY Ethics, Skills, & Values (2012)*. He has been featured in *Time Magazine, Publisher's Weekly, Utne Reader, Portland Mercury, Oregonian, Broken Pencil, Bulletproof Radio, Readymade, Punk Planet, Spectator* (Japan), *G33K* (Korea), and *Maximum Rocknroll*. He lives in Portland, Oregon.

Elly Blue, 2018